T0271298

Organizational Myopia

Could the terrorist attacks on the Twin Towers have been avoided? What about the control failures in the recent global financial crisis? Behind these apparently very different events, it is possible to identify a common element of organizational myopia – a syndrome that severely limits the capacity of organizations to foresee the effects of their own decisions and to recognize signs of danger or opportunity. *Organizational Myopia* explores the barriers that impede organizations from identifying an effective response to the problems that they have to confront. Using real-world cases, the author investigates the mechanisms that generate myopia in organizations at the individual, organizational, and interorganizational level in contexts that are complex, uncertain, ambiguous, and changeable. This book will help readers understand how to limit the origins of myopia and therefore increase the capacity of organizations to anticipate and contain unexpected events.

MAURIZIO CATINO is Associate Professor of Sociology of Organizations in the Department of Sociology and Social Research at the University of Milan–Bicocca, Italy, and Visiting Scholar in the Department of Sociology at New York University. He has published several articles on the dark side of organizations, human error in complex systems, and organizational theory. He is the author of *From Chernobyl to Linate: Technological Accidents or Organizational Errors?* (Bruno Mondadori 2006), and *Understanding Organizations* (Il Mulino 2012). He served as policy advisor for many public and private institutions, including the Italian Parliamentary Commission on Medical Errors and the Italian Air Force.

Organizational Myopia

Problems of Rationality and Foresight in Organizations

MAURIZIO CATINO

University of Milan–Bicocca, Italy

CAMBRIDGE
UNIVERSITY PRESS

CAMBRIDGE
UNIVERSITY PRESS

University Printing House, Cambridge CB2 8BS, United Kingdom

One Liberty Plaza, 20th Floor, New York, NY 10006, USA

477 Williamstown Road, Port Melbourne, VIC 3207, Australia

314-321, 3rd Floor, Plot 3, Splendor Forum, Jasola District Centre, New Delhi - 110025, India

79 Anson Road, #06-04/06, Singapore 079906

Cambridge University Press is part of the University of Cambridge.

It furthers the University's mission by disseminating knowledge in the pursuit of education, learning and research at the highest international levels of excellence.

www.cambridge.org
Information on this title: www.cambridge.org/9781107027039

© Maurizio Catino 2013

This publication is in copyright. Subject to statutory exception and to the provisions of relevant collective licensing agreements, no reproduction of any part may take place without the written permission of Cambridge University Press.

First published 2013
First paperback edition 2014

A catalogue record for this publication is available from the British Library

Library of Congress Cataloging in Publication data
Catino, Maurizio.
    Organizational myopia : problems of rationality and foresight in organizations / Maurizio Catino.
      pages   cm
    Includes bibliographical references and index.
    ISBN 978-1-107-02703-9
    1. Organizational learning.   2. Organizational behavior.   I. Title.
    HD58.82.C38   2013
    302.3´5–dc23   2012036678

ISBN 978-1-107-02703-9 Hardback
ISBN 978-1-107-44721-9 Paperback

Cambridge University Press has no responsibility for the persistence or accuracy of URLs for external or third-party internet websites referred to in this publication, and does not guarantee that any content on such websites is, or will remain, accurate or appropriate.

Contents

Figures

Tables

Abbreviations and acronyms

AA	American Airlines
CAIB	Columbia Accident Investigation Board
CCM	Control Center Management
CIA	Central Intelligence Agency
CONR	Continental NORAD Region
CONSOB	Commissione Nazionale per le Società e la Borsa
FAA	Federal Aviation Administration
FBI	Federal Bureau of Investigation
FED	Federal Reserve System
FEMA	Federal Emergency Management Agency
GAO	Government Accountability Office
HRT	High Reliability Theory
IBL	Individual Blame Logic
LFT	Latent Factors Theory
NASA	National Aeronautics and Space Administration
NAT	Normal Accidents Theory
NCCFC	National Commission on the Causes of the Financial Crisis in the US
NCTA	National Commission on Terrorist Attacks
NEADS	Northeast Air Defense Sector
NORAD	North American Aerospace Defense Command
NSA	National Security Advisor
NSC	National Security Council
OFL	Organizational Function Logic
RAF	Royal Air Force
SEC	Securities and Exchange Commission
SOA	Sarbanes-Oxley Act
SWFs	Sovereign Wealth Funds
UA	United Airlines
WTC	World Trade Center

Acknowledgments

I have been working on the theme of organizational myopia since 2006, and a first version of this book was published in Italian by Il Mulino (Bologna) in 2009. The current book is a largely revised and updated version of my original work, with new chapters, new cases, and a more advanced analytical framework.

I owe a debt of gratitude for our conversations and for helping me on this project to Delia Baldassarri, Paul DiMaggio, Luca Lanzalaco, Antonio Mutti, Marta Tienda, Diane Vaughan, and two anonymous reviewers. Last but not least, I wish to thank Paula Parish, editor at Cambridge University Press, and the editorial team for working with me to substantially improve the quality of the manuscript.

Introduction

Brazil, 1956. Government authorities are concerned about the fact that the country's domestic bees population, necessary to pollinate various types of food crops (melons, almonds, etc.) does not effectively perform the expected task because these bees do not cope well with the tropical climate. Moreover, they do not produce much honey.

The geneticist Warwick Kerr is appointed by the government to find a way of increasing the bees' efficiency, including by crossbreeding them with other species of bees. Kerr travels to Africa and returns with seventy-five queen bees of an African variety (the highly aggressive *Apis mellifera scutellata*) together with their colonies. These bees are placed in special hives in a laboratory in Rio Claro, in the state of São Paulo, and are kept under strict surveillance. For a year, Kerr attempts to obtain a hybrid that is both docile to keep and active in pollinating, but he does not succeed.

One day a careless beekeeper erroneously removes the queen excluders and lets twenty-six queen bees escape, together with their swarms. Subsequently, these African queen bees crossbreed with the local European bees, resulting in a hybrid that differs greatly from the government's requirements: the new breed is certainly highly productive – in fact, it adapts well to the tropical climate – but it is extremely aggressive and dangerous both for humans and animals. In a short time, the inhabitants and the beekeepers in the Rio Claro area notice a significant change in the behavior of bees. Attacks on human beings become more frequent and increasingly disruptive, while a number of dogs are actually killed by the bees. From the point of view of their venom, African bees are no more dangerous than European bees, but these new Africanized hybrids are much more inclined to attack humans. The bees that migrated from Asia to Europe encountered a temperate climate and a favorable environment that made them docile and peaceful and, for this reason, easily domesticated. In contrast, the marked aggressiveness of African bees derives from the fact that in migrating from Asia to Africa, the bees encountered very hostile conditions. As a result, they became nomadic to be able to keep pace with the flowering of plants. They also came to be very wary of humans because they were in the habit of plundering their honey. Only the most aggressive bees managed to survive, with the result that with the passing of the generations, they became even more aggressive.

By 1986, many years after the breakout from Kerr's laboratory in Rio Claro, the aggressive Africanized bees had crossed Central America and arrived in Mexico. The United States has invested millions of dollars to try to find a solution to the problem and to prevent the bees from entering their territory, but their efforts have been in vain: the bees have overcome the biological barriers that were created and are now advancing at a rate of about 500 kilometers a year. After eighty generations, there are now billions of these aggressive bees, and they have killed livestock and people. Today, they are present in many states in the United States, where they have supplanted the existing bees species. Moreover, it is believed that, with the intense traffic of cargo and container ships in the Atlantic, they will arrive sooner or later in Europe as well. On the positive side, however, these bees, as well as being very active in the pollination process, produce a great deal of honey. Indeed, Brazil, after adopting special protective measures and locating the beekeeping industry a long way from inhabited areas, has become one of the largest honey producers in the world.

Could an event of this kind have been foreseen? Was the initiative of Kerr and the Brazilian government a myopic action, in the sense that the medium- to long-term consequences of the importation of African bees were not foreseen? Yes, it probably was.

Could the terrorist attacks on the Twin Towers have been avoided? What about the *Challenger* and *Columbia* accidents, the two US space shuttles that exploded in flight? Behind these apparently very different events, it is possible to identify a common element: *organizational myopia*. It is a syndrome that severely limits the capacity of organizations to foresee the effects of their own decisions and to detect signs of danger. Ultimately, it can lead to failures and even disasters.

The theme

In recent years, the topic of organizational myopia has become increasingly important in management practices and in the field of organization studies. It is crucially related to the problem of how organizations can foresee the future in contexts that are more and more complex, uncertain, ambiguous, and changeable.

The term *myopia* refers to a defect in sight that results in a blurred vision of objects located at a distance from the eyes. What is involved is a dysfunction in refraction in which the image of distant objects is formed in front of the retina, thereby rendering them indistinct, whereas the vision of the same objects at a short distance remains clear. In an extended sense, myopia means a lack of clear-sightedness and foresightedness, a restricted view of things. A myopic person, then, is someone who is shortsighted, lacking in perspicacity and long-term vision (the term derives from the Greek word μυωπία, muōpia, from myein "to shut" and ops "eye").

By organizational myopia, we mean a limited capacity on the part of an organization to evaluate the facts as they actually are and in terms of their possible evolution. Organizational myopia manifests itself in particular in the form of two distinct mechanisms relating to the incapacity of an organization or interorganizational system:

1. to detect signs of potential danger, which can undermine its survival or compromise its normal operation; and
2. to detect potential opportunities, which can improve reliability and resilience of the organizational system, favoring its long-term survival and adaptation to environmental changes.

Myopia in complex high-risk organizational systems lies at the basis of many disasters. The main consequence of organizational myopia is the persistence in an organization of beliefs and practices that lead to decisions whose effects result in a higher probability that a negative event will take place. The concept of organizational myopia has analogies with Turner's (1976; Turner and Pidgeon 1997) concept of "failure of foresight" and Wilensky's (1967) concept of "large-scale failures of intelligence" in that it draws attention to failure and/or incapacity on the part of organizations to foresee the future. By organizational intelligence, we mean the search for reliable and complete information and the capacity on the part of an organization to make sense of it. For example, in the aftermath of a disaster, public inquiries often focus on certain causal factors that, though never having been taken into consideration beforehand, seem, after the event, very clear, self-evident, and capable of explaining it. So inevitably the question arises: Why wasn't anything done before? On the one hand, it is necessary to keep in mind certain cognitive mechanisms (e.g., hindsight bias) that, *after* the event, make what was *previously* complex look as though it were simple and straightforward. On the other hand, it is necessary to explain – based on the hypothesis that no one wanted to deliberately cause the disaster – the reason for the previous inaction.

The phenomenon of organizational myopia is potentially interesting for anyone involved with organizations. Its range of action goes far beyond high-risk organizations, to include a range of social, economic, and political phenomena, such as long-term consequences of political decision making, climate change and global warming, technological and financial innovations, and so on. Finally, myopia in regard to ill-defined and unclear threats strikes companies of all types. The top managers of the pharmaceutical company Merck, for example, under-estimated the reputational consequences for the company of certain preliminary and scarcely reliable data on the painkiller Vioxx, that is, to the effect that it was associated with cardiovascular risk. Similarly, the managers of Kodak ignored the initial faint signs of decline in the use of film, while the bicycle manufacturer Schwinn underestimated the threat posed by the mountain bike, which in the course of time would turn out to cast a shadow over the traditional bicycle. Indeed, companies like Digital, Xerox, Delta, Kmart, and General Motors have all unexpectedly seen radical changes in their fortunes since the time in 1982 when Peters and Waterman, in *In Search of Excellence*, classed them as *excellent*.

"There's nothing as blinding as success," said Robert Haas, chair-man of Levi Strauss & Company (*New York Times*, June 25, 2000), referring to the perverse effects of *organizational hubris*. By organ-izational hubris, we mean that mix of confidence and excessive pride that derives from past successes, the uncritical acceptance of praise and the idea that one is in some way exempt from the rules. A form of arrogance, this attitude is often a prelude to organizational decline, accidents, and disasters. Underestimating competition – considering past successes and consolidated positions a guarantee of success in the future – lay at the heart of the inertia of Levi Strauss in the face of the emergence of new rivals. This was also the case with other big companies such as IBM, Digital, General Motors, and many others (Sheth 2007). As far back as 1960, Theodore Levitt, in an article for the *Harvard Business Review* titled "Marketing Myopia," pointed out how every industrial sector goes through a period of rapid expansion, after which there comes into play a vicious circle. The operators, after a certain period of success, become convinced that there are no threats or alternatives to their product and that their continued expansion is guaranteed. Lulled into this state of false security, they concentrate on exploiting the benefits of mass production and economies of scale through high production volumes and low costs. Over the medium to long term, however, the pursuit of these objectives has the combined effect of blocking innovation, which in turn produces stagnation and decline.

The book

This book provides an account of the various mechanisms that underlie organizational myopia, considering a variety of cases from different contexts. Its aim is to make sense of this phenomenon both with respect to micro-level behavior and to macro patterns occurring at the organizational and interorganizational level. Broadly speaking, this book constitutes an enquiry into the theme of the *dark side* of organizations and the *unintended consequences* (Merton 1936) of organizational behavior.

We argue that organizations that develop a systematic capacity to identify, evaluate, and react to ill-defined threats manage to avoid the emergence of serious problems much better than those that fail to develop such a capacity. Many risks bring with them "recovery windows" (Roberto 2009), a period between the appearance of the first signs of danger and the occurrence of the adverse event itself, a space during which one or more members of the organization have an opportunity to take cognizance of the signs and eliminate or contain the threat. Not to read such signs is a sign of myopia.

The book is divided into five chapters. The first one, "Cases of Myopia," presents three instances of myopia that occurred in different contexts. I start with the myopia of a society, investigating the case of *Easter Island* and the disappearance of the Moai civilization due to the inhabitants' incapacity to anticipate the consequences of their aggressive deforestation. I then study the myopia of a country, analyzing the *9/11 terrorist attacks* and the behavior of the US defense system, both with respect to the failure of intelligence in foreseeing the attacks, and with respect to its capacity in dealing with it and containing its effects. Lastly, we discuss the myopia of an organization, studying the *Challenger* and *Columbia space shuttle disasters* and NASA's difficulty in identifying and learning from weak signs of danger. This chapter also contains a number of other cases including war battles, the problem of the tragedy of the commons, and a few instances of positive myopia, such as the case of a paper mill in Karnaphuli in East Pakistan.

In the second chapter, "Uncertainty and Predictability in Organizations," we discuss various difficulties that organizations may encounter in foreseeing nonroutine or unexpected events and, more generally, problems of uncertainty in complex environments. Expectations in this context play a double role: on the one hand, they reduce complexity; on the other hand, they may be biased and lead to erroneous conclusions. The chapter introduces two alternative theoretical approaches to the predictability of unexpected events: the *predictable surprises* approach, according to which some events are unexpected but essentially predictable, and the *bolt from the blue* (or *black swan*) approach, according to which such events are unpredictable or at the most predictable only by virtue of hindsight bias, that is, predictable only ex post. In the first framework, if the occurrence of unexpected events is not predicted, this is due to executive failure. In the second framework, most events are very difficult to identify, imagine, and obviate because of a set of variegated, interacting, cognitive, organizational, and political factors. These two models are put to a test in the case of the financial crisis of 2007, and a third, midway model is introduced, that of a *gray swan*, which identifies a category of events that are predictable within limits.

The third chapter, "The Mechanisms of Organizational Myopia," outlines an analytical model of organizational myopia distinguishing among three levels at which myopia can occur: the individual, the organizational, and the interorganizational. The *micro*-individual level refers to biases, heuristics, and other cognitive errors that may affect decision-making processes. At the *meso*-organizational level, myopia is favored by the inadequacy of the way in which organizations analyze threats, integrate information, create incentives for action, and learn from experiences. Finally, the *macro*-interorganizational level refers to the environment in which organizations operate and encompasses many organizations and institutions, such as the government, regulators, corporations, interest groups and lobbies, and so on. The model is then applied to understand the mechanisms that contributed to auditing companies' failure of control in Enron, Parmalat, and other similar cases, which constitute an interesting and understudied case of gatekeepers' failure.

The fourth chapter, "Anticipating Risk: The Problem of Learning," explores how organizations learn from errors and failures, especially from unusual and rare events. Anticipating risk and reducing accidents is not an impossible mission, in particular if there is an incubation period that allows the organization to detect weak signs, to prevent critical events, and to contain their consequences. The chapter contrasts two different approaches to the understanding of the origins of organizational accidents. The *individual blame logic* approach aims at finding the guilty individuals, and its logic of inquiry is driven by the question of who caused the accident. In contrast, the *organizational function logic* approach focuses mainly on organizational factors and asks, What factors favored the accident? How and why did the defense system fail? In this chapter, I maintain that organizational learning is favored by an organizational function logic in which the reporting of failures is incentivized and people are not punished for unintentional errors.

The fifth chapter, "Implications for Organizational Design," highlights the importance of detecting and making sense of weak signs and of cultivating imagination in organizations as fundamental ingredients for expanding organizational intelligence. Here we present the characteristics of High Reliability Organizations (HROs), a type of mindful organization that, in combating organizational myopia, is better able to confront unexpected events.

Finally, in the Epilogue, relying on the analytical categories discussed in the previous chapters, I introduce a classification of different forms of organizational myopia based on the predictability of the event and the possibility of dealing with it either ex ante, ex post, or both (manageability). We identify four types of organizational myopia:

1. *Systemic myopia* occurs when the events are *potentially predictable* and *manageable both ex ante and ex post*. Events are potentially predictable if there is a *direct* and *clear* causal link between signs and event and if before it takes place, there is an *incubation period* in which signs make possible its detection. If events are potentially predictable and manageable by the organization both ex ante and ex post, the organization is victim of systemic myopia

if it fails (a) to detect signs before the event (failure of anticipation) or (b) to contain its consequences, despite the presence of a recovery window (failure of containment). Myopia here is a systemic condition of an organization, as in the case of man-made disasters and organizational accidents, such as the British Petroleum oil spill, the *Columbia* shuttle disaster, and the Enron financial misconduct.

2. *Foresight myopia* occurs, instead, when events are *potentially predictable*, but were manageable only ex ante, as in the case of the *Challenger*'s O-rings, or only ex post, as, for example, in the Chernobyl accident.

3. *Unavoidable myopia* concerns events that are *hardly predictable* because *no preceding signs exist* whatsoever, or there is an *indirect* and *unclear* causal link between signs and event, or the event has never occurred before and there is no model to refer to. The organization could act only ex ante or only ex post and was not able to do so. It is the most justifiable of the four forms of myopia, because there was no opportunity for the organization to implement mindful either preventive action or suitable methods of containment. A classic example of unavoidable myopia is the Three Mile Island nuclear plant accident.

4. Finally, *preventive and reactive myopia* occurs when events are *hardly predictable*, but the event was manageable both ex ante and ex post. The organization could have implemented anticipatory preventive measures (for example, forest maintenance, preemptive fires, antiseismic construction, etc.) but did not do so (failure of anticipation). In addition, the organization was also unable to contain the consequences of the event (failure of containment). The 9/11 terrorist attacks fall into this category.

If it is true that an organization cannot avoid accidents and unexpected events, it is also true that an organization can contain the consequences and the frequency with which they occur. This book pursues two objectives. First, starting out from the analysis of a number of cases (Chapter 1), the book contributes to the construction of an organizational theory of myopia, identifying the various mechanisms that generate it (Chapters 2 and 3) and make it difficult to learn from failures (Chapter 4). The aim here is to explore the barriers that at various levels impede and prevent organizations from identifying an effective response to the problems that they have to confront. Second, the book considers the implications of organizational myopia for organizational design, discussing some possible lines of action aimed at limiting its scope and increasing the capacity of organizations to anticipate and contain unexpected events (Chapter 5).

1 | *Cases of myopia*

1.1 Myopia of a society: the trees of Easter Island

Easter Island (called Rapa Nui, meaning "great island/rock" in the language of the natives) is located in the South Pacific and is triangular in shape. One of the world's most remote and isolated islands, it covers an area of 171 square kilometers and reaches a maximum height of 509 meters. It lies approximately 3,600 kilometers west of the coast of Chile, and its closest inhabited neighbors are Polynesia's Pitcairn Islands, 2,075 kilometers to the west. In administrative terms, it is a separate province of the Chilean region of Valparaíso. It was first colonized by the Polynesians at a time when it was covered by an immense forest of palm trees.[1]

Until about the thirteenth century, the population remained small in number and substantially in equilibrium with the natural resources of the island. Europeans discovered its existence thanks to the Dutch explorer Jacob Roggeveen on April 5, 1772, Easter Day. The island was christened with the name that it has kept to this day. The territory had presumably been inhabited since around the tenth century, but even now, it is a mystery how the Polynesian inhabitants of Pitcairn Islands were able to accomplish a journey of at least two weeks in small canoes, carrying with them seeds, chickens, and drinking water.

Nowadays, the island is a flat, vegetationless expanse, but this was not always the case. In the past, it was covered with a variety of plants and trees, including especially a type of giant palm tree that grew in many parts of the territory, but of which there is no trace today. Instead, there are giant stone statues (known as *moai*) and around three hundred stone platforms (known as *ahu*) on which they stood. Both the *ahu* and the *moai* face inward, to the island's interior, probably toward the clan that was responsible for erecting them. The *ahu* is

---

[1] For more details on the Easter Island case see *Twilight at Easter*, in Jared Diamond's *Collapse: How Societies Choose to Fail or Succeed* (2005).

a rectangular platform, made of rubble fill held in place by four stone retaining walls of graybasalt. They are up to 4 meters in height and up to 150 meters in width, with an overall weight of between 300 and 9,000 tons. The *moai*, instead, are monolithic statues; that is, they are carved out of a single block of volcanic tuff. Some have a squat cylinder (*pukau*) on their heads that is made from another type of reddish tuff, which has been interpreted as a headdress or hairstyle once common among the island's men.

There are 887 statues on Easter Island, half of them still in the quarry of one of the island's three volcanoes, Rano Raraku, where almost all the statues were made. Fifty, however, were made in other quarries using a different type of tuff from that of Rano Raraku. The statues have an average height of 4 meters and a weight of around 10 tons, with the highest measuring 10 meters and weighing 75 tons. In the Rano Raraku quarry is a half-finished statue that was never erected, with a length of 21 meters and a weight of around 270 tons, because it was probably too high and heavy to be transported and set in place on an *ahu*. The construction of the statues began in the eleventh century and came to an end in the seventeenth century: the meaning of the *moai* is, however, still far from clear and many theories exist. According to the most popular explanation, the statues represent dead ancestors or important members of the community and were dedicated to them. The statues' size grew over time, likely to indicate the importance of the clan that built them. However, this race to build the biggest statue came to a sudden halt, leaving scholars with many questions concerning the end of the *moai* society.

The island is still inhabited today, but the civilization of the *moai* has vanished, as have the trees: Does a possible nexus exist between these two facts? The statues were created in the Rano Raraku quarry and then erected in various parts of the island, up to 14 kilometers in distance from the workplace. To transport and raise the statues, the inhabitants devised a method that involved two parallel wooden tracks held together by fixed wooden crosspieces. It is estimated that a group of fifty to seventy people, working five hours a day and moving the sled forwards 4.5 meters with every pull, could transport a 12-ton statue over a distance of 14 kilometers in one week.

The construction of the statues required a great deal of wood: to build the tracks, to create poles for levers with which to raise the statues, and also to make long, robust cables using the trees' fibrous bark. In addition, the activity of building, transporting, and raising the statues consumed a huge amount of energy and increased food requirements by around 25 percent in the three centuries of the most intense activity. This led to the extensive exploitation of vegetation, in particular the giant palms: the trees were used both for the erection of the *moai* and for the cremation of the dead. They were also cut down to make space for vegetable gardens, to build canoes used to navigate the open seas, and to provide firewood, among other activities. Finally, the palms were also fed upon by a species of rat, accidentally introduced by the first colonizers to arrive on the island. Over a few centuries, therefore, the indiscriminate use of the trees resulted in the total deforestation of the island, which proceeded in parallel with the epoch of the erection of the *moai*.

The consequences of this deforestation were disastrous not only for the environment, but for the population as well. Without trees, it was impossible to build new canoes for fishing. Moreover, the trees protected the interior of the island from wind and salinity, enabling agriculture. In the absence of this protection, cultivation was threatened, and the availability of food resources was reduced. The population also had less protection from the cold because it became impossible to build new shelters, and the exposed land was more vulnerable to landslides. In addition to all this, many animal species, including the birds that had become a vital food resource, became extinct. The balance based on the clan system and the role of the priests was overthrown by a rebellion led by warrior chiefs, who removed the priests and elite from power, and precipitated a civil war, following which the *moai* were demolished. Finally, there was a demographic collapse, and the practice of cannibalism became widespread.

In sum, after reaching a peak, with around 15,000 inhabitants, the Easter Island civilization went into swift decline, coming to an end around the seventeenth century, because of the deforestation caused by the construction of the statues. This is the case of a society that self-destructed through the extensive exploitation of resources. Two factors help explain this dramatic outcome. First, *landscape amnesia* prevented the inhabitants from being aware of the progressive destruction of the vegetation: year to year, the deforestation increased only marginally, thus making it difficult for the inhabitants to notice the change. However, taken as a whole over decades, the impact of deforestation was dramatic. Second, *collective myopia* hindered the comprehension of the long-term effects of the construction of the statues. The *moai* society did not realize the extent to which it was using natural resources, particularly in an isolated territory and with geological features that were highly vulnerable to this type of exploitation.

1.2 Myopia of a nation: the 9/11 terrorist attacks

The 9/11 terrorist attacks against the United States seem an incomprehensible event if we consider the asymmetry of the forces involved: on the one hand, nineteen Islamic terrorists members of al Qaeda, trained in Afghanistan and, on the other hand, the world's most powerful nation, which spends billions of dollars each year on national security. The former managed to evade the security systems of three of the United States' biggest airports, hijack four airplanes, and destroy the Twin Towers and part of the Pentagon with three of the planes. The fourth plane was headed towards Washington, DC, with the probable aim of attacking either the US Capitol or the White House. In an extremely limited amount of time, four or five hijackers on each flight took control of four long-range domestic flights by using knives, pepper spray, and threats. By turning off the transponder, they made it extremely hard for the air traffic controllers to track their route. The result: nearly 3,000 dead, billions of dollars of damage, and a defense system that was revealed to be highly defective.

The terrorist attacks took place in a short time; its preparation had lasted years. To understand the event, we should distinguish between two different phases – the hijacking and the preparation phase – and answer the following questions: *Could the US defense system have managed the hijacking in a different way? Could the al Qaeda suicide mission have been foreseen?* Let's start from the first question.[2]

Could the US defense system have managed the hijacking in a different way?

There are three main organizations responsible for the US air defense: for the air traffic control, the Federal Aviation Administration (FAA);

---

[2] The analysis of the 9/11 terrorist attacks is mainly based on *The 9/11 Commission Report. Final Report* of the National Commission on Terrorist Attacks on the United States (NCTA 2004).

for the military air defense, the North American Air Defense Command (NORAD); and for the president and the government. The FAA is responsible for regulating the safety and security of civil aviation. Its primary task is to maintain a safe distance between airborne aircrafts. The FAA is articulated in twenty-two control centers that receive information and make operational decisions independently. The coordination is guaranteed by one command center (the national control operations center). NORAD is a binational command that was established by the United States and Canada in 1958. Its mission is to defend the airspace of North America and to protect the continent. In the United States, NORAD is divided into three sectors. On 9/11, all the hijacked aircrafts were in NORAD's Northeast Air Defense Sector, known as NEADS.[3]

Let us now consider the timeline of the events and how the defense system responded to these events (Tables 1.1–1.4). Later, I compare this response with the procedures of the defense system in force in 2001.

Table 1.1 shows the timeline of the events for the first flight, AA11. Only 27 minutes passed from the moment of the first communication concerning the hijacking of flight AA11 until its collision with the North Tower of the World Trade Center in New York City.

In the case of the second flight, UA175, 11 minutes passed from the moment of the first communication of its hijacking until its collision with the South Tower of the World Trade Center in New York City (Table 1.2). Because of its total concentration on Flight AA11, the air traffic control did not even notice flight UA175's disappearance. The air force was not notified at all.

The third flight, AA77, vanished from the radar of the air traffic control and was identified thereafter by Dulles control center, but the FAA did not ask the air force for assistance and did not report anything to the military authorities before the crash (Table 1.3). At 9:21 AM, FAA misinformed NEADS (NORAD) about the number of aircrafts. NEADS acted on the confusion that AA11 was still airborne, while instead this flight had crashed in the first tower. NEADS scrambled Langley Air Force base to intercept this *phantom aircraft*. The confusion increased. Here's an extract of FAA's report to NEADS:

[3] NEADS reports to CONR (Continental NORAD Region), CONR to NORAD.

FAA:	Military, Boston Center. I just had a report that American 11 is still in the air, and it's on its way towards – heading towards Washington.
NEADS:	Okay. American 11 is still in the air?
FAA:	Yes.
NEADS:	On its way towards Washington?
FAA:	That was another – it was evidently another aircraft that hit the tower. That's the latest report we have.
NEADS:	Okay.
FAA:	I'm going to try to confirm an ID for you, but I would assume he's somewhere over, uh, either New Jersey or somewhere further south.
NEADS:	Okay. So American 11 isn't the hijack at all then, right?
FAA:	No, he is a hijack.
NEADS:	He – American 11 is a hijack?
FAA:	Yes.
NEADS:	And he's heading into Washington?
FAA:	Yes. This could be a third aircraft.

Table 1.1. *American Airlines 11 (AA11), flying from Boston to Los Angeles*

7:59	Takeoff
8:14	After last routine radio communication, the hijacking begins[4]
8:19	Flight attendant notifies American Airlines (AA) of hijacking
8:21	Transponder is turned off
8:23	AA attempts to contact the cockpit
8:25	Boston Center becomes aware of hijacking
8:38	Boston Center notifies NEADS of hijacking
8:46	NEADS scrambles Otis fighter jets in search of AA11
8:46:40	AA11 crashes into WTC (North Tower)
8:53	Otis fighter jets airborne
9:16	AA headquarters aware that flight 11 has crashed into WTC
9:24	NEADS scrambles Langley fighter in search of AA11

Note: NEADS = Northeast Air Defense Sector (NORAD); WTC = World Trade Center.

---

[4] "We do not know exactly how the hijackers gained access to the cockpit; FAA rules required that the doors remain closed and locked during flight ... Perhaps the terrorists stabbed the flight attendants to get a cockpit key, to force one of them to open the cockpit door, or to lure the captain or first officer out of the cockpit. Or the flight attendants may just have been in their way" (NCTA 2004, p. 5).

Table 1.2. *United Airlines Flight 175 (UA175), flying from Boston to Los Angeles*

8:14	Takeoff
8:42	Last radio communication
8:42–8:46	Likely takeover
8:47	Transponder code changes
8:52	Flight attendant notifies UA of hijacking
8:54	UA attempts to contact the cockpit
8:55	New York Center suspects hijacking
9:03:11	Flight 175 crashes into WTC (South Tower)
9:15	New York Center advises NEADS that Flight 175 was the second aircraft crashed into WTC
9:20	UA Headquarters aware that Flight 175 has crashed into WTC

Note: WTC = World Trade Center; NEADS = Northeast Air Defense Sector (NORAD).

Table 1.3. *American Airlines Flight 77 (AA77), flying from Washington, DC to Los Angeles*

8:20	Takeoff
8:51	Last routine radio communication
8:51–8:54	Likely takeover
8:54	Flight 77 makes unauthorized turn to south
8:56	Transponder is turned off
9:05	AA Headquarters aware that Flight 77 is hijacked
9:25	Herndon Command Center orders nationwide ground stop
9:32	Dulles tower observes radar of fast-moving aircraft (later identified as AA77)
9:34	FAA advises NEADS that AA77 is missing
9:37:46	AA77 crashes into the Pentagon
10:30	AA Headquarters confirms Flight 77's crash into Pentagon

Note: FAA = Federal Aviation Administration; NEADS = Northeast Air Defense Sector (NORAD).

Obviously, the true situation was still not clear to the main authorities involved (FAA and NORAD-NEADS), and indeed, the confusion intensified as the number of aircraft involved increased: although two planes had struck the World Trade Center towers, the FAA headquarters in Washington informed the Boston center that AA11 was still

Table 1.4. *United Airlines Flight 93 (UA93), flying from Newark to San Francisco*

8:42	Takeoff
9:24	Flight 93 receives warning from UA about possible cockpit intrusion
9:27	Last radio communication
9:28	Likely takeover
9:34	Herndon Command Center advises FAA headquarters that UA93 is hijacked
9:36	Flight attendant notifies UA of hijacking; UA attempts to contact the cockpit
9:41	Transponder is turned off
9:57	Passenger revolt begins
10:03:11	Flight 93 crashes in field in Shanskville, PA
10:07	Cleveland Center advises NEADS of UA93 hijacking
10:15	UA Headquarters aware that Flight 93 has crashed in PA; Washington Center advises NEADS that Flight 93 has crashed in PA

Note: NEADS = Northeast Air Defense Sector (NORAD).

airborne (NCTA 2004, p. 26). Moreover, even when it considered the possibility of a *third aircraft*, it did not refer to AA77. Finally, at 9:34 AM, NEADS contacted the FAA to look for flight AA11, which, in reality, had already crashed 48 minutes before (at 8:46 AM, in fact).

The fourth flight, UA93 (see Table 1.4), ploughed into an empty field in Shanksville, Pennsylvania, at 580 miles per hour, about 20 minutes' flying time from Washington, DC. The heroic revolt of alerted, unarmed passengers prevented the hijackers from crashing the airliner into their intended target (probably a symbol of the US government). In this case, the chain of command was activated swiftly following the communication between Cleveland center and FAA headquarters, and the FAA set up a line between the various centers and the command center. The FAA did not, however, seek the help of the military, who were informed only in the aftermath of the crash.

The 9/11 terrorist attacks took place in a time interval that ran from 7:59 AM (the takeoff of the first plane) to 10:03:11 AM, when the last of the four planes crashed (see Table 1.5), a total time of just

Table 1.5. *Summary of the hijacking timelines*

	Takeoff	First communication	Awareness of hijacking	Collision	Time between awareness and collision
AA11 (WTC Tower North)	7:59	8:19	8:25	8:46:40	21 minutes
UA175 (WTC Tower South)	8:14	8:52	8:55	9:03:11	8 minutes
AA77 (Pentagon)	8:20	/	9:05	9:37:46	32 minutes
UA93 (Shanksville)	8:42	9:36	9:34	10:03:11	29 minutes

Note: WTC = World Trade Center; / = data not found.

2 hours, 4 minutes, and 11 seconds. If we take into consideration the moment at which the air traffic control (or the airline) became aware that the planes had been hijacked, then the overall time for the reaction is reduced to 1 hour, 38 minutes, and 11 seconds. Awareness for the first two airplanes emerges a few minutes after the first communication is received, whereas for the remaining planes, awareness of hijacking derives from the aircrafts' suspicious behavior.

What could have been done in such a short time? To answer this question, we should consider the air defense procedures that were in place in 2001.

Air defense system procedure

NORAD carried out military exercises dealing with terrorist attacks, but never simulated (or even conceived of) a *suicide mission* involving the hijacking of passenger aircraft. Thus, there were no guidelines for this type of event. The FAA and NORAD protocol in case of hijacking requires that:

1. pilots notify the controller of the hijacking;
2. the controller notifies supervisors;
3. supervisors inform Control Center Management (CCM);
4. CCM informs FAA headquarters in Washington;

5. the director of the FAA Office of Civil Aviation Security takes on the role of hijack coordinator;
6. hijack coordinator contacts Pentagon to ask for military escort aircraft;
7. Pentagon seeks approval from the Secretary of Defense;
8. if approved, orders are transmitted down NORAD chain of command;
9. Pentagon helps FAA coordination with the military.

The implicit assumptions of the protocols in place on 9/11 for the FAA and NORAD to respond to a hijacking presumed that:

- the hijacked aircraft would be readily identifiable and would not attempt to disappear;
- there would be time to address the problem through the appropriate FAA and NORAD chains of command;
- the hijacking would take the traditional form: that is, it would not be a suicide hijacking designed to convert the aircraft into a guided missile (NCTA 2004, p. 18).

In addition, the assumption was that information would be clear and not ambiguous, subject to interpretation and requiring time for clarification and confirmation.

Unfortunately, on the morning of 9/11, the existing protocol was unsuited in every respect for what was about to happen. Despite some violations of procedure (in the case of flight AA11, the Boston air traffic controllers informed NEADS directly without first passing through the FAA) and unscheduled shortcuts, the military aircraft took off after everything had already occurred and, moreover, in a situation of complete lack of clarity in terms of what was actually happening. When Vice President Dick Cheney's order to "intercept" the commercial flights was issued is not clear; there was confusion within NORAD relating to the nature of the order. Finally, whether the pilots received the order is not clear.

What happened on 9/11 showed (a) the weakness of established routines in unexpected circumstances, such as suicide missions; (b) how human mistakes create a sequence of interdependent failure; (c) the problems of coordinating between large organizations that rarely operate together on a daily basis; (d) the difficulty of operating on an extremely tight time schedule; and (e) that the defense system was not prepared and the personnel were not trained for events of this type.

As stated by the 9/11 Commission:

> The details of what happened on the morning of September 11 are complex, but they play out a simple theme. NORAD and the FAA were unprepared for the type of attacks launched against the United States on September 11. They struggled, under difficult circumstances, to improvise a homeland defense against an unprecedented challenge they had never before encountered and had never trained to meet. (NCTA 2004, p. 45)

Therefore, the response to the initial question – *could the US defense system have managed the hijacking in a different way?* – can only be a negative one, given the procedures and coordination rules in force at the time. The homeland defense system was not prepared for an attack of this kind and could not have handled the situation in a more effective way than it in fact did. As Lagadec (1993, p. 54) affirms, "the ability to deal with a crisis situation is largely dependent on the structures that have been developed before chaos arrives. The event can in some ways be considered as an abrupt and brutal audit: at a moment's notice, everything that was left unprepared becomes a complex problem, and every weakness comes rushing to the forefront."

Lagadec continues (1993, p. 66), saying, "The ability to learn quickly is precisely what is called for in a crisis." Yet, to learn quickly in a crisis, it is necessary to have already learned enough earlier. This leads us to the second question.

Could the al Qaeda suicide mission have been foreseen?

If the defense system could not avoid or contain the damage in such a short time (1 hour, 38 minutes, and 11 seconds), could it have forecast a threat of this type and made suitable arrangements to counter it? There was a great deal of relevant information that could (or should) have alerted the US defense system. In fact, many reports warned of an attack on the United States. Why were these not heeded? Were the 9/11 terrorist attacks a bolt from the blue or an avoidable failure? The answer to these questions is more complex than the answer to the preceding one (if the event could have been handled in a different way). It is necessary to take into account (a) the nature of the

information available and (b) the modalities of operation, organization, and coordination of the various organizations dedicated to US
homeland defense.

In 1997, the Gore Commission, which was set up in July 1996 in
response to an airplane accident which was mistakenly interpreted as
a terrorist attack,[5] produced a report containing twenty recommendations for the implementation of new measures to provide safeguards
from terrorist attacks. These recommendations asked for the use of
more efficient instruments for the identification of terrorists at airports
and a more selective screening of passengers. The Gore Commission
displayed a great deal of concern in relation to the dangers of sabotage and the use of explosives on airplanes, even though it did not
devote particular attention to the possibility of suicide hijackers. In
brief, the report of the Gore Commission displayed a very high awareness that the threat of terrorism was changing and growing. Many of
the recommendations were not implemented, due to pressure from the
air industry lobby or bureaucratic sluggishness. In 1998, several US
terrorism experts, reanalyzing recent terrorist threats regarding airplanes and events that had taken place in various countries,[6] presented
the FAA with a list of worrying scenarios, including the possibility of
suicide missions with cargo aircraft against nuclear power plants, the
Twin Towers, the White House, the Pentagon, and other objectives. In
1999, during the hijack of a plane belonging to an Indian airline in
Kandahar, Afghanistan, the terrorists used knives that were not picked
up at check-in, and cut the throat of one passenger, leaving the victim
to bleed to death, as did the Twin Tower terrorists. The possibility that
terrorists might therefore take control of a plane's pilot cabin due to
the ease with which the cockpit door could be opened was something
that had been known for years.

There were many signals relating to possible terrorist attack during the first few months of 2001. CIA director George Tenet noted
that "the system was blinking red" (NCTA 2004, p. 254) during the
summer months. From January to September 2001, there were more

---

[5] On July 17, 1996, TWA 800, a Boeing 747-131, exploded and crashed into the
Atlantic Ocean near New York, killing all 230 people on board. Despite initial
thoughts of it being a terrorist event, the government's conclusion was that
TWA 800 accident was caused by mechanical failure.

[6] Such as threats to the Eiffel Tower in Paris or the small plane that crashed into
the White House in 1994.

than forty reports regarding Osama Bin Laden in the President's Daily
Brief, the report that the president receives each day from the CIA concerning the principal threats to national security (NCTA 2004).[7] Many
other signals came from other agencies and in the spring of 2001, the
level of reporting on terrorist threats increased dramatically:

- On June 22, 2001, the CIA warned of a possible attack on American
  soil.
- On June 25, 2001, a message on an Arab television station announced
  important surprises against the United States and Israel.
- On June 28, 2001, National Security Council (NSC) Counterterrorism
  coordinator Richard Clarke sent a memo to National Security Advisor
  Condoleeza Rice regarding the increasing alarm relating to a possible
  attack by Bin Laden and al Qaeda.
- On July 2, 2001, the FBI sent out a red alert message to law enforcement agencies to watch out for any kind of suspect activity. A spec-
  tacular attack on the United States was feared, but there was also
  the possibility of one abroad.
- On August 6, 2001, the CIA briefing mentioned a potential attack in
  the United States, but notwithstanding the large number of threats,
  there was no specific information regarding time, place, method,
  and target.

Going back to the fundamental question, *Was the attack on the Twin
Towers foreseeable?* Some believe that it was not, or at least only with
great difficulty and a robust hindsight bias (NCTA 2004). According to
many others, it was indeed predictable on the basis of the information
available (Bazerman and Watkins 2005; Perrow 2007). Mohamedou
(2007) states that the story of al Qaeda and its conflict with the United
States and its allies indicates that the events of 9/11 were not wholly
unpredictable. The attack was a military operation that had been
planned since 1996 and had been carried out by a commando team
trained in the context of a war that had been officially and publically
declared in 1996 and then again in 1998. Incorrect security policies
and a profound organizational hubris (arrogance) led to the homeland
defense system's undervaluation of the clear messages sent out in the

---

[7] Each President's Daily Brief consists of a series of six to eight relatively short
articles or briefs covering a broad array of topics. CIA staff decide which
subjects are the most important on any given day.

preceding decade. Perrow (2007) states that not having predicted and avoided the attack on the Twin Towers is a manifestation of the failure of the George W. Bush administration. Bush's responsibility, maintains Perrow, lies in the fact that his administration had ignored clear documentation provided by the defense system regarding terrorist threats and was thus unprepared for the eventual attack. As Clarke testified, "I believe the Bush administration in the first eight months considered terrorism an important issue but not an urgent issue."[8] The threat of Osama bin Laden and al Qaeda was not considered as a political priority.

Bazerman and Watkins believe that the events of 9/11 were predictable in that they were *predictable surprises*. They define a predictable surprise "as an event or set of events that take an organization by surprise, although leaders had all of the information necessary to anticipate the events and their consequences" (Bazerman and Watkins 2005, p. 366). Various official reports from the GAO (Government Accountability Office, the investigative branch of the US Congress) produced in 1987, 1990, and 2000 had identified the possible threat to air security, both from the use of explosives and from terrorism. Bazerman and Watkins (2005) believe that a key responsibility of leaders is to identify and avoid predictable surprises. Leaders must have the vision and courage to understand the barriers (cognitive, organizational, and political) that hinder a situational awareness and act to overcome them. The political and administrational elite is therefore responsible, in accordance with the two authors, for not having acted to avoid 9/11 and for not having confronted or having known how to confront a predictable surprise. The event was foreseeable in that the work of the Gore Commission had supplied a great deal of evidence regarding the risks and the vulnerability of US security. These risks, however, were not adequately analyzed by the successive Bush administrations.

In his testimony, Clarke said that "he thought that warning about the possibility of a suicide hijacking would have been just one more speculative theory among many, hard to spot since the volume of warnings of al Qaeda threats and other terrorist threats was in the tens of thousands – probably hundreds of thousands" (NCTA 2004,

---

[8] Mr. Richard A. Clarke, Eighth Public Hearing, Panel III, Wednesday, March 24, 2004, p. 104.

p. 345). Yet the possibility of a suicide hijacking was imaginable, and imagined, observes the NCTA.

If terrorist threats were imaginable and imagined, the questions to answer become why was the defense system not adequately alarmed and why did it not improve security conditions, as indicated by the Gore Commission? Was it only an executive and political failure?

To try to explain why the attacks were not predicted, two interrelated levels must be taken into consideration: the individual (cognitive) and the organizational and interorganizational level (in Chapter 3, this analytical model will be looked at more closely in terms of the different levels and factors which can foster organizational myopia).

Individual and cognitive factors: the failure of imagination

The idea of a suicide attack with commercial aircrafts on American territory was outside the cognitive schemes of the defense system. The event closest to it in time was the Japanese attack on Pearl Harbor in December 1941, or other similar events such as the German invasion of the Soviet Union in 1941, the North Korean invasion of South Korea in 1950, or the Yom Kippur war in 1973. But these were morphologically different events and far from recent.

The information existed, but crucially, a model for the event was lacking. Hijacking was traditionally regarded as an instrument to obtain money, political recognition, the freedom of political detainees, or a mixture of all three. Moreover, the last hijacking had taken place ten years before, and there was no longer any particular fear regarding this type of event. The traditional conception of hijacking led to the undervaluation of the memo from the FBI in Minneapolis concerning Zacarias Moussaoui, arrested for an immigration visa violation.

Moussaoui had entered the United States in February 2001 and had begun flight lessons at Airman Flight School in Norman, Oklahoma. He resumed his training at Pan Am International Flight Academy in Egan, Minnesota. His behavior was suspect for many reasons. He had joined the school on his own initiative, while the students who followed flight training for Boeing 747s normally arrived in groups, sent there by airline companies. In particular, he wanted the instructors to teach him how to takeoff and land a Boeing 747 aircraft, even though he did not work for a commercial airline and had little knowledge of flying. He said he did not intend to become a commercial pilot but wanted the training as an *ego-boosting thing* (NCTA 2004, p. 273). The FBI agents discovered that Moussaoui possessed jihadist beliefs; he had $32,000 in his bank account with no explanation of where the money came from; he had traveled to Pakistan and became extremely worried when the agents asked him if he had visited nearby countries while in Pakistan (this country was one of the main routes used in order to reach the training camps in Afghanistan). "The agent concluded that Moussaoui was an Islamic extremist preparing for some future act in furtherance of radical fundamentalist goals. He also believed Moussaoui's plan was related to his flight training" (NCTA 2004, p. 273).

The undervaluing of the Moussaoui case can be seen as a missed opportunity. At the time, the fact that an Islamic person was attending a course to become a pilot of a commercial aircraft and that his behavior was far from convincing was not deemed worthy of any particular attention. This information was not adequately related to other threats in order to build a plausible scenario for a new threat. This was because the cognitive frame[9] of the US defense system did not include the representation of the *aircraft as weapon*.

It should be specified that many of the alarm signals and much of the information preceding 9/11 were vague, imprecise, and confused, with information and messages regarding false threats. Parker and Stern (2005) highlight many cognitive factors at an individual/cognitive level that constituted serious obstacles to recognizing meaningful information: cognitive overload, interpretive ambiguity and receptivity fatigue, the signal-to-noise problem, and the cry-wolf phenomenon. Many of these factors and biases are analyzed in Chapter 3.

One problem at an individual/cognitive level pertains to the so-called routinization of tension (Betts 1982, 2007). There had been many fears of possible terrorist attacks previously in 2000, but numerous cases turned out to be false alarms. This led to the so-called cry-wolf phenomenon, where the great number of false alarms reduced sensitivity to warnings. The agencies were inundated with data, but the information was nebulous and the 9/11 Commission found that it was difficult to conclude with any certainty if the threats reported were in reality specifically connectable to the Twin Tower attacks. Post facto,

---

[9] Cognitive frames are the mental structures, beliefs, and tacit assumptions that simplify and guide people toward the understanding of a complex reality.

it is easier to say that certain information was signal and other was noise. Unfortunately, this is much harder to determine ex ante.

Betts (1982, 2007) points out how detecting alarm or danger signals beforehand may, on the one hand, have the positive effect of dissuading the attackers from proceeding with their plan but, on the other hand, may have the negative effect of being read as a false alarm, if the attack itself is never verified.

Myopia at an individual level is related to the fact that if no model for an event exists, then the event is extremely difficult to predict; it is a problem of expectations and *sensemaking* (Weick 1995). Pieces of information flow in and their importance can only be registered if a *frame* exists to give sense to their multiplicity. Without such a frame, information can appear irrelevant: the frame of the defense system did not foresee the use of an airplane as a weapon and was thought to be well equipped and adequate for any new threats. It is true that the idea of a suicide hijacking had also been imagined by Richard Clarke, but he imagined aircraft *with* explosives, not aircraft *as* explosives (Weick 2005a).

Paradoxically, the fact that the FBI had arrested the Islamic terrorists responsible for the World Trade Center bombing on February 26, 1993, in a short time helped reinforce the idea that the system was well-defended and that things would also run smoothly in the event of an attack: "there were no new menaces for the defense." This was certainly a failure of imagination: "the methods for detecting and then warning of surprise attack that the US government had so painstakingly developed in the decades after Pearl Harbor did not fail; instead, they were not really tried. They were not employed to analyze the enemy that, as the twentieth century closed, was most likely to launch a surprise attack directly against the United States" (NCTA 2004, pp. 347–8). The theme of imagination is discussed also in Chapters 3 and 5.

Organizational and interorganizational factors: the failure to connect the dots

The *organizational* level refers to the logic of the functioning of single organizations, to the modality of division and organization of work, integration, and coordination. Finally, the *interorganizational* level refers to the complex network of relations between the various agencies and organizations charged with internal security, to the modalities of communication and sharing of information. At these levels, organizational and governmental decision making is seen as organizational output, dependent upon the goals, structures, preferences, power, norms, rules, routines, and interests of the organizations involved (March and Olsen 1989; Allison and Zelikow 1999). Such a perspective highlights the extremely politicized nature of organizational life and the impact that inter- and intra-agency parochialism, rivalry, and competition can have on the decision-making processes and on the evaluation of information and threats. The approach focuses on the interaction between multiple agencies and organizations in a pluralistic politico-administrative environment (Allison and Zelikow 1999).

The problem of terrorism regards many different organizations such as the State Department, the Defense Department, the Justice Department, the Transportation Department, the NSC staff, the CIA, the NSA, the armed services intelligence agencies, the FBI, the FAA, the customs and immigration services, and numerous state and local police jurisdictions. In turn, these organizations are made up of several subunits. In order to discover terrorist plans beforehand, it is necessary to integrate all source intelligence: to connect the dots, in other words. Unfortunately, complex organizations develop a set of mechanisms that tends to isolate the dots. Organizational fragmentation and organizational structure, particularly if they are maladapted to a particular mission, can create minor and ruinous problems in cooperation, coordination, and policy attainment (Parker and Stern 2005).

As the NCTA affirmed, there were "*structural barriers to performing joint intelligence work*. National intelligence is still organized around the collection disciplines of the home agencies, not the joint mission. The importance of integrated, all source analysis cannot be overstated. Without it, it is not possible to 'connect the dots.' No one component holds all the relevant information" (NCTA 2004, p. 408).

Sandy Berger, national security advisor to the Clinton administration, stated, "we've learned since 9/11 that not only did we not know what we didn't know, but the FBI didn't know what it did know." It is a clear affirmation of an organizational problem relating to the management and circulation of information. The National Commission on Terrorist Attacks (NCTA) points out that while terrorists evolved and adapted, the homeland defense system moved with the slow trudge of bureaucracy. Faced with an evolution of threat represented by al Qaeda, the defense system maintained its bureaucratic organization.

It was difficult to share information, perform reliable analysis, and coordinate actions in order to respond to threat.

Agencies were in fact inundated with a multitude of signals, but the problem was how to distinguish relevant information from noise. It was certainly not possible to verify and go more deeply into all the pieces of information and all the weak signals. There were ten missed operational opportunities to assemble enough of the puzzle pieces gathered by different agencies to make some sense of them and then develop a fully informed joint plan (NCTA 2004). An example of organization failure, coordination problems, lack of information sharing, and unreliable interorganizational learning is the case of unusual people taking flying lessons. Some FBI agents were suspicious about this. As the NCTA stated:

In July 2001, an FBI agent in the Phoenix field office sent a memo to FBI headquarters and to two agents on international terrorism squads in the New York Field Office, advising of the "possibility of a coordinated effort by Osama Bin Laden to send students to the United States to attend civil aviation schools." The agent based his theory on the "inordinate number of individuals of investigative interest" attending such schools in Arizona. The agent made four recommendations to FBI headquarters: to compile a list of civil aviation schools, establish liaison with those schools, discuss his theories about Bin Laden with the intelligence community, and seek authority to obtain visa information on persons applying to flight schools. His recommendations were not acted on. ... No managers at headquarters saw the memo before September 11, and the New York Field Office took no action. ... If the memo had been distributed in a timely fashion and its recommendations acted on promptly, we do not believe it would have uncovered the plot. It might well, however, have sensitized the FBI so that it might have taken the Moussaoui matter more seriously the next month. (NCTA 2004, p. 272)

The raw data was there, but organizations failed to make sense of it, they "failed to transform it into meaningful information, one might say, and to further transform the information into evidence to support decisions and actions" (Bardach 2005, p. 353). Organizations failed to connect the dots. "Information was not shared, sometimes inadvertently or because of legal misunderstandings. Analysis was not pooled. Effective operations were not launched. Often the hand-offs of information were lost across the divide separating the foreign and domestic agencies of the government" (NCTA 2004, p. 353). The agencies worked as specialists, without sharing information, even if this regarded similar cases. *Information jealousy* was widespread and reinforced by a reward system that favored those who solved cases (and why, therefore, should someone give assistance to someone else if this meant threatening the former's possibility of success, visibility, power, and money?). The consequence was the absence of *joint operations* between the various agencies: each one went its own way. Competition prevailed over cooperation and not only at an interorganizational level (between the FBI and the CIA, for example) but also at an intraorganizational level, within the same agency, as in the case of the FBI and its various field offices. The FBI was divided into fifty-six territorial offices, and each one made decisions based on local, rather than national, priorities. The individual offices were therefore reluctant to deal with problems that were not under their own control and authority. The organizational reforms introduced in 1993 by director Louis Freeh had led to a huge decentralization of operations, giving more power to territorial offices and increasing the importance of working by projects. Any student of management would hold this to be the best possible choice. The problem is that if processes of differentiation are not combined with correspondingly adequate levels of coordination and integration (Lawrence and Lorsch 1967; Snook 2000), then the differentiation becomes pathological and dysfunctional throughout the entire system.

The importance of organizational coordination[10] is well-known in organizational theory (Thompson 1967; Lawrence and Lorsch 1967). Heath and Staudenmayer (2000) define *coordination neglect* as the failure to effectively integrate and distribute tasks undertaken by different members of an organization. "When individuals design organizational processes or when they participate in them, they frequently fail to understand that coordination is important and they fail to take steps to minimize the difficulty of coordination" (Heath and Staudenmayer 2000, p. 157).

Pushing operations and decisional levels lower had led to a lack of general vision, the *big picture*, in the system. The powerful move to decentralize and work by project cases reduced, or even obstructed,

---

[10] Coordination here is understood as the effective regulation of interdependence between a variety of actors and/or organizations.

the possibility of linking the collective awareness of the agents in
the field with national priorities. FBI agent training was inappropriate, with only three days out of a sixteen-week course dedicated to
combating terrorism. The scarce availability of translators also made
investigative activity regarding potential Arab terrorists difficult. The
absence of a system of efficient *knowledge management* meant that
the information and knowledge (of interrogators and investigations)
were not adequately integrated and diffused. An important aspect
was that the FBI focused primarily on investigating crimes after they
had occurred, a reactive case-based approach, and not on gathering intelligence proactively to prevent crimes before they happened.
Finally, the FBI also tended not to share information with other
organizations due to the fear of losing the opportunity of solving a
crime.[11]

The CIA also exhibited many of the problems already seen relating
to the FBI, such as *information jealousy* and the scarce circulation of
knowledge. Both the CIA and the FBI had developed their central capabilities around traditional missions and threats. Their current security
culture was developed and established during the Cold War, and they
had never evolved their organizational and cognitive schemata to confront the new challenges and threats posed by Islamic terrorism. Since
the end of the Cold War, both the CIA and the FBI failed to adapt to
the growth of terrorism. Reconstructing the histories of reforms in the
two agencies and the efforts of counterterrorism in the decade 1991–
2001, analyzing government documents and conducting more than
seventy interviews with high-level defense figures in the government,
Zegart (2007) demonstrates how political leaders were well aware
of the terrorist threat and of the need to reform the defense system.
Resistance within the intelligence system, political interests, and bureaucratic careerism, with the fragmentation of the federal structure,
fostered an unjustified organizational inertia with regard to change.

---

[11] "There were other legal limitations. Both prosecutors and FBI agents argued
that they were barred by court rules from sharing grand jury information,
even though the prohibition applied only to that small fraction that had been
presented to a grand jury, and even that prohibition had exceptions. But,
as interpreted by FBI field offices, this prohibition could conceivably apply
to much of the information unearthed in an investigation. There were also
restrictions, arising from executive order, on the commingling of domestic
information with foreign intelligence" (NCTA 2004, pp. 79–80).

These were determining factors in the failure to take advantage of the many opportunities to prevent the 9/11 terrorist attacks.

The problems therefore regarded both the functioning of individual agencies and the coordination between them. At an organizational level, these included an inability to pay attention to anomalies, difficulty in relating local inquiries to national priorities, low circulation of information, information jealousy, and a case-based organization that involuntarily rewarded non-collaboration. The same problems were displayed at an interorganizational and system level, with one further dilemma: the personnel at the base of the hierarchical chain spent their time gathering information relating to threats, but often their limited awareness of the big picture hindered them from collocating this information in an adequate and mindful frame. In contrast, the personnel at the top of the hierarchy could see the big picture clearly but had no time to give sufficient attention to the information percolating up from below.

It is a classic organizational and informational problem. Kelman (2005) highlights several problems with the handling of information. For example, in the case of private enterprise, analysis of the environment is carried out by top management, assisted by a small staff, whereas in the case of the US government and administration, there is a multiplicity of actors involved at a variety of levels. The overall picture is certainly far more difficult to reconstruct and less easy to share. In the case previously analyzed, the defense system found itself facing the terrorist threat in a situation in which information was known to one organization but completely unknown to another, or was known in various parts of the system but not in a comprehensive manner. In other cases, information was known to a single person but was not brought together with other information, even when its importance became evident (as in the memo regarding Zacarias Moussaoui). Finally, taken as a whole, the great amount of information available was not understood, in that it was not possible to collocate it within an adequate interpretive context. Instead, it was analyzed and weighed according to schemata that were already in use.

The problems that emerged, states the *9/11 Commission Report* (NCTA 2004), were symptoms of the government's general inability to adapt itself to dealing with the new problems and challenges of the twenty-first century. Public organizations failed to adapt their core capabilities to the changing environment of new terrorism. The organizational hubris of the US defense system, based on the myth of invincibility, was reinforced by the successes preceding 9/11. This hubris, combined with a defense model still based on the opposing factions of the Cold War, fostered organizational myopia in relation to giving the correct importance to signals and threats and to predicting what was going to happen.

Cognitive factors at an individual level contributed to myopia, rendering it extremely difficult to make sense of new threats. Organizational and interorganizational criticalities made the US defense system vulnerable to terrorist attacks. The agencies operated like a set of specialists in a hospital: each one ordered tests, looked for symptoms, prescribed solutions, but what they did not do was work together as a team. Structural barriers existed to cooperative work: the agencies were organized around discipline and not around shared participation in a joint mission; their attention was focused principally on what they found, forgetting that the priorities were national ones (NCTA 2004). At a macro-level, the system failed to adapt its abilities to the discontinuous environmental changes that increased with the emergence of anti-Western terrorism.

Parker and Stern (2005, p. 324) observe that "vigilant response to threat depends upon individuals who perceive, feel, and act. These individuals are enabled and constrained by the multilayered and highly complex institutional structures in which they are embedded."

In conclusion, we must be extremely cautious in holding certain strategic surprises to be predictable only because information relating to their possible manifestation was present. People tend to overestimate the ability to predict a determined result once they have become aware of the result itself. Once we know what has occurred, there exists a greater propensity to state that this was in fact predictable. Fischhoff (1975; Slovic, Fischhoff, and Lichtenstein 1982) calls this behavior *hindsight bias*, in other words, a retrospective distortion of judgment. As Roberta Wohlstetter (1962, p. 387) affirms, it is "much easier after the event to sort the relevant from the irrelevant signals. After the event, of course, a signal is always crystal clear; we can now see what disaster it was signalling since the disaster had occurred. But before the event it is obscure and pregnant with conflicting meanings."

1.3 Myopia of an organization: NASA and the space shuttle accidents

At 11:38 AM (East Coast time) on January 28, 1986, the *Challenger* space shuttle, launched from Cape Kennedy by NASA, exploded. It was a tragedy, not only for the loss of lives but also for the heavy blow dealt to NASA and the space industry, the shattering of an omnipotent technological myth. The presidential inquiry commission led by William Roger verified that the technical cause of the accident was the breaking of the O-rings. The O-rings join segments of the solid rocket boosters (SRBs) and prevent leakage of hot gases during take-off. The accident was caused by the fact that one ring had not held and the released fuel gas had, like a blowtorch, perforated a component, triggering a sequence of events that brought about the accident less than two minutes after the launch. The technical design of the shuttle provided for two gaskets, guaranteeing safety through redundancy, so that if the first O-ring was damaged, the second would nevertheless halt the escape of the rocket fuel. But the cold weather of the preceding days, particularly the night before the launch, had hardened the rubber of both rings, eroding them.

The NASA personnel were aware of the possible consequences of cold on the O-rings. On the evening prior the launch, people from NASA and SRB manufacturer Morton Thiokol (the company that had manufactured the O-rings) participated in a teleconference to discuss whether to postpone the shuttle launch. During the teleconference, Morton Thiokol engineer Roger Boisjoly argued that the shuttle's O-rings might not perform well at low temperature.

They concluded that it was best to postpone the launch until environmental conditions had improved, with a higher external temperature. But the NASA management expressed a great deal of perplexity about the postponement, emphasizing the fact that several delays had already taken place. Moreover, they maintained that no formal univocal correlation had been established concerning the relationship between external temperature and the grip of the O-rings. Morton Thiokol had at first opted for a postponement, but in the end, its management did not recommend against launch: the company's vice president stated that "we have to think like managers and not like engineers" and said he was in favor of the launch. The Morton Thiokol's official position had therefore changed, and the launch for the day after was approved.

The checks carried out on the shuttle during the night and in the early morning resulted in a further delay, but, at 8:30 AM, the astronaut crew entered the pilot's cabin and at 11:38 AM, *Challenger* took off. The explosion occurred seventy-two seconds later. The commission of inquiry decided that the responsibility for the event was NASA's, because it had launched the shuttle in conditions that were not safe.

The tragic decision was motivated, according to the commission, by the consequences, both economic and in terms of visibility, which other delays in launching would have had on public opinion, among the mass media and politicians. The commission verified that the O-ring problem was not a new one and that a substantial amount of evidence about it had existed since 1977, but NASA had decided to go ahead with the missions while seeking for a solution at the same time. In addition, the commission underlined how the doubt displayed by Morton Thiokol had not been sufficiently taken into account. It also emphasized that the decision-making process had not been correct and how the middle-ranking hierarchy of the Marshall Center had not adequately informed the NASA management about the O-rings' technical defects. The commission concluded that if the technical cause – the *first-order cause* – lay in the defects and the erosion of the O-rings, the real causes were due to the economic difficulties and management aspects that had resulted in a violation of safety standards. This point of view was greeted with wide consensus and was in almost complete agreement with what newspapers and other mass media had been maintaining for a long period. What had in fact taken place was effectively demonstrated by the famous American physicist Richard Feynman who, during a press conference, placed a piece of O-ring rubber in a glass of zero-degree water in order to show how the rubber lost its elasticity due to the cold – a characteristic that NASA should have been very familiar with.

In 1986, the pressure on NASA and the expectations were extremely demanding, as was the launch schedule forecast for the *Challenger* shuttle. The previous launch had been delayed: the timetable was changed three times, and the management had second thoughts at the last moment. The *Challenger* launch that lead to the accident had itself been delayed four times. NASA needed to demonstrate its efficiency and find a way to balance its budget. The basic accusations that were therefore made to the NASA chiefs were the following: they had given in to the pressure of productivity and had knowingly carried out a launch in dangerous conditions in order to keep in line with the pre-established program. There emerged a clear position of moral condemnation towards the top level of management at NASA, responsible for an accident that could have been avoided and that demonstrated the *banality of bad organization* by a small group of unscrupulous people: the NASA and Morton Thiokol managers, bureaucrats without a conscience who had sacrificed safety in the name of efficiency and visibility.

But is this really how it was? Why should a complex organization, with a high degree of economic and human resources, with the best minds available concentrated within the Marshall Center, be so blind as to commit such an evident and enormous mistake (if mistake indeed it was)? As George Hardy, NASA's vice director, said, "I would hope that simple logic would suggest that no one in their right mind would knowingly accept increased flight risk for a few hours of schedule" (Vaughan 1996, p. 49).

Perhaps the explanation in the newspapers and the description of the commission of inquiry (the Rogers Commission) had ignored some deeper aspects of the problem. Perhaps it was not simply a matter of the violation of standards by a reckless group of directors and technicians, even though this was the main official conclusion.

After the *Challenger* tragedy, NASA adopted the ritual measures typical of post-accident situations: those held to be responsible for the event were removed, and some procedures and decision-making processes were partially revised. No modifications were made, however, to the structural conditions and environment external to NASA, relating to the organizational field. Political pressure, objectives of efficiency in conditions of scarce resources, and the culture of the organization itself were never called into question. The organizational and cultural factors later analyzed by Diane Vaughan (1996) that were the basis of the *Challenger* accident were left unchanged and, seventeen years later, these conditions would be recognized as causative factors in the *Columbia* accident. In fact, on January 16, 2003, history repeated itself. The *Columbia* shuttle was launched into space: the 113th flight in the Shuttle Space Program and the 28th for the *Columbia*. Eight-one seconds after the launch, when the shuttle was at a height of approximately 65,000 feet and a speed of around 2,500 kilometers per hour, a fragment of foam insulation broke off from the shuttle's bipod ramp and hit a tile on the left wing's thermal shield, causing a small breach in the thermal protection system. The incident was undervalued by NASA and no proposal was put forward to remedy the situation.

On February 1, 2003, returning to Earth after the sixteen-day space mission, *Columbia* disintegrated over the skies of Texas. The seven crew members died, and the shuttle, which had cost almost $2 billion, was destroyed. The breach in the thermal protection system had allowed red-hot air to penetrate the insulating shield and progressively melt the aluminum structure. This had weakened the structure, caused the craft to lose control, broken the wing, and finally brought about the collapse of the shuttle itself. There was no possible way for the crew to survive. The fate of *Challenger* had depended on a rubber gasket (the O-ring) ruined by use and the cold; the fate of *Columbia* had been decided by a small piece of foam that had damaged the shuttle's cockpit. The disastrous consequences of both these events were not foreseen.

By their very nature, high-risk technologies are exceptionally difficult to manage. Space shuttles in particular are highly complex, composed of more than 2.5 million different pieces and more than 1,000 valves. NASA itself is also highly complex, a matrix organization employing over 24,000 people. Numerous organizational units spread over a variety of sites and complex channels of information and communication. To some extent, it could be regarded as a bureaucratic and hierarchical organization. Immediately after the event, NASA set up the Columbia Accident Investigation Board (CAIB), formed by members of NASA, aviation experts, an ex-astronaut, some civil investigators, and two professors of engineering. The main questions to answer were why had the accident happened, who was responsible, and what had to be done.

Over the next seven months, the CAIB staff, consisting of more than 120 people, worked with approximately 400 NASA engineers, examining thousands of documents and interviewing and listening to the testimony of hundreds of witnesses, until, on August 26, 2003, the board made its report on the accident public. Why had NASA not foreseen the technical problems of the O-rings and the detached piece of foam, events which had already occurred more than once? Why had NASA undervalued the information immediately following the launch of *Columbia* relating to the conditions of the thermal shield? The two cases reveal profound similarities, despite the different types of technical faults. They also demonstrate NASA's myopia in predicting the events caused by a series of organizational failures, as is maintained in the investigation report concerning *Columbia* (CAIB 2003). The myopic analysis of the *Challenger* accident, wholly focused on individual responsibility, had not taken into account the organizational and cultural factors behind the disaster, meaning that these remained unaltered within NASA's organizational system up until the *Columbia* disaster. The CAIB concluded that "both accidents were failures of foresight ... the causes of the institutional failure responsible for *Challenger* have not been fixed and if these persistent, systemic flaws are not resolved, the scene is set for another accident" (CAIB 2003, vol. 1, p. 195). There were echoes of the *Challenger* event in what happened to *Columbia*. Starbuck and Milliken (1988) maintain that the decision to launch the *Challenger* was made based on the success of previous launches rather than on a systematic evaluation. The past established the premise of the future, and each launch reduced, in the perception of the decision makers, the possibility of negative eventualities in following launches. Diane Vaughan (1996), after studying this accident for nine years, analyzing thousands of internal documents, and listening to recordings of the teleconferences, was able to demonstrate that, in contrast to what the commission had reported, the accident was in reality one that conformed fully to the regulations and was not a violation of existing safety standards. The paradoxical conclusion was that the *Challenger* disaster was, in fact, respect for the regulations, and not their violation, which had caused the accident. There could have been no more worrying a conclusion. As it will be discussed later, Vaughan maintains that the accident was caused by perfectly rational actions, and not by errors or violations, or by irrational, impulsive, self-interested, or amoral acts. The decision to launch *Challenger* was made *in conformity* with the decisional model adopted by NASA. It was therefore that cultural and organizational model, established progressively over time, and not individual people, which had triggered the event.

Vaughan began her research by analyzing the reasons for the accident as they had been explained by the board of inquiry. At first, she was convinced that the conclusions were correct, but during the research, she verified the fact that no regulation had been formally violated. The previous launches and all the activities connected with them featured great care and scrupulousness in relation to safety, rather than hazard or exposure to risk. The reality consisted of ongoing tests, verifications, and new investments to improve safety, not attempts to minimize costs. And in terms of cost-benefits logic, a launch failure was in fact far more expensive, where visibility was concerned, than was a success, quite apart from the massive economic consequences. If, therefore, it was neither a matter of immoral conduct nor a violation of regulations, the deeper causes and factors had to be sought in the history and the culture of the organization in order to understand what had happened. It was necessary to investigate into how a certain culture had progressively developed through decisions and actions.[12]

The accident analysis has to explain the *failure of foresight* (Turner and Pidgeon 1997), the mechanisms of *myopia*, which make an organization blind to evaluations, anomalies, and warnings of danger. Vaughan studies the organization in depth, above all the history and the culture of NASA, pointing out how they were the result of decisions and actions made by people and how they in turn constituted forms of conditioning for the actions of those who had contributed to their definition. The cultural and organizational reality of NASA was socially constructed (Berger and Luckmann 1966), and risk and safety, far from being objective scientific categories, were based on collectively constructed regulations (Douglas 1985). Risk and danger were not a property of technical systems but were defined and interpreted by the social system based on beliefs held by people, previous experience, and the requirements of the context. Risk was socially constructed, and there were certain phases to identify and absorb it (from the warning of potential risk, to its identification, its evaluation, and its acceptability, up to action). All decisions were based on the idea that conformity was the rule, in contrast to violation or inaccuracy. In reality, as Vaughan acutely points out, following procedures did not guarantee total safety, and simply going ahead along those lines certainly did not exclude a possible accident. On the one hand, procedure was a modality to minimize risk; on the other hand, it constituted a system that made it possible to act as if everything was correct even though this was not in fact the case. The organizational and cultural aspect prevailed over human error: "the *Challenger* disaster was an accident, the result of a mistake. What is important to remember from this case is not that individuals in organizations make

---

[12] Vaughan calls her research method *historical ethnography*, inspired by Darnton's *The Great Cat Massacre* (1984).

mistakes, but mistakes themselves are socially organized and systematically produced" (Vaughan 1996, p. 394).

Vaughan (1996, p. 410) shows "how disastrous consequences can emerge from the banality of organizational life" and the explanation for all this may be found in three elements intrinsic to NASA: (1) normalization of deviance, (2) the culture of production spread throughout the institutional environment, and (3) the structural secrecy of the circulation of information deriving from the vast and complex organizational articulation. Each of these aspects is worth looking at more deeply.

Normalization of deviance

It is necessary to address matters at an organizational level to identify what Vaughan (1996, 2005), in relation to the two accidents, calls *normalization of deviance*. "The explanation of the *Challenger* launch is the story of how people who work together develop models that make them blind to the consequences of their actions" (Vaughan 1996, p. 409). Normalization of deviance is what preceding warnings and evaluations should have helped avoid. Small changes, which were slight deviations from the normal course of events, gradually became the norm, providing a basis for accepting further deviances and so forth, in an increasing crescendo.

When the shuttle *Columbia* was launched, the few, not particularly clear, photos taken during the flight show that from the day after the launch, several pieces of foam had broken off. Ten percent of flights had had similar problems, but this time, greater damage seemed to have been caused with respect to the previous flights. The engineers at the Marshall and Kennedy Centers, not in fact directly involved in this launch, presented a request for further images of the impact directly to the Department of Defense. They did this without following procedures and going over the heads of the mission management team. This course of action did not conform to NASA regulations and procedures. It was an act that irritated the administration, which promised to take corrective measures to make it impossible for engineers of an *inferior status* to behave in such an insubordinate manner. The foam break-off was literally a first warning signal that was ignored and incorrectly interpreted. Three different groups at NASA requested further images in order to analyze more closely what had occurred, including photos from external sources, but the mission management team rejected further verification. Better images might have shown the size and location of the damage, and engineers might then have been able to improvise a reentry route or repairs to increase the likelihood of the shuttle's survival. Every safe return of a shuttle with the foam damaged had reinforced the belief that the problem did not constitute a real threat.

This failure of imagination was due to a categorization that influenced the inference process of the decision makers. NASA personnel made a distinction between *in-family* and *out-family* problems (CAIB 2003). An in-family event was "a reportable problem that had already been previously experienced, analyzed and understood" (CAIB 2003, p. 122). The problem was, as is shown later, that the foam break-off was interpreted by management as an in-family and not an out-family problem.

According to Weick (2005a, p. 426):

For something even to qualify as "reportable" people need to have words already in hand to do the reporting. And those same words can limit what is first seen and then reported. Whatever labels a group has available will color what they perceive, which means there is a tendency to overestimate the number of in-family events that people feel they face. People don't first recognize something and then label it as an in-family event. Instead, they have categories of in-family events which punctuate a stream of experience into familiar events and a residual. The world is thereby rendered more stable and certain, but that rendering overlooks unnamed experience that could be symptomatic of larger trouble. The problem here is a failure of imagination, a failure that is common in organizational life.

Once this conviction was in place, it was easy for the management to treat the requests from the engineers for more information from the photos as their professional desire to learn more, rather than an imperative for the success of the mission.

The everyday work practices of NASA personnel were characterized by a high level of uncertainty and unique technical conditions. It was not possible to refer to other concurrent experience, but only to their own history. Risk was therefore a constant and uneliminable condition that could be met with sure, shared, and codified regulations, such as the process of risk acceptability and verification of flight feasibility. To arrive at a situation of acceptable risk, it was required to follow five rules:

1. warn of potential risk;
2. draft a formal document for the identification of risk;
3. describe and prove the possibility that an accident can happen;
4. draft a second document of risk evaluation and, finally, of the acceptability of the risk; and
5. decide to react.

Every anomaly that was identified had to be absorbed through this process: work groups developed an acceptable scientific paradigm that expanded incrementally including recurrent anomalies (Vaughan 1996). In the case that the possibility of a breakdown was not completely null, after a formal evaluation, it could become an acceptable risk only if all the procedures to avoid it had been identified and if the management accepted the risk on the basis of a careful analysis. Risk was therefore ever present in the everyday functioning of the organization and, through shared procedures, from *uneliminable* risk became progressively *residual* and then *acceptable*: regulations, procedures, and beliefs transformed uncertainty into certainty.

   All work required to continue had to be considered at least as acceptable risk. Another procedure consisted of the verification of flight feasibility, which was carried out through an overhaul of the craft before the launch. This overhaul was the responsibility of a mixed commission composed of NASA top-level personnel, engineers from the companies that had built parts of the shuttle, and representatives of the committee running the mission. The overhaul lasted two weeks and was extremely scrupulous, but, as Vaughan points out, it was far from ensuring the total elimination of uncertainty and risk. In general, risk was negotiated between the different parties based on a variety of points of view. Disputes arose between the *practical* party, concerned with the economic aspects, and the *purists*, concerned with quality. These decisional structures therefore established what was and was not a risk through a process of incremental negotiation. Because the conviction existed that no object is completely perfect and absent of potential risk, what was important to ensure was that any eventual defects were residual, improbable, or wholly uneliminable. In the past, it had been discovered that exhaust gas had eroded the rubber of the O-rings, but without causing an accident. The evaluation of the O-rings therefore fell wholly within the decisional process. The safest alternative was to completely redesign the rocket, which would have entailed twenty-seven months of work and an increase in the budget of several million dollars. In addition, there was the guarantee of redundancy: if one O-ring broke, there was always another. The acceptance of possible erosion signified the confirmation of the process of normalization of deviance. In her analysis, Vaughan highlights how the regulation developed after the practices, rather than the opposite. In its implementation, the engineering work consisted of progressive experimentation in conditions of uncertainty. The shuttle and its operations had been pushed to the maximum in terms of level of performance, and the engineers found themselves forced to develop a *promiscuous* technology in which it was necessary to continuously make decisions in situations of uncertainty, if not ignorance. In these conditions, an acceptable risk became a question of social negotiation rather than an objective characteristic of technical systems (Short and Clarke 1992).

NASA treated shuttle launches as operational, not experimental. Design problems and unpredictable flight conditions led to anomalies in many areas during every mission. Because anomalies were the norm, neither the erosion of the O-rings nor the break-off of the foam was considered as a sign of danger before (in the case of the O-rings) and after the launches (in the case of the foam). The model of treatment of information had consequences on how the NASA technicians defined and redefined risk. When anomalies were revealed, the engineers saw the danger signs as ambiguous, because in the past, anomalous incidents were followed by missions with no resultant damage. This succession of events reassured the technicians that the problems were in fact not so serious and that the danger signs were weak. The parameters of risk evaluation defined these situations as not alarming, not dangerous. Danger signs, in other words, became routine: they occurred so often that they became a sign that the machine was operating as expected (Vaughan 2005). The result was the production of a cultural belief that the problems did not constitute a threat to the safety of the flight, a belief that was reinforced by the successful return of every mission. Flying with defects became normal and acceptable, rather than deviant, which is how it appeared to those outside NASA after the accidents. It is an example of the mechanism of normalization of deviance.

The culture of production

While the normalization of deviance concerns the micro-level of analysis, the culture of production involves macro and interorganizational aspects. The first consideration to make is that NASA, though to a large degree autonomous, operates in a world conditioned by various kinds of pressure deriving from the US Congress's control of funding. Political evolution had progressively brought about a change of priorities in how NASA acted: the launches, from purely scientific missions, now had to take into account business requests and opportunities. The *Columbia* mission was, state Cabbage and Harwood (2004), far more a matter of politics than of pure science. In the decade preceding the *Columbia* disaster, the space flight program operated in conditions of an increasingly restricted budget, with access to funds 40 percent lower than those in the past. As a result, there was little margin in the budget to deal with unexpected technical problems and to make improvements to the shuttle (CAIB 2003).

An external, capitalist culture with an eye for business began to pervade a world dominated principally by scientific, or at the most military, priorities. The hours and rhythms of work intensified. Deadlines became inflexible. This new culture of production, not generated from within, contributed, in Vaughan's opinion, to reinforce the normalization of deviance. The start of the space station construction program led to further pressure on the space shuttle program, required to respect the scheduled launch timetable. A delay in launch timing would have consequences on the space station project and would increase costs. The two programs' interdependence, following the *Challenger* accident, had grown enormously, making the relationship between the shuttle and space station projects a completely inextricable one. Launch risk was evaluated based on the consequences that would arise for the safety of the space station program and the rotation of the crew on the station (Farajoun 2005). All this led to an undervaluation of the risks. NASA management began to focus less on failures and problems relating to safety and more on the requirements and demands of the space station program. After the *Columbia* accident, NASA was most severely criticized for not having learned from the 1986 *Challenger* disaster. The CAIB report (2003) states that the break-off of the insulating foam, with the resultant breach of the thermal protection system, was not the only cause of the *Columbia* accident, just as the erosion of the O-rings was not the only reason for the *Challenger* event; in both cases, the NASA organizational system had failed. The CAIB report also asked why NASA had continued the launches, knowing of the problems relating to the possible break-off of foam. Why did the NASA managers believe that this event would not compromise safety conditions? Why, despite the fact that these problems had been known since the investigation following the *Challenger* disaster, had NASA minimized the possibility of these accidents in the future? Many risks, therefore, had already existed at NASA before the *Challenger* launch, and continued to exist even after the *Columbia* disaster. This is one of the report's main conclusions. The report itself went beyond the immediate causes of the event, directing its analysis towards political, budget, and management decisions that had an impact on the space shuttle program and on the structure, culture, and safety of the system. Although NASA described itself as an organization with a *badgeless* culture, where skill counts for more than hierarchy does and everyone is responsible for the result, hierarchy and power were still important factors in its everyday operations. It was a hierarchical system with invisible ranking and an informal and rigid chain of command, with strictly controlled modalities of communication (Mason 2004). The most important point of the CAIB report was to highlight, apart from the technical aspects briefly described earlier, the organizational and cultural causes. The NASA culture was responsible for the tragedy because it had not taken fully into account – in fact, had even impeded – signs of danger and dissent, nourishing complacence towards existing risk. And all this had been aggravated by the fact that seventeen years before, a similar event had taken place.

At the beginning, the NASA culture was something completely different from the era of the *Columbia* accident. The founding culture, promoted by Wernher Von Braun, a legend in the aerospace world, was generated by a military legacy that made discipline a core cultural element. It was a culture with a deep respect for risk and which gave great emphasis to technical skills and factors in decision making. The new concept of mission and the new model of management began in 1972, when President Nixon pushed NASA to make an important cultural change: from a culture of excellence to one of production. This transformation progressively gave precedence to management culture over technical culture, with a careful eye on cost and image, becoming more sensitive to external pressures. "Faster, better, cheaper" was the slogan of Dan Goldin, NASA administrator from 1992 to 2001. The business world and its ideology had thus eroded the technical supremacy, which had guided the organization's development since its origins. Efficiency and cost reduction, these were the signs perceived by NASA technicians, not those relating to safety. The

technical core, says Thompson (1967), had become more exposed to
environmental, economic, and political pressures, with no compen-
satory attention and care left over for safety problems. Parallel to
the spread of this new culture of production, the decisional structure
had also changed, becoming ever more hierarchical. The decisional
process was divided into levels with a strong concentration of power
at the top, which made open communication and the circulation of
information difficult. Anyone who pointed out possible dangers was
seen as a troublemaker and risked losing their position. Whereas the
old (sixties and seventies) culture would respond quickly to signs of
weakness, the new culture of production tended to normalize deviance by eliminating dissonant signs from the reference frame. It was
a decisive transformation of organizational culture, a change in the
values, standards, and practices that governed the running of the
organization. The culture of production, the hierarchy, the difficulty
in information, the communication processes, and the undervaluation
of skills with respect to hierarchy were latent conditions and factors
in the accident: they rendered the organization blind and deaf to the
danger signs and the evaluation of risk relating to the grip of the
thermal shield's tiles. This organizational myopia and deafness were
fostered by hubris, the organizational arrogance that had spread as
a result of the excellent results of the previous years and that had
hardly even been dented by the accidents that had occurred (with
Challenger and before that with Apollo program). The myth of invulnerability guided decisions. But this attitude of omnipotence becomes
extremely dangerous when the technology involved is complex and
uncertain. As Mason (2004) states, this attitude of omnipotence is
very dangerous when technology is complex, uncontrollable, and,
in the last analysis, unpredictable, and especially when the fundamental standards of interrogation and inquiry have been replaced by
standards of silence, self-protection, and managerial efficiency. This
type of behavior nourishes organizational arrogance. It consists of an
exaggerated pride, a sense of omnipotence based on previous success
that reduces the ability to learn from errors or signs of weakness that
go against the dominant vision. Managers in this situation tend only
to listen to those who confirm their own opinions. The CAIB report
found many echoes in this of the numerous failures that emerged
following the *Challenger* accident and that were still present in the
NASA organization.

The sense of overconfidence (or *can-do attitude,* as the report calls it) led to problems not being sufficiently considered, in particular those problems that could impede the launch and that were raised by low-status individuals in the organizational hierarchy. Along with organizational and communication problems relating to structure and hierarchy, other problems existed that were more a matter of mind-set and culture. For example, the reports compiled by the Debris Assessment Team (DAT – the ad hoc team created to evaluate the damage caused by the foam) contained interesting data, but salient information was lost step by step as they proceeded towards the upper levels. In presentations, these data were displayed in a synthetic form, and any unclear information was cut out. As a result, those very elements of doubt that should or could in fact have caused alarm bells to ring for the management were eliminated. In addition, evaluating the edited information created a *framing effect*, an anchorage in past experience, where foam break-off had not caused any vital damage. The evaluation of the problem thus underwent a transformation, diminishing its importance from a situation of potential risk that could compromise the mission to a routine maintenance problem. Finally, the engineers and the managers responsible for the mission respected different kinds of risk culture. For the former, risk consisted of anything that might threaten the safety of the mission; for the latter, the managers, risk meant any problem or inconvenience that might threaten future NASA projects. The engineers lacked precise and sufficient information to demonstrate the true level of danger, partly because, in the past, when a similar foam break-off had occurred, it had not led to any serious damage. This therefore left the managers of the program in the driving seat of the decisional process, able to state that the hazards related to the foam break-off were secondary problems and, as such, were not linked to the safety of the mission.

Structural secrecy

The third element in the explanation of the two disasters can be found in a characteristic of the NASA communication system that contributes to the normalization of deviance, a way of *not seeing*: structural secrecy. With this term, Vaughan (1996, 2005) refers to a situation in which the structures of an organization and their regulatory relationships impede the awareness and understanding of what is happening, obscuring the seriousness of the problem from those who are responsible for supervision. Secrecy is built into the structure of organizations. The more an organization grows in size, the more activities and actions that occur in one part become unknowable and unobservable by the other parts. The division of work into subunits, hierarchy, and geographical dispersion reduce awareness of tasks and aims. The communicative process was inefficient not through the intention of the personnel but because of the organizational characteristics of NASA. How did this happen?

It was a routine fact for problems to arise, and when this happened, the workgroup decided how to act based on previous experience and decisions taken in the past. Every decision confirmed the one before. The problem that emerged was filed according to a preset format and thus lost its unusualness. This helps to explain why something that appeared of little importance before the accident became a determining factor in the board of inquiry afterwards. In the case of *Challenger*, the wear and tear on the gaskets in previous launches was always due to a variety of causes (or at least this was the conclusion of the inquiry) and even in the launches in which they were damaged to a greater extent, they still carried out their function without breaking completely. Signs of anomaly, as with the O-rings for example, were weak and ambiguous and did not necessarily reinforce one another.

A second aspect of structural secrecy derives from NASA's organizational articulation. Work was divided into numerous, physically dispersed organizational units. The entire launch project required the involvement of a host of subcontractors and highly specialized skills: this made it extremely difficult to have a comprehensive vision of the process, except in terms of macro-phases, and the end result was a certain opacity. The fallacious assumption that had bolstered NASA's reorganization strategy (involving privatization and outsourcing) before the *Columbia* accident was that the reduction of safety staff would not cause reductions in the overall safety of the shuttle space program, since the contractors would shoulder more responsibility relating to safety. This fallacy, together with the existence of technical specialism and categorizations, produced a lack of comprehension and evaluation of specific information in certain contexts or could lead to their omission if they did not fit into preset categories. Organizational complexity thus made horizontal communication difficult. Finally, another source of structural secrecy was present in the relationship between controllers and controlled. The inspection system supervisors were required to seek out possible points of weakness in the launch and, having once identified them, were responsible for halting operations. These supervisors, however, depended on the information communicated to them by those they supervised, and this seriously reduced their ability to individuate invisible events that the latter had already missed.

NASA, in particular the part involved with the space shuttle program, is a huge and complex organization that operates with high-risk technology in high-risk environments. It emits ambiguous signals, engages in extreme activities, and pursues high-risk objectives in order to satisfy a large number of subjects from different organizational and institutional environments. At the same time, during the periods of the two disasters, with significant constraints upon its budget and downsizing of personnel, it was under a great deal of pressure in terms of deadlines, leadership changes, and technological, political, and financial uncertainties. The CAIB (2003) concludes that both accidents were failures of foresight in a situation involving an inadequate and fallacious safety culture – a "broken safety culture" (CAIB 2003, p. 184). The centralization of the safety system in the quality assurance organizational unit was one of the major factors in the decline of safety at NASA, due to its lack independence and sufficient influence. As seen earlier, there were three factors that, combining together to create systemic effects, produced a situation of myopia at the basis of the *Challenger* and *Columbia* disasters. These were a decision-making model that normalized technical anomalies, creating the cultural belief that the launch was safe; a culture of production that forced the launches to proceed rather than incur delays to verify any eventual anomalies; and structural secrecy, which hindered in-depth awareness amongst NASA top-level personnel relating to the true state of problems. The *Columbia* disaster demonstrated that NASA had not been able to draw the right lessons from the *Challenger* accident (Starbuck and Farajoun 2005; Mahler 2009).

The two disasters were the result of systemic myopia, therefore, and not a matter of human error or hazard guided by management interests, as maintained by the commission following the *Challenger* event. The latter theory, that the launch was forced to take place by unscrupulous directors under pressure from program deadlines and against the will of the engineers, is thus overturned by the former.

The engineers were in fact in agreement with the idea that the situation was one of acceptable risk, that evidence not to go ahead with the launch was insufficient, and that the temperature was not in the end unduly low – in the past, similar conditions had not created any problems and the redundancy of the O-rings guaranteed safety. The decision to launch was shown to be mistaken after the fact, but the engineers' analysis was reliable, even though made in a context of extreme uncertainty. The launch fit perfectly into a decisional mechanism formed over time – a mechanism that rendered this particular decision a perfectly safe one. This is perhaps the most important paradox that Vaughan points out: scrupulous research into the minimization of risk unwittingly creates the very event that is to be avoided. It is not a matter of the banality of evil, as the first commission maintained with reference to the *Challenger* launch, but, as Vaughan argues and as the CAIB report on *Columbia* confirms, of the banality of organizational life. Technology without risk does not exist, and the evaluation of its functioning and of its possible risks is always a question of human judgment. NASA was in fact characterized by a high-level culture of reliability and decentralization; two elements that High Reliability Organization theorists establish for reliable organizations. This does not, however, stop accidents from happening.

The conclusions that were developed from the *Challenger* case in relation to the possibility of preventing accidents and learning from them are fairly pessimistic and in line with the ideas of the Normal Accident Theory: "while management and adequate organizational design may reduce accidents in certain conditions, they can never eliminate them completely" (Vaughan 1996, p. 416). It was NASA's organizational and safety culture that fostered the accidents, a culture that had evolved according to a variety of pressures imposed by technical requirements: an exceptional can-do culture of invincibility, within which efficient engineering controls were substituted by an organizational hubris and by a sense of overconfidence that created a context for normalization of deviance (Vaughan 1996) and anomalies. The conflict between engineers and managers, between efficiency and safety, led to many mistaken decisions and an undervaluation of danger signs. In a hierarchical organization such as NASA, the managers had the final say, and in particular, in conditions of stress and pressure of time, they tended to direct the engineers while paying little attention to messages that were at odds with their intentions. The organization's bureaucratic-hierarchical

culture emphasized the chain of command and control based on procedure and limited efficient communication about technical problems.
Potential danger signs were undervalued and contrasting opinions and
doubts either went unheeded or failed to arrive at the highest levels of
the hierarchical chain. In this way, many danger signs were simply lost;
relevant information that might have later altered the course of events
was available but not taken into account, such as the messages of alert
concerning the state of the O-rings for *Challenger* and the damage provoked by the foam break-off for *Columbia*.

It is the culture itself, therefore, that has to be the basis for the
design of a new NASA, one more reliable and less exposed to the possibility of accidents. The CAIB report states that the safety conditions
to allow NASA to continue its space exploration program simply do
not exist, at least if it does not take up the numerous recommendations
that would bring about a real cultural and organizational revolution
aimed at creating a new type of organization. NASA has to become
a highly reliable organization: "high-reliability theory is extremely
useful in describing the culture that should exist in the human space
flight organization" (CAIB 2003, p. 181). In such a new organizational
structure, errors and failures would be a cause for true preoccupation,
there would be high sensitivity towards operations and skills rather
than to rank, and divergent opinions would be encouraged and carefully evaluated, without simplifying cuts or omissions. This would
bring about changes in the hierarchical structure, with a robust promotion of the culture of communication in relation to risk and signs of
weakness and the constitution of an independent technical authority
for safety programs. But a serious problem still remains. Even if the
culture did change in a positive way, the managing of policies and
resources is still determined by external subjects, such as Congress.
Even with a new organizational culture, one more careful and less
myopic with respect to safety conditions, external conditioning, and
pressures would remain unaltered.

1.4 Other cases of myopia

The tragedy of the commons

Large-scale instances of myopia regards the handling of *common-pool
resources*. Common-pool resources are both natural (water, air,

fisheries, pasture, climate, etc.) and artificial (streets, parking areas, bridges, energy, etc.) and both renewable and nonrenewable. They are characterized by two conditions: (1) the exclusion of an individual from exploiting the goods is very difficult (non-excludability) and (2) the consumption by one actor reduces the possibility of use by others. The handling of these resources presents a particular public goods dilemma known as the *tragedy of the commons*, from the title of an article published in *Science* in 1968 by the biologist Garrett Hardin. In this article, Hardin refers back to the pessimistic predictions of Thomas Malthus regarding the relationship between the limitations of resources and population growth. Hardin explains his thesis through the case of shepherds with free access to public pasture, where the pasture for each farmer's sheep reduced the availability of grass for the sheep belonging to others. Each shepherd used the public pasture to feed his flock; by increasing the number of animals, it was possible to increase his income. The other shepherds thought and did the same. Each shepherd was in fact encouraged to increase the size of their flock; resources, however, were limited. The advantages were internalized by each individual sheep owner while the cost (the consumption of resources) was distributed amongst the various participants. This leads to a situation in which there are too many animals for the size of the pasture and some of them would starve to death. This is an example of *selfish-actor* myopia. As Hardin (1968, p. 248) states, "each man is locked into a system that compels him to increase his herd without limit – in a world that is limited. Ruin is the destination toward which all men rush, each pursuing his own best interest in a society that believes in the freedom of the commons."

The *tragedy of the commons* has come to symbolize the environmental degradation to be expected whenever many individuals use a scarce resource in common (Ostrom 1990). In these situations, rational actions have involuntary consequences, *adverse effects*, which make the situations worse for everyone (Elster 1989). Perfectly rational individuals can produce, in particular situations, results that are not collectively rational (Coleman 1990). The question put by Hardin paved the way for a new stream of research on how to *govern the commons* (Ostrom 1990). The pursuit of short-term interest by a group of *appropriators*, acting as rational myopic egoists, produces long-term damage, compromising, even definitively, their own activity. To govern common-pool resources, the incentives that lead individuals to *free ride* (Olson 1965) must be modified.

Two opposing solutions were initially formulated. The first required the institution of an authority that regulates use with mutual coercion (Hardin 1968), a sort of *bureaucratic Leviathan*. In Hardin's original view, there is no easy answer to the public goods problem, if not the institution of an external authority, which, resorting to coercive measures, can force the actors to be less myopic and more prudent, fostering behavior that increases collective gain. The second presupposed that resources would be privatized (Sinn 1984; R.J. Smith 1981) so that each actor would have an interest in their maintenance and would be discouraged from displaying wasteful behavior. Each solution has its pros and cons. Both require a huge amount of information and control, and neither completely eliminates the possibility of destructive voluntary behavior by actors interested in short-term advantages.

Ostrom (1990) posits the existence of alternative solutions to both privatization and externally imposed regulations. She points out that the problem that users of a limited resource must face is that of setting up an organizational structure that encourages the choice of cooperative strategies. The *third way* suggested by Ostrom is based on the possibility of maintaining over time the rules and forms of self-government regarding the selective use and sharing of the resource. All the users, recognizing that they share similar interests, must commit to respecting established quotas as *sustainable exploitation*, controlling transgression and in this way fostering the development of cooperative behavior (Ostrom 1990).

Dietz, Ostrom, and Stern (2003) summarize the major conclusions from this scholarships as follows: the management of common resources is easier (a) if the resources and their uses can be monitored by the community; (b) if the rates of change are modest in the resources, in the populations that use them, in technology and in social and economic conditions; (c) if the community maintains frequent face-to-face communication and close-knit social networks that increase the potential of reciprocal trust (social capital), making it possible to lower costs of monitoring and control; (d) if access to resources is forbidden to external agents; and (e) if the users of the resources themselves support monitoring and respect for the rules.

Many of the problems regarding common resources discussed by Ostrom were analyzed by Diamond (2005) in his study of the collapse of societies, as in the case of the inhabitants of Easter Island, where the management of common resources was absent and the continuous and myopic exploitation of timber led the civilization to destruction. Similar problems face the new commons today, for example, the use of parking areas, water management, the problems of pollution, and the dissipation of resources. As highlighted in the report on the effects of climate change by Nicholas Stern (2006), former chief economist with the World Bank, costs to stabilize the climate are significant but manageable, while further delay will be far more costly and above all dangerous.

In all these cases, the problems of short-term preference myopia and the difficulties in evaluating options for a long-term prospect are evident. What emerges is the importance of finding forms of self-organization and design solutions (both institutional and self-governing) that make it possible to overcome myopic attitudes that may be destructive in the use of resources.

When numbers do not mean strength

Quintessential examples of organizational myopia are revealed by errors in military strategy. A typical case of myopia is that of continually changing tactics without having either a clear basic strategy or a precise objective. The selection and maintenance of an objective, holding firm to a planned strategy (except of course when unexpected failures arise, which require its sudden alteration), and the concentration of forces are fundamental principles of military strategy. They were principles that were not followed by the German Strategic Command in the case of the Battle of Britain, the conflict between the German and British air forces in 1940. The changing of tactics, with no clear strategy and without carefully verifying the evolving circumstances of the situation, reduced the relevance of the German air force's numerical superiority compared with that of the British and canceled out the advantage of surprise that was in Germans' favor.

If the powerful German air fleet had defeated the numerically inferior British air force, then history might have been very different indeed. Why did this not happen?

The German air force, the Luftwaffe, was three times the size of the British equivalent, the Royal Air Force (RAF). Moreover, the Luftwaffe was far better trained and had the advantage of surprise. And yet, this was still not sufficient. Resources alone are not enough and do not guarantee success. The way in which they are used is as important as the numerical aspect (Grattan 2005). The defeat, as will be seen, was due to a lack of clear strategy and organizational ability. "My planes will destroy the RAF in four days!" announced Hermann Göring, minister of aviation, commander in chief of the Luftwaffe and Reichsmarschall. It was a prophecy that could not have been more wrong. The initial conviction of an easy victory led to continual changes of tactics for the Luftwaffe. Göring, like Hitler, committed an error in evaluating the relationship between the two forces, overestimating their own and underestimating the British: an excess of presumption, of hubris, which would prove fatal for Germany.

At the end of June 1940, Germany controlled Western and Southern Europe down to the Pyrenees. The Führer was convinced that Britain would agree to sign a peace treaty: however, to his great astonishment, the suggestion was vigorously rejected by the British government at the beginning of July 1940. A war with Great Britain was not on the agenda, and in addition, it would need to be launched quickly before weather conditions worsened and made it impossible for German troops to land on the British coast. Military strategy at that time was based around the ideas of the Italian Emilio Douhet, who believed that the war of the future would be decided by bombers, by destroying enemy defenses, by weakening the morale of citizens, and by the opposing forces paving the way for invasion by the attacking army. There was one major obstacle: the RAF, the British air force. As had emerged a few months previously during the Norwegian campaign, if the adversary controlled the air space, the infantry's freedom of action was greatly limited. Therefore, the initial phase of the war would have to involve the destruction of the RAF by the Luftwaffe, after which it would be possible to send troops on to British soil. Although it was certainly an unforeseen problem in Hitler's plans for expansion, it was not, however, envisaged as a particularly troubling one. The main problem was time: it had to be done soon.

In terms of strategy, German military movements depended on the autocratic behavior of their leader, who often made decisions on his own, without listening to opposing opinions or paying attention to warning signs. English strategy was a much simpler affair, since alternatives did not exist: the first move had to come from the enemy. The Germans, however, losing sight of the objective, carried out four tactical changes: (1) first, they attacked the British coastal convoys, confronting the RAF over the English Channel in July; (2) they began the main assault in the month of August and then (3) shifted attacks (from August 23, 1940, to September 3, 1940) to the RAF's fighter airfields in the south of England; and (4) finally, from September 7, 1940, they began to bomb London. It was a series of moves that owed more to the search for the killing blow than to the careful evaluation of the consequences of each single action. In fact, during the first two phases, the attacks on the coastal convoys, radar stations, and RAF bases, the Luftwaffe was making good headway and might have defeated the combat forces in southern England in a matter of six weeks. But Göring decided to change the objective, giving the RAF time to reorganize.

Certain limitations in terms of information and tactical errors characterized the German strategy: it was taken for granted that the battle in the air would be quickly over; information regarding the productive capacity of the British aeronautical industry greatly underestimated the real rates of production; the existence of the British radar system was ignored; the number of aircraft was confused with their power; tactics were changed without any modification being made to strategy. It is useful to take a closer look at each single element. Aviation minister Hermann Göring was convinced that the air battle would be a short one and stuck to this belief to the end, even when it became obvious that there were clear contradictory signs. Department 5 of the Luftwaffe's information service underestimated the production capacity of the British aeronautics industry: a report on July 16, 1940, estimated production at between 180 and 330 fighters each month – the real figure, however, was between 446 and 496, that is, 30 to 50 percent more than the number hypothesized. This mistake in evaluating the actual production capacity of the British reinforced the conviction that they could not fight back for long. A further aspect involved the British radar system, the existence of which was ignored by the German report of July 1940. The British had a prewarning system that made it possible for Fighter Command to send up interception aircraft while at the same time alerting other squadrons. In addition, the Germans were erroneously convinced that every British squadron was responsible for protecting the area in which it was based, underestimating the mobility of the air fleet. Another point regarded British aircraft technology. Compared to German planes, the British Hurricanes and Spitfires were more agile in maneuvering and offered greater protection to their pilots. Agility in the air combined with coordination between squadrons made possible by the efficiency of the radar system meant that the British air force could afford a fighting power superior to the amount of aircraft actually in their possession. This was helped by the centralized command and control system that doubled the combat impact of the fighters. The ability to coordinate allowed the British to overcome the numerical superiority of the Germans, on the one hand, canceling out the advantage of surprise (with radar) and, on the other hand, increasing response capacity to the German attack (with centralized command).

The Luftwaffe, in other words, made the decision to attack Britain in a situation of inadequate information and fallacious convictions: the island's anti-air defenses are hopelessly insufficient as to power, equipment, training, command, and the condition of airfields; the Luftwaffe is utterly superior to the RAF, ran a German report of July 16, 1940. When the war began, the Luftwaffe could count on 2,500 aircraft against the 700 British fighters. German superiority, however, was only apparent. The German twin-engine heavy fighter, the Messerschmitt Bf 110, turned out to be a fiasco, too slow and cumbersome to be anything but easy prey for the more maneuverable British fighters. For four weeks, the German air fleet tried to win mastery of the skies, but with no evident results, and with serious losses on both sides. This situation forced the Luftwaffe to change tactics. On August 12, 1940, it attacked the RAF command and the radar station between Portland and the Thames estuary, the objective being to clear a path for the German bombers. This action brought concrete results, and the British radar system was greatly compromised, even though it was partially rebuilt later. The Luftwaffe, however, believed that such tactics were leading nowhere, and instead of continuing these attacks against radar positions, they suspended such incursions and thus, perhaps, lost a real chance of victory against the British air force. The German command instead opted for a decisive battle on August 15, 1940, when the Luftwaffe carried out 2,199 incursions against 974 carried out by the RAF. The rapid coordination ensured by radar made it possible for the RAF to inflict heavy losses on the German pilots. Göring therefore ordered the fighters to escort the bombers rather than to fly in front, but this defensive maneuver canceled out the German fighters' tactical advantage. Losses were significant on both sides, and the numerical inferiority of the British began to trouble Churchill deeply, as he feared the battle would be lost.

At this point, however, the Germans committed another tactical mistake: feeling that the path they were on was not going anywhere in terms of immediate advantages, the German command once again changed tack and decided to attack London, halting the bombing of airfields and British factories. This was their crucial error, one that originated from the desire for a quick finish to the conflict and from imprecise reporting from the German information service that had underestimated existing British forces. Göring believed that bombing London, as well as avenging the attack on Berlin carried out by British bombers on August 26, 1940, would force the British high command to use their remaining air reserves. But he underestimated a vital detail: to bomb the English capital, the German planes would have to use up almost all their fuel, leaving only ten minutes of autonomy available for air combat over the city. In the battle on September 15, 1940, the Luftwaffe lost fifty-six planes against the twenty-six lost by the British. At this point, Hitler realized he could not conquer British air space before the arrival of the bad weather and that this would therefore leave no useful time to land troops: he therefore decided to postpone the invasion of Great Britain indefinitely. In the Battle of Britain, in the end, the Luftwaffe lost many more aircrafts than the RAF: 1,651 compared to 1,085.

The weak link in the Battle of Britain was strategy. As seen in the preceding explanation, from July to October 1940, the Luftwaffe's strategy altered four times and lacked a coherent design: it was a continuous sequence of tactical shifts with no clear strategic direction. Just when the German attacks seemed to be beginning to produce significant results, Göring changed the objective. In his treatise *On War*, von Clausewitz (1832 [1944]) wrote that war is a zone of uncertainty, unpredictability, and chaos. In situations of this kind, the winner is the one who commits fewer errors and who does not commit the final error, the decisive one. This premise helps mitigate that excess of presumption, of ex post rationality, based on that we are more intelligent than the actors who made (erroneous) decisions ex ante. Even with this proviso, the case has much to teach us regarding three aspects of strategic decision making: (1) the fallacy of original convictions, (2) the modality of decision making, (3) continuity in the implementation of strategy.

With regard to the first aspect, the fallacy of original convictions, Göring's certainty that the RAF would be defeated in a short time was the fallacy that gave rise to the decisions that followed. This original conviction constituted the *sensemaking framework* within which successive strategic choices and sequence of continual changes would be articulated. Never questioning the soundness of this certainty was perhaps the fundamental error.

In terms of the second aspect, the modality of decision making, we know that Hitler himself was making strategic decisions and that there was very little likelihood that these could be discussed with other officers. Hitler's decision making was an intuitive one, something that became problematic in situations of uncertainty. Being right in preceding circumstances does not mean that this will always be the case. "Nothing creates blindness more than success," stated Robert D. Haas, chairman of Levi Strauss & Company, describing the inability of his company to recognize the radical changes that were taking place in the external environment and the arrival of new competitors: previous success does not, in other words, guarantee success in the future. "A system where dynamic inputs create constant outcomes induces a potentially dangerous form of organizational blindness," affirms Snook (2000, p. 214).

Danny Miller (1992) defines this situation as the *Icarus paradox*, pointing out how the victories won by an organization and its particular strengths can lead the decision makers to excess that brings about failure. Organizational hubris renders the decision makers myopic and deaf, fostering overestimation of their own resources and undervaluing those of the adversaries: factors that are extremely risky in situations of uncertainty and imprecise information. In fact, intuitive strategic thinking requires rigorous and rational verification before implementation.

Finally, coming to the third aspect, continuity in the implementation of strategy, the Luftwaffe altered its objectives so many times during the Battle of Britain that it wasted resources and nullified the advantage of surprise. If this may appear quite rational from one point of view (avoiding repetition of error), from another, it is obvious that continual and sudden changes make it difficult to fully evaluate the results of actions underway, dissipating the forces in the field. What needed to be changed were not the objectives (coast, radar stations, London) but the original conviction of short-term victory. Rigidity in this particular area impeded recognition of a winning strategy.

An authoritarian and intuitive leadership that does not verify the rational implementation of objectives with colleagues, that is blind due to success achieved in the past and deaf to dissenting voices and warning signs, is the sure prelude to disaster. As will be seen later, High Reliability Organizations (HROs), which operate in conditions of high risk and extreme uncertainty, have developed management modalities and practices in order to deal with the unexpected. Collaborative leadership, learning from adverse events, the valorization of expertise rather than hierarchy, and strategy sharing to limit damage caused by errors are some of the elements that make it possible for these organizations to tackle the unexpected, minimizing adverse events and the negative outcomes of their own actions. German organization and strategy as described previously were the complete opposite of this.

A diametrically opposed error is that of maintaining static tactics when confronting an evolving situation. For instance, during the First World War, in the battle of Caporetto (Italy), the Italian high command demonstrated a static and dated method of conducting the battle, while the German troops adopted a far more flexible fighting strategy. Despite the presence of relevant information, the Italian high command's insistence on going ahead with predetermined tactics led to defeat with considerable loss of life amongst the soldiers (Zaccuri 1993). The case displayed the evident detachment between the assumptions of those conducting the battle and what was in fact the reality of the situation. The defeat was determined by the maintenance of a static strategic frame in relation to an evolving situation.

1.5 Positive myopia and the principle of the hiding hand

From the examples presented so far, it might be deduced that myopia is always involuntary and negative, but, in reality, this is not always the case. There is a beautiful story by the Austrian poet Ingeborg Bachmann, "Miranda" (in *Three Paths to the Lake*, 1972) in which the extremely myopic main character goes around without glasses as a form of defense against the world. Miranda's denial is her strategy for protecting herself from a destructive reality. Although this untreated myopia hinders her from seeing the danger signals present in her sentimental life, it also helps her to tolerate certain problems, which are only seen in a rather blurred manner.

There are events in which "the unanticipated consequences of purposive social action" (Merton 1936) could have positive effects, improving the situation for everyone. One example is Adam Smith's idea of the invisible hand. Forms of ignorance regarding the limits of awareness of problems can be a positive factor for the realization of activities that in an ideal situation with full awareness of the problems would not be undertaken. Some analogies can be found between the form of positive myopia and the concept of *serendipity*[13] (Merton and Barber 1992), defined as the ability to draw profit from the unforeseen by accident and sagacity. Serendipity indicates that mixture of intuition and luck that helps to arrive unintentionally at positive results. It is a situation in which an unforeseen, anomalous, or strategic element provides the opportunity for the development of a new theory or the expansion of an existing theory. It is not simply a question of luck, because the accidental discovery still depends on a scientist's particular catalogue of qualities, such as determination, assiduity, courage, curiosity, and imagination. There is nothing fortuitous in accidental discoveries, state Merton and Barber.

In order to indicate exactly this type of situation, Hirschman (1967) formulates *the principle of the hiding hand*. He provides an interesting example of positive myopia and serendipity with a case concerning the construction of a paper mill in Karnaphuli, in East Pakistan. The paper mill was one of the earliest large-scale industrial enterprises built in Pakistan following the separation from India, set up by a state agency to make use of the immense bamboo forests present there. The paper mill started to operate in 1953 and the management passed into private hands in 1959. But just as things seemed to running perfectly, a serious problem arose: the bamboo began to flower. This was an absolutely unforeseen event, perhaps even wholly unpredictable, given the state of knowledge as it was then. In fact, the bamboo was known to flower every fifty or seventy years. Due to the paucity of observations, the life cycle of the many varieties of bamboo was not fully known. Suddenly,

---

[13] The word *serendipity* was invented by Horace Walpole in 1754, referring to the Persian fairy tale *The Travels and Adventures of Three Princes of Sarendip* (Sarendip or Serendip is an old name for Sri Lanka, also known as Ceylon). In this tale, the three princes were always making discoveries by accident and through the sagacity of things that they were not looking for. Robert Merton adopted this term to explain phenomena relating to inventions and scientific discoveries.

there was a complete lack of raw material, since the flowering not only provoked the death of the plant but also rendered the dead bamboo unusable. Moreover, after the flowering, it was necessary to wait a number of years before the bamboo grew back to a commercially exploitable height. So, the factory, after just seven years of activity, found itself with a dramatic shortage of raw material. Bamboo paste was temporarily brought in from other areas, but this proved to be far too expensive an operation. A research program was quickly launched, therefore, in order to identify other fast-growing species that might to some extent replace the unreliable bamboo as the principal raw material base for the mill. The crisis therefore had an unexpected yet positive effect, leading to a diversification of the mill's raw material base. Experimenting with a variety of species that turned out to be more suited in terms of the performance required, and by identifying new and better raw materials, they were able to bring a resolution to the crisis. The paper mill, it might be said, was lucky. Its planners overestimated the availability of raw material, and the mill avoided the disastrous consequence of this prediction thanks to the availability – unexpected and not previously evaluated – of alternative raw material.

Studying the case, Hirschman (1967, p. 10) wonders "whether this experience really was a matter of pure luck or whether there are reasons to expect some systematic association of such providentially off-setting errors." Something similar occurred in other situations, such as in successful irrigation and irrigation-hydroelectric projects. When a river that had to provide sufficient water for a number of different uses (agricultural, industrial, and urban) could not meet all these needs, this scarcity of water was solved by making use of other sources that the planners had not taken into consideration: groundwater lifted by tubewells, better regulation of the river through upstream dams, or the deviation of water from rivers farther away.

It should be obvious, states Hirschman (1967, p. 11):

that overestimates of the availability of a given material resource are always going to be offset by underestimates of alternatives or substitute resources; but if we generalize a little more, we obtain a statement that no longer sounds wholly absurd: on the contrary, it is quite plausible and almost trite to state that each project comes into the world accompanied by two sets of partially or offsetting potential developments: (1) a set of unsuspected threats to its profitability and existence, and (2) a set of unexpected remedial actions that can be taken should a threat become real.

On the basis of many projects analyzed, Hirschman points out, it emerges that if the planners of complex projects had known beforehand all the difficulties of the initiative, the problems, and the unforeseen costs that they would be forced to meet, then they would probably not even have begun to work on them.

Pessimistic evaluation would have won out over creative, political, administrative, and technical capacity. Full foregoing awareness of all the problems would have had a negative effect on the realization of the projects, impeding innovations with perhaps important consequences.

Just as creativity tends to be underestimated, maintains Hirschman, it is similarly necessary to underestimate the difficulties of the tasks that must be faced in order to facilitate the realization of initiatives that otherwise might never be undertaken. This is *the principle of the hiding hand*, a kind of invisible or unseen hand that conceals difficulties to a positive end. Innovation is sometimes created by false steps and errors of evaluation rather than by the accurate planning of rational behavior.

Errors in calculation or pure ignorance (Sawyer 1952) are at the base of many projects in the field of transport and in the exploitation of new resources in the United States of the nineteenth century. Without these errors, many positive projects would never have been realized. The principle of the hiding hand states therefore that the overestimation of benefits matches the planners' underestimation of their own ability to solve problems. This must be compensated for by the underestimation of the problems and threats that might arise in the course of the project. It is a mechanism that forces those averse to risk to accept risk and, during the process, transforms them gradually into people less averse to risk. The hiding hand is a way to induce action through error, where the error is an involuntary underestimation of the costs, threats, and difficulties involved in the realization of a project. The overestimation of benefits plays a positive role in fostering the realization of initiatives and projects that would not otherwise be undertaken.

It is important, however, that operational difficulties do not emerge too quickly; otherwise, it might seem more opportune for the planners and managers to halt the initiative rather than to face up to the difficulties and seek creative solutions. The tendency to deal with the difficulties will be proportional with force already expended, whether financial or of another kind. Whenever costs and future difficulties have been perfectly evident from the beginning, a strategy to stop these from discouraging the initiative is that of overestimating the prospective benefits. This necessitates a magnifying glass for benefits in order to provoke an action that otherwise might not be initiated. Hirschman (1967, p. 31) puts it like this:

Extravagance in promising future benefits can thus often be found and may play a useful role in those development projects that require difficult initial decisions, be it a change in existing institutions or a fiscal sacrifice demanded of some or all of the citizenry. Actually the promise of some sort of utopia is most characteristic of larger-scale undertakings such as the launching of social reforms or of external aggression because they are likely to require heavy initial sacrifices.

A certain amount of hubris might actually be positive. In his article "The Hubris Hypothesis of Corporate Takeovers," Richard Roll (1986) locates the determining element of many mergers in the excessive certainty of high-level managers, even in the presence of evidence to the contrary. Because it is extremely difficult for managers to organize a merger during their careers, the opportunity of one may result in an underestimation of the risks and an emphasis on benefits. They convince themselves of the excellence of the initiative and of the fact that the data against it do not reflect the effective value of the two companies brought together.

In conclusion, the extravagance of future benefits, a certain ignorance of operational conditions, and assured myopia play a positive part in balancing out the tendency to overestimate costs and threats and to under estimate the creative ability to face up to them. As long as it takes place over short periods, underestimating costs and problems in ignorance compensates for that other myopia that underestimates the creative ability to tackle them. Positive myopia is a useful mechanism that facilitates the realization of complex projects in conditions of uncertainty and also facilitates innovation. It therefore becomes comprehensible how individuals may benefit from their mistakes: by making mistakes, they also make innovation possible.

2 | *Uncertainty and predictability in organizations*

2.1 Risk and uncertainty in complex non-ergodic systems

A common problem in many social sciences, just as in the theory of organizations, is the absence of *cardinal laws* comparable to those of physics: this is due to the *non-ergodic* nature of the world (North 2005). An ergodic[1] science is founded on a structure with a constant and therefore timeless basis. A non-ergodic world, in contrast, is a world in continuous transformation. As Davidson (1991, p. 132) states, an ergodic stochastic process implies that "the average calculated from past observations cannot be persistently different from the time average of future outcomes." Economists are divided on whether economic systems are ergodic: Samuelson (1969) maintains that the hypothesis of ergodicity is essential to economic theory whereas North (2005) argues that this hypothesis is simply ahistorical. Social sciences, like organization theory, do not have the basic principles that render knowledge ergodic, and thus cannot facilitate the identification of the *right path* to take in conditions of uncertainty.

Organizations, just like human societies, are not immutable with respect to the categorizations and institutions that interpret them, since these impose a certain direction. Certain strategies exist however to reduce conditions of uncertainty through an increase in information, the expansion of awareness within the existing institutional framework, the modification of the institutional framework, the re-elaboration of beliefs, and so on (North 2005). For example, increasing information regarding accidents in a specific activity, such as maritime or road traffic, has led to a greater ability to predict events, thus transforming uncertainty into risk, to the benefit of insurance companies. In fact, greater information allows insurance companies to better price their insurance policies.

---

[1] The term *ergodic* is used in statistical mechanics to indicate some properties of physical systems.

The characteristic of non-ergodicity assumes particular relevance since, even though actors may have a perfect perception of their environment and institutions may be optimal at a specific moment, both can turn out to be anything but adequate when the human environment changes over time. This is the problem tackled in the analysis of the cases of the 9/11 terrorist attacks and NASA, in which both systems dealt with a new environment using obsolete and inadequate systems of beliefs and institutions.

Simple organizational environments, featuring a low number of elements with limited variation and limited interaction between them, are characterized by stability and clear, easily identifiable cause-effect relations. But organizational environments undergo constant change, and managers and decision makers are continually confronted by the problems of maintaining stable levels of performance and evaluating whether environmental changes require changes in strategy and organization. Chaotic environments (Snowden and Boone 2007) feature cause-effect relations that are impossible to determine because they change continuously and there are no manageable models: the events of 9/11 belong in this category. Interpreting the environment is an extremely ambiguous task rendered even more complicated by the high cost of any eventual errors (Milliken 1990).

Risk and uncertainty

Economic and social theory has long analyzed the concepts of risk and uncertainty. Over the centuries, the significance of the term *risk* has undergone profound changes. The notion of risk appeared for the first time in the Middle Ages, when maritime insurance became a common occurrence (Ewald 1991). At that time, the term was used to refer to the dangers of navigation and was associated prevalently with natural events such as storms, floods, and epidemics, which were difficult to both control and avoid. From the sixteenth century onwards, the term expanded to social contexts, while since the nineteenth century, it has always been more associated with people and their conduct (Ewald 1991). Risk gradually took the place of the concept of fortune or fate (Giddens 1990).

The concept of risk is in itself neutral. It can indicate situations of potential gain and situations of potential loss. Today, however, the concept of risk invariably refers far less to opportunity for gain and increasingly to opportunity for loss. In everyday language, the term *risk* tends to be used above all to indicate threat, hazard, danger, and harm. Risk is defined in statistical terms as the probability of an event multiplied by the magnitude of losses or gains associated with the event. In accordance with the classical notion of probability, the concept of risk is applicable to those situations in which the possible outcomes and their respective probabilities are known with certainty (Bernoulli 1713). By employing the mathematical theory of probability, it is possible to carry out a risk analysis. It is, for example, possible to calculate the probability of winning at a certain game, of obtaining a certain number when throwing dice, and so on.[2]

Risk can therefore be based on technico-scientific estimates, but its evaluation can also depend on human perception. For example, objectively speaking, although a specific means of transport, such as an airplane, is safer than another – the car, for instance – the fear generated by the former may be superior to that generated by the latter. This perception would translate in actual behavior, inducing individuals to use riskier means of transportation because they are perceived as being safer.

Knight (1921) makes a distinction between the concept of risk and the concept of uncertainty. A situation of risk arises if it is possible to assess the probability of certain events that makes it possible to quantify the cost of insurance against them. One example of this is car accidents, for which insurance companies are able to calculate, based on a series of historical statistics, the probability of their occurrence. With conditions of uncertainty, on the other hand, it is not possible to assess the probability of certain events: it is a matter for expert intuition and evaluation. This is exemplified by a financial crisis, in which it is not possible to predict the moment, place, magnitude, or effects with a reasonable level of accuracy.

Keynes (1921) proposes a highly relevant theory of risk and uncertainty, whereby the subjects have a central role in estimating the

---

[2] According to the Frequentist concept, the distribution of probability can be deduced by what has occurred in the past, in other words, by historical precedents. This is a criterion adopted by life insurance companies, for example, which defines the value of the premium to be paid based on the mortality rate. They are not able to predict the future health conditions of a person who takes out a policy, but they can establish the price based on actuarial tables that indicate with extreme precision the overall distribution of human mortality.

probability of real events, even though their estimates depend on reality itself. Keynes distinguishes among three situations in which individuals assess risks. In the first, evaluation is certain; for example, there exists a specific probability of winning in a specific prize draw. In the second, it is possible to provide a quantitative estimate – for example, 20 percent of the airplanes of company Alpha are more than thirty minutes late. In the third, it is not possible to make any concrete prediction; for example, it is not possible to say that a financial crisis will come to an end on day X. Situations of the third type are characterized by an absolute or radical uncertainty. Radical uncertainty is therefore that type of uncertainty that cannot be transformed into calculated risk nor be evaluated in a statistico-mathematical manner.

Disregarding the classical distinction between risk and uncertainty, a more recent conception of risk sustains that it is not primarily a probabilistic concept (March and Shapira 1987) and that risk is used to refer to situations in which the chance or probability that a threat or danger will result in adverse consequences cannot be formally calculated (Hutter and Lloyd-Bostock 1990; Hutter and Power 2005a; Hutter 2010).

From a macro-perspective, society today is often described as a risk society (Beck 1986) precisely in order to indicate its pervasiveness in every social environment. Risk has become ubiquitous (Hood et al. 1992). Several social and cultural theories and perspectives on risk have been developed.[3] According to cognitive science, risk is conceived as an objective phenomenon. It is assumed to exist in reality, and it can be assessed by determining the real probability of an adverse event multiplied by the magnitude and severity of its consequences. By comparison, in the cultural-symbolic perspective, risk is never fully objective or knowable and is contingent on individuals' belief systems and their moral and political positions (Douglas 1966, 1985, 1992; Douglas and Wildavsky 1982; Beck 1986). Ewald (1991, p. 199) maintains that "nothing is risk in itself; there is no risk in reality. But on the other hand anything can be at risk; it depends on how one analyzes the danger, considers the event." Power (2007, p. 4) sustains a broadly constructivist approach to risk management: "managing risk depends critically on management *systems of representation*,

---

[3] For a summary of the debate, see Douglas (1985); Lupton (1999); Taylor-Gooby and Zinn (2006); and Ghephart, Van Maanen, and Oberlechner (2009).

and on instruments for framing objects for the purpose of action and intervention."

Recently, there has been a shift in the conception and study of risk in contemporary society: "real hazards and dangers are produced and yet risk is commonly linked to decision making in organizational or organized contexts" (Ghepart, Van Maanen, and Oberlechner 2009, p. 149). Organizations, not individuals, are the critical agents of the so-called risk society. Risks are increasingly produced by organizations, and organizations are often impacted by risks: "organizations are both centers for processing and handling risks and potential producers and exporters of risk" (Hutter and Power 2005b, p. 1). As the study of organizational disasters highlights, accidents are organized (Turner 1978; Vaughan 1996; Turner and Pidgeon 1997; Reason 1997; Perrow 1999). This leads to the assumption that organizing and risk are two sides of the same coin (Hutter and Power 2005a).

Accepting risk is part of accepting organizations, writes Douglas (1992). It is therefore important that the study of risk becomes a relevant theme in organization studies. It is important to have a better understanding of the role of organizations in producing, managing, preventing, and transforming risk. Institutions and organizations need to be understood as fundamentally oriented to transforming risk (Ghepart, Van Maanen, and Oberlechner 2009). Organizations never encounter risk as a pure given, but attention must be triggered, interpreted and coordinated (Hutter and Power 2005a).

Power (2007, p. 6) affirms that "uncertainty is therefore transformed into risk when it becomes an object of management, regardless of the extent of information about probability ... When uncertainty is organized it becomes a risk to be managed." Understanding risk means understanding both the social construction of risk and the social construction of ideas regarding the organizational management of risk.

In his work *Organizations in Action*, Thompson (1967) identifies uncertainty as the fundamental problem for complex organizations and considers dealing with uncertainty to be the essence of the administrative process. The concept of uncertainty has been central to organizational theory, particularly for those theories that, since the sixties, have given top priority to the relationship between organizations and the external environment (Lawrence and Lorsch 1967; Thompson 1967). Galbraith (1977) affirms that uncertainty is the difference between the quantity of information required and the quantity of information possessed by an organization. Uncertainty means that the decision makers do not have sufficient information regarding environmental conditions and that because of this, it is difficult to predict external changes. In conditions of uncertainty, for the organization there is an increase in the risk of failing to respond to environmental demands and an increase in the difficulty of calculating the costs and probabilities of various decisional alternatives (Koberg and Ungson 1987; Milliken 1987). Environmental uncertainty, or *perceived* environmental uncertainty, has been an important problem for organizational theorists, in particular for those who have dealt with aspects of organizational design (Burns and Stalker 1961; Lawrence and Lorsch 1967; Thompson 1967; Galbraith 1977). Burns and Stalker (1961) define uncertainty as the ignorance of the person who faces a choice. Such uncertainty may concern the future in general as well as this person's ignorance of the consequences of the possible lines of action that might be followed.

For Thompson (1967), there are three types of source of uncertainty for organizations. The first and most important regards the scarce awareness of the relations between cause and effect (generalized uncertainty). The second regards organizational dependence on an environment that might not be cooperative. The third source of uncertainty is internal and pertains to the way in which the various components of an organization depend on each other. The ability of an organization and a society to manage and respond to different types of uncertainty is not simply a function of the correct application of techniques but also regards the creation of practices that guide the management's attention, define objectives, coordinate actions, and distribute responsibility (Scheytt et al. 2006).

Milliken defines uncertainty as the inability perceived by an individual to accurately predict something within or external to the organization (Milliken 1987) and identifies three different types of environmental uncertainty that can be dealt with by the managers of an organization when trying to understand and respond to external environmental conditions (Milliken 1987, 1990). The first type of uncertainty pertains to the lack of awareness regarding how environmental components may change (*uncertainty of state* or *perceived environmental uncertainty*). This type of uncertainty partly depends on the characteristics of the environment in which the organization operates. The second type of uncertainty regards the ability of an individual to predict the impact of environmental changes on the individual's organization, in terms of the nature of the impact, its severity, or its timing (*uncertainty of effect*). And, finally, the last type of uncertainty (*uncertainty of response*) pertains to the awareness of which response options are available and the value and utility of each one. In this case, an uncertain response depends on the scarcity of awareness regarding the options and the inability to predict the possible consequences of each response. What differentiates the three types of uncertainty is the type of information that the managers and decision makers hold to be insufficient. In the case of environmental uncertainty, managers hold that information about the nature of the environment is lacking; in the case of uncertainty of effect, managers are aware of environmental transformation but are not able to evaluate its effects on their own organization; and finally, with uncertainty of response, the managers perceive a lack of information regarding possible response options and regarding the value and utility of each course of action in terms of the desired organizational objectives (Milliken 1987). In situations of uncertainty regarding the state of the environment and the nature of environmental changes, managers find it difficult to identify threats and opportunities, as was the case in the evaluation of terrorist threats before 9/11. High levels of uncertainty can paralyze the process of strategy planning, reducing the possibility of prioritizing threats and of taking the remedial actions necessary.

One way to reduce conditions of uncertainty consists of defining rules to restrict flexibility of choice (Heiner 1983). Such rules are *institutions* that can improve the ability of an agent to control his environment (North 2005). The establishment of an institutional framework as a contingent response to various levels of uncertainty is an essential component of every society. At the base of this process is the human attempt to structure the environment and render it more predictable (North 2005). In a more strictly organizational context, Daft and Weick (1984) structured the process of interpretation of the environment and the reduction of uncertainty into three moments. First, the managers must evaluate an environment and gather data regarding potential factors of change. Second, they must analyze and interpret the collected information in order to identify threats and opportunities. Third, they must act based on their interpretations.

Uncertainty and ambiguity

The theme of myopia, as we have seen, is strictly connected to that of risk and uncertainty. It might be worthwhile here to distinguish between two concepts, uncertainty and ambiguity, which are often regarded as synonymous. In situations of ambiguity, people are confused through an excess of possible interpretations of the events in which they are involved, whereas in situations of uncertainty, people have *no* interpretation of events. They are therefore two completely different kinds of situation: on the one hand, there is an excessive number of interpretations and on the other hand, a total lack. Martin (1992) states that people judge events to be ambiguous when they are highly complex or paradoxical, or when there is an element of obscurity – for example, when they are difficult to decipher or when their interpretation leads to contradictory conclusions. For March (1994), ambiguity refers to lack of clarity or coherence in reality, causality, or intentionality. Ambiguous situations, as March maintains, cannot be codified in a precise fashion within exhaustive and exclusive categories. It follows that, in ambiguous situations, the presuppositions for rational decisions are not completely satisfied. In such situations, in fact, more information does not represent a remedy for an imperfect vision of the real world. The increase in information does not reduce equivocality, but interpretative frames are necessary to reduce ambiguity. It is a problem of sensemaking (Weick 1995). Uncertainty, then, differs from ambiguity first because of the absence of interpretation: in uncertain situations, in fact, adequate interpretations of reality are lacking. In contrast, in ambiguous situations, people are confused by the excessive number of interpretations. In uncertain situations, as opposed to ambiguous situations, the increase in information can reduce uncertainty, transforming it into risk (Stinchcombe 1990).

Another difference is between ignorance and confusion: to remove ignorance, more information is required; to remove confusion, a different type of information is necessary, such as that created by face-to-face interaction (Weick 1995). To resolve confusion, mechanisms are required that make debate and clarification possible, rather than a search for more information (Daft and Lengel 1986). Errors can occur when the need for more information (ignorance, uncertainty) is mistakenly understood as a need for different types of information.

In conditions of extreme uncertainty, the nature of organizational planning significantly changes. In such cases, argues Clarke (1999), rational planning becomes very difficult and is more than anything a rhetorical exercise, justified as a reasonable promise that risk and danger can be controlled. The leaders of high-risk organizations, such as nuclear power plants, chemical plants, or defense systems, for example, rarely admit that uncertainty cannot be measured or predicted by rational calculation. In situations such as these, planning carries out a function that is more symbolic than truly operational in the sense that the plans represent something else with respect to a real ability to anticipate future events, and be ready to tackle negative events. These types of symbolic plans have been called by Clarke (1999) *fantasy documents*, that is, rhetorical instruments that have a political usefulness in reducing uncertainty for organizations and experts.

According to Clarke (1999, p. 2), "organizations and experts use plans as forms of rhetoric, tools designed to convince audiences that they ought to believe what an organization says. In particular, some plans have so little instrumental utility in them that they warrant the label 'fantasy document.'" In conditions of low uncertainty, planning is possible, whereas in conditions of high uncertainty, it is fairly complex and, in Clarke's view, becomes a rhetorical activity, a sort of – false – promise by planners to reassure by maintaining that critical situations can be controlled.

Clarke states, for example, that the plans to face the consequences of a nuclear war are fantasy documents in that the knowledge and experience necessary to know what might really need to be done are simply not available. In this sense, plans understood as fantasy documents are imaginative fictions embodying what people hope will occur when things go wrong. Fantasy documents are symbols of rationality that organizations use to indicate that they are able to control danger, even though in reality this is not in fact the case. They have the function of symbolizing rationality and control, of transforming uncertainty into risk, but from a reassuring symbolic and communicative point of view rather than from a real one. As specified, in the first place, Clarke refers to high-risk contexts when speaking of a symbolic use of planning. The opposite of the fantasy document is the frank admission that risk and danger exist. Admitting this means admitting that there are new dangers and new costs for which no certain control exists. But, in Clarke's opinion, this frankness in admitting the existence of organizational risk that cannot be controlled is not particularly widespread. Few organizations would put leaders prepared to be so open in the highest positions, and few organizations, concludes Clarke, exist in an environment that accepts such explicit announcements of limit and impotence.

2.2 Organizations and the future

Giddens (1990) argues that while for premodern society "the future is something that just happens," which individuals can only influence in a limited manner, in modern society, the future is something that must be accurately deliberated, influenced, and ideally planned. This is even truer with regard to organizations and management. The philosopher Alfred North Whitehead, in a famous lecture at Harvard Business School in 1931, identified in the *activity of prediction* a crucial element in the sphere of economic thinking. Anticipating many of the next few decades' themes of organizational theory, Whitehead stated that economic organizations needed to foster prediction in order to deal with the inexorable changes generated by the modern age (Whitehead 1967).

The problem of the future's predictability is increasingly a pressing preoccupation for companies. A survey carried out amongst the managers of various companies (E. Davis 1995) indicated that handling continuous and sudden change is the most important problem for managers and organizations. In order to survive, organizations must increasingly learn to traverse temporal, geographical, and cultural confines (Daft 2004). The establishment of meticulous plans, the use of sophisticated risk management techniques, and the development of ever-more-complicated revisional systems are aimed at reaching this objective. However, as research demonstrates, strategic planning is becoming increasingly limited (Mintzberg 1994; Mintzberg, Ahlstrand, and Lample 1988). Not being able to control the environment, states Mintzberg, one's strategic planning depends on the ability to predict its configuration during the implementation of the plans. If the environment remains unchanged, no problems are presented for the plans. If the environment undergoes modification, on the other hand, one's planning must be able to predict these changes, and this problem is not easy to solve, particularly when the changes do not demonstrate features of regularity and cyclicity. Given, therefore, that the activity of planning is not able to control the environment, it must be based on known trends, recurrent and reliable tendencies. This can only function though in stable and predictable situations (which we have defined as *ergodic*) in the presence of a structure with a constant and therefore timeless base. As Hogarth and Makridakis (1981) note, however, long-term predictions (two years and longer) are notoriously imprecise, and the hypercompetitiveness of the relevant environments of many organizations tends to present a very different situation, one of a continuously changing world (*non-ergodic*). Narayanan and Fahey (2005, p. 38) affirm that "the future is a *cognitive construction*. Because the future has not yet happened, it must be conceived, imagined, or otherwise created as an explicit cognitive act by one or more individuals." The future may be cognitively inaccessible due to incompleteness of information.

Organizations are increasingly limited in terms of predicting change, especially change that is radical and discontinuous. Tsoukas and Shepherd (2004) propose a model for the analysis of future and uncertain events based on knowledge, more specifically, on knowledge to predict the event and knowledge to deal with it. How organizations deal with the future, state the two authors, depends on how they answer the following two questions: (1) the extent to which there is a stock of knowledge on which to draw for undertaking action and (2) the extent to which there is knowledge for anticipating important events. In other words, up to what point does an organization know what is going to happen and up to what point do they know how to tackle it, should it occur. Different methods are obtained based on how these questions are answered, methods that the organizations can adopt to deal with the future.

When there is a high level of knowledge to predict events and a high stock of knowledge to be able to tackle them (Figure 2.1, quadrant 1), organizations use the classic predictive methods. Some events can be predicted based on extrapolations from the past, based on information that the organizations possess. In this case, the future is no different from the past. It is configured as a model that is repeated over time, as in the case of the seasonal oscillation of the sales of various goods and services. When certain events can be predicted but there is no stock of knowledge to deal with them (quadrant 2), prediction is of little use, and in these cases, analogical reasoning is the method most employed. For example, when models from distant countries are used

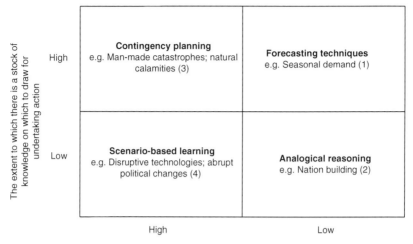

Figure 2.1 Organizations and the future: a typology
Source: Tsoukas and Shepherd 2004, p. 4

in the construction of new political institutions, as happened in Iraq. Building institutions, especially of a democratic type that yet at the same time reflect the values and culture of the local population, is an objective that brings with it great uncertainty. How to create functioning market economies and liberal democracies in the ex-communist countries, for example, is another aspect that does not seem a likely candidate for a short-term solution. Even with all its limits in terms of comparison, however, the analogy of the development of capitalism in other countries does help to generate lessons regarding what to do.

In cases in which the knowledge to predict certain events is low, but there is an adequate stock of knowledge to deal with them (quadrant 3), organizations tend to use the *contingency planning* technique. In these situations, even though prediction is not sufficient, an adequate stock of knowledge is still present to handle these events. For example, it is very difficult to predict the *when* of a terrorist attack but the possible consequences can be dealt with and the damage minimized.

Finally, the last and most complex category involves the combination of a low level of knowledge regarding prediction of events and a low stock of knowledge on which to draw to deal with them (quadrant 4). In these situations, it is very difficult for managers and policy makers to deal with events that they know little about in terms of the likelihood of their happening and of their dynamic – the attack on the Twin Towers being a perfect example. Rapid price increases, dramatic political changes, substantial technological innovation, sudden changes in styles of consumption – these are all events that are difficult to predict and there is no knowledge base developed to anticipate them. In these cases, *scenario-based learning* is the most productive method.

Michael Porter (1985) considers the construction of scenarios not as prediction but as a possible architecture of the future. Using stories, scenario-based learning provides operators and managers with instruments to connect data and information spread out over time. Plausible future scenarios need to be connected through narrative to current tendencies and past experiences. This type of learning does not eliminate uncertainty, but rather, it recognizes its irreducible nature and, as a consequence, accepts the unpredictability of environmental changes (Van der Heijden 1996). In accordance with this perspective, uncertainty is not so much a threat as an opportunity to be given shape. In this case, a foresighted organization is an organization that has refined its ability to see, observe, and perceive what is happening both internally and externally. Organizational awareness is fostered by the fact that the members of the organization become skilled and expert in perceiving the changes in the external environment. It is a matter of individual and organizational ability in seeing the differences: changes, even small ones, and weak, apparently insignificant signals. By preparing scenarios for different possible futures, an organization can verify the plausibility of possible environmental changes and the way in which these will have an impact on the organization. Working on these scenarios enables managers and professionals to investigate the future, even though the specific scenarios analyzed never in fact occur. Tsoukas and Shepherd (2004, p. 10) state that "foresightfulness becomes an *organizational skill* when future-oriented thinking ceases to be a specialized activity undertaken by experts and/or senior managers, in which they engage from time to time in order to deal with something called 'the future,' but acquires the status of expertise that is widely distributed throughout the organization and is spontaneously put to action."

Referring to the use of ICT (Information and Communication Technologies) in the financial sphere, Ciborra (2006) highlights certain collateral effects connected to the use of new technologies, a kind of *risk duality* deriving from technological networks. On the one hand, these technologies have made it possible for financial risk management to develop and evolve, creating greater technical interconnectedness in financial markets. On the other hand, they have increased the operational risk in these markets, in that they have increased the areas of ignorance in the interconnections created. The paradox that emerges is that risk management increases knowledge and safety, which then pushes the risk level of the operations farther away, reducing the capability of control because of the level of interconnection created. The result being that more knowledge is less control. It is a problem for the regulators and for those interested in systematic risk management, and not only in the financial sector. The level of myopia is shifted into systematic, increasingly interconnected dimensions.

To conclude, the future is unpredictable and open, without end, unknowable. It follows that organizations must pass from a *forecasting* logic to a *foresight* logic, cultivating this ability at all organizational levels (Tsoukas and Shepherd 2004). This is possible, because "foresight is essentially about *re-education of attention* and … it can be systematically cultivated through visual strategies that privilege *peripheral* rather than *frontal* vision as the basis of human understanding" (Chia 2004, p. 22).

2.3 Predictable surprises versus bolts from the blue

The question of the predictability of various types of events, such as those described in Chapter 1 (e.g., 9/11 terrorist attacks, the NASA space shuttle disasters), or others, such as the Enron scandal (2001) and the recent world financial crisis (2007), has given rise to a range of contrasting viewpoints. According to some scholars, events of this kind are unexpected but essentially predictable. If their occurrence is not predicted, this is the responsibility of some actors; what is involved are executive failures – the inability of political and organizational leaders to prevent the events. According to others, such events are unpredictable or at the most predictable only by virtue of hindsight bias, that is, predictable only ex post. The types of events in question are impossible to identify, imagine, and obviate because of a set of variegated, interacting, cognitive, organizational, and political factors. It is possible to take a wide range of measures to counteract unexpected events and limit their damage, but it is not possible to eliminate them completely. We refer to the former position as the *predictable surprise* position (Bazerman and Watkins 2004, 2005; Parker and Stern 2005) and the latter as the *bolt from the blue* or the *black swan* position (Betts 1978, 1982, 2007; Handel 1980; Kam 1988; Vertzberger 1990; Taleb 2007). Let us examine these two theories in detail.

Predictable surprises

A predictable surprise can be defined as "an event or set of events that take an individual or group by surprise, despite prior awareness of all the information necessary to anticipate the event/s and their conse-quences" (Bazerman and Watkins 2004, p. 1). Predictable surprises – as demonstrated by many of the examples cited in this book – occur regularly in both private and public organizations. Proponents of the predictable surprise perspective argue that, precisely because such sur-prises are in fact predictable, business, organizational, and/or political leaders have a responsibility to identify and prevent them.

As we saw in Chapter 1, some scholars (Bazerman and Watkins 2005; Mohamedou 2007; Perrow 2007) maintain that what was involved in the case of the 9/11 terrorist attacks was a predictable surprise. In fact, in the years leading up to the attack, a number of offi-cial reports had identified a range of possible threats to aviation secu-rity, recommending among other things a series of additional security measures against Islamic terrorism. These recommendations, however, were ignored. Bazerman and Watkins (2005) argue that in situations of this kind, leaders have a responsibility to recognize and understand the barriers (cognitive, organizational, and political) impeding a full comprehension of the issue in question and to take action to overcome them. In their view, then, so far as the specific case of the 9/11 terror-ist attacks is concerned, the political and administrative elites of the time should have been held responsible for not having dealt with or not knowing how to deal with what was a predictable surprise. In the case of the collapse of the energy giant Enron, many of the inad-equacies of the corporation's financial control system had been known for a considerable amount of time. As early as in 2000, a number of economists had signaled to the Securities and Exchange Commission (SEC) that the rapid growth in consultancy activities from the nine-ties on the part of the world's five largest auditing firms – namely,

Arthur Andersen, Deloitte & Touche, Ernst & Young, KPMG, and Pricewaterhouse-Coopers – had meant that it had become practically impossible to guarantee impartial financial audits (see Chapter 3). The interlinking between (partisan) consultancy activities and (impartial and independent) auditing activities had had the effect of rendering the latter of the two activities null and void. The Big Five had been drawing more and more of their profits from their work as consultants. As a consequence, to give negative assessments in their guise as auditors would have jeopardized their consultancy activity and the continuity of their contracts in general. The inevitable result was the collapse of Enron and Arthur Andersen and the firing of thousands of people.

A surprise is considered to be predictable when "leaders unquestionably had all the data and insight they needed to recognize the potential for, even the inevitability of, a crisis, but failed to respond with effective preventative action" (Bazerman and Watkins 2005, p. 4). Events are not simply either predictable or unpredictable; rather, they are collocated along a continuous axis of predictability. The Enron case is characterized by a number of elements of predictable surprise: in the first place, its leaders were aware of the problem – a problem that had been getting worse over time and that would clearly not come right by itself but one that if confronted would have involved certain costs in the short-term future for only probable (i.e., not necessarily guaranteed) benefits in a distant future; second, the natural human tendency to maintain the status quo did not encourage those involved to focus on the problem and adopt remedial action; and, finally, the impact of private interests' influence may have on people's preparedness to face the problem and adopt corrective measures.

The concept of predictable surprise is diagnostic in nature; its utility is not to explain events ex post but to postulate that events with certain characteristics are predictable. The attack on the Twin Towers and other targets or the Enron financial scandal were, according to the proponents of this position, predictable surprises because in the period leading up to them were a large number of warning signs that could and should have been recognized and on the basis of which remedial measures should have been put in place. From this point of view, a consideration of the phenomenon of hindsight bias would not undermine the conclusions reached in that this phenomenon would not be relevant to the particular class of events in question, that is, predictable surprises. Not all surprises can be considered to be predictable. Predictable surprises are only those in relation to which the threat, first, ought to have been identified because the conditions for its recognition existed beforehand. Second, the threat ought to have constituted a high-priority item on the agenda of decision makers. Third, the threat ought to have prompted and effective counteraction. The predictable surprise of the 9/11 terrorist attacks may also be seen as a market failure arising out of the deregulation of the American aviation industry. In fact, the linking of managers' earnings to a quarterly evaluation of stock prices induced many companies to keep costs low over the short term even at the price of compromising security and reliability.

Aviation security, however, is a collective good (Bazerman and Watkins 2005); everyone benefits from it, but no one – neither individual nor company – has strong incentives to realize it. In short, the incapacity of the US government to promote simple measures to improve aviation security was due to a range of factors: the failure of the decisions of key individuals in posts of command, the lack of courage on the part of political elites, problems of organizational coordination, and the reluctance of the aviation industry lobbies to accept the introduction of security policies that would have led to increased costs and been met with the disapproval of their clients. All in all, then, an extremely serious charge.

The hindsight bias problem

The proponents of the theory of predictable surprise, then, maintain that many of the events we have discussed could have been predicted by the political, organizational, and financial elites in question. Certainly, there can be no doubt that a series of factors of various kinds made it difficult to anticipate them. Nonetheless, according to the scholars in question the fact remains that these events were predictable and that they ought to have been prevented. But is this really true? "In composing this narrative, we tried to remember that we write with the benefit and the handicap of hindsight bias," affirms the *9/11 Commission Report* (NCTA 2004, p. 339) regarding the possibility of predicting the notorious suicide attacks against the Twin Towers and other targets. Roberta Wohlstetter (1962), referring to the attack by the Japanese on Pearl Harbor in 1941, argues that it is much easier to identify significant warning signs and to distinguish them from insignificant ones after a given event has taken place. Naturally, after an event a sign is always clear, but before the event, it remains opaque and subject to multiple and at times contradictory interpretations.

One phenomenon of particular interest consists in the manner in which people attribute sense to events that have already taken place, representing them as the (almost) inevitable consequences of conditions and factors present right from the beginning. Fischhoff (1975; Slovic, Fischhoff, and Lichtenstein 1982) refers to this attitude as hindsight bias, that is, retrospective distortion of judgment, on account of which individuals, once they have been made aware of a given result, are induced to overestimate the possibility of its being foreseen. Once we know what has happened, we have a greater propensity to affirm that such an occurrence was predictable. Hindsight bias is based on a presumed capacity to understand the relations between events in a situation ex ante. The retrospective observation of an event tends to presume that it was clearly predictable. What is involved is a form of narrative fallacy that points to our limited capacity to observe sequences of events without interpolating an explanation or some type of relationship among them. Explanations help to keep facts together and to give sense to them. This propensity becomes negative, however, when it produces the impression that we have understood something when we have not, as when it leads one to incorrectly formulate the conclusions of the analysis of an accident in the form of an ex post rationalization.

Before an event, the future seems implausible; after it, the past seems incredible (Woods and Cook 1999, 2002). Before an accident, individuals, especially if subjected to pressures and deadlines, can misinterpret warning signs. If these signs are weak or contradictory, people may attribute little importance to them, judging that the future appears implausible. There is a difference between the rationality before and during an event and the apparently wiser rationality subsequent to it. The fact that one possesses an awareness of the results of past events influences the way in which one considers them. It is as though we possessed a *superior rationality*, which does not derive from the fact that the analyst is more intelligent but from the fact that he or she envisages a more precise pathway and is better able to see the interconnections among events. The person who describes facts that have occurred is not more intelligent, then, than the person who has experienced them. Moreover, it is by no means the case that such an observer, put in the prior circumstances in question, would have demonstrated the same apparent wisdom that he or she makes claim to after the event. Possessing knowledge of facts that have occurred, then, significantly influences the way in which these facts are subsequently considered.

Fischhoff (1975) tested his theory on two groups of students. He provided these two groups with an account of a nineteenth-century English colonial war, an event that was little known. One group was informed of the actual outcome of the conflict while the other was not. Both groups were asked to evaluate four different possible outcomes. The students who were aware of the actual outcome of the war maintained with greater conviction the probability of the result than did the others. The knowledge of the results of the conflict on the part of one group, then, influenced in a decisive manner the choice between the four possibilities. In other words, knowing what has occurred modifies one's perception of previous events and of causal history. The phenomenon of hindsight bias is characterized by two elements:

• the "it was perfectly clear" effect, on account of which analysts emphasize what individuals should have known and predicted;
• the nonawareness of the influence that knowledge of the results exerts on perceptions of the facts that have occurred.

Post facto, the facts, then, appear more linear, more evident, and less ambiguous, contrasting, and undefined than they probably did to the actors involved in the events themselves. Labeling a past action as erroneous is at times (very often, one might say) a judgment based on a different perspective and on different information available after the event has taken place. It should be acknowledged, however, that the proponents of the predictable surprise theory are aware of this effect and that they argue that the cases analyzed by them are not vitiated by such a mechanism. In fact, however, many of their descriptions and their conclusions seem to be. Taking up the facts and putting them in a sequential order to demonstrate their predictability is an operation that, to say the least, is rather dubious from a methodological point of view. The facts do not present themselves in this way to actors; rather, they are immersed in a sea of contrasting information and are in the presence of other types of threats. This, at any rate, was what happened in the case of the 9/11 terrorist attacks. In this case, moreover, the US defense system, still based on the Cold War model (NCTA 2004), was characterized by a state of organizational and interorganizational fragmentation that made it difficult for the flow of information to circulate.

Wagenaar and Groeneweg (1987), analyzing a selection of one hundred naval accidents, point out how they seem to be the result of extremely complex, unpredictable coincidences. This unpredictability is determined both by the large number of the causes involved and by the fragmentation of the information distributed among the various participants. The authors argue that accidents take place not because people gamble and lose but rather because the people involved do not in fact believe that the accident that is about to occur is in fact possible. These considerations induce one, then, to moderate any attitude of severity or excessive censure in relation to the behavior of organizations, but above all, they encourage us to seek modes of organization that might render more evident in advance what is destined to become limpid later.

Bolts from the blue

A more pessimistic position is put forward by those scholars who hold that events such as those cited until now are very difficult to obviate because of a complexity in the factors at play that makes it impossible to predict them. What is involved from this point of view is a *bolt from the blue* or a *black swan*. The latter expression came into being in consequence of the fact that before the discovery of Australia (in the first decades of the seventeenth century), it was believed that all swans were white, as indeed all the empirical evidence at the time confirmed. When the first black swan was discovered, it was necessary to consider as erroneous what had been viewed as a truth until then. The metaphor of the black swan – present in the works of John Stuart Mill, Karl Popper, and Charles Sanders Peirce – has been taken up again recently by Nassim Nicholas Taleb (2007) to denote an event that has devastating consequences, that is rare, and that is almost impossible to predict. In accordance with this perspective, anticipating the unexpected and predicting surprises are impossible because of the infinite number of weak warning signs present in the environment and the limited capacities of existing technologies that do not make it possible for organizations to effectively identify such signs (Mintzberg 1994).

Predicting surprises is a problem to which scholars of military strategy have dedicated particularly close attention. We have already discussed some aspects of this theme in Chapter 1. According to the most widely shared point of view, surprises occur in the military field because military intelligence systems fail to capture warning signs. Logically, it follows from this that the problem would be resolved if these systems were perfected in such a way that they were able to identify even weak warning signs. But the fact of the matter is that in many important military cases (Betts 1982, 2007), the failure of intelligence services to collect information was only a secondary element in the failure to foresee future events. In many cases, for example, the leaders of states under attack were fully aware of the incumbent threats but still did not react in the way that was subsequently revealed to have been necessary. The failure to perceive threats or to react to them undermines defense efforts. Referring specifically to the military field, Betts (1978) maintains that it is completely illusionary to believe that military operations can be avoided by making recourse to better forms of organization or by way of more adequate regulations or new procedures. The quality of the intelligence of military systems can only be improved marginally not radically. A surprise military attack is an attack launched against an opposing force that shows itself to be insufficiently reactive in terms of its potential to mobilize its own resources. Surprise is defined here as the incapacity of the party attacked to foresee the attack because of errors in evaluating how, when, where, and if the enemy would attack (Betts 1982, 2007). Surprise is by its very nature impossible to predict. If an attack is identified beforehand and countermeasures are put in place, it is no longer a surprise. In this way, successes in identifying warning signs may be indistinguishable from failures.

The analysis of cases of military attacks (Betts 1982, 2007) underlines the essential arbitrariness of prediction; in many situations, the awareness of the danger had the effect that the threat disappeared or that is was directed toward other objectives. Warning signs of a possible attack were present before the attack on Pearl Harbor, the Nazi invasion of the Soviet Union, and the North Korean attack on South Korea, but in each of these cases, there were two problems: the first was that the relevant information did not go up the chain of command in an efficient and effective manner and, the second, that the warning signs were not taken into consideration in an adequate manner because they were fragmentary and contradictory compared with the prevailing strategic assumptions and evaluations (Betts 1978). A further issue to take into account is the fact that the routinization of tension and the prevalence of false alarms desensitizes observers and distracts them from perceiving imminent dangers, rendering unrealistic the rule of "when in doubt, react," for warning signs are continuous and sudden attacks invariably follow periods of prolonged tension. Decision makers are accustomed to living in environments characterized by states of constant alert with the result that warning signs lose relevance and informative force. Failures to predict events, then, could be due not so much to the cognitive rigidity of those who identify signs and make decisions as to the ambiguity present in every piece of data and every item of information examined. One could, moreover, doubt the credibility of the source that furnishes evidence on threats, especially if it is a person that has already given rise to false alarms.

Predicting and protecting oneself from surprises is difficult for reasons that are deeply rooted in human psychology, in political uncertainty, in military complexity, and in organizational intractability: "But there are no significant cases of bolts from the blue in the twentieth century. All major sudden attacks occurred in situations of prolonged tension, during which the victim state's leaders recognized that war might be on the horizon. Surprises succeeded despite ample political warning and, paradoxically, in some cases because of it" (Betts 1982, p. 18). Surprises occur notwithstanding the presence of multiple warning signs. Nonetheless, a wide range of organizational problems can make it difficult to adequately identify significant information and defuse its explosive potential, as we have seen in the case of the 9/11 attacks.

An effective process of identifying threats should make provision for a certain number of phases, including (1) the acquisition of information on the threats; (2) the decision to institute a state of alarm in consequence of the threats; (3) communication about the situation with the relevant decision makers; (4) the discussion on the part of the authorities about the threats, the evaluation of them and the consequent decision to respond; and (5) the implementation of the authorization to respond in conjunction with the military command. Logically, these phases form a sequence. But the presence of ambiguous messages, as well as various factors of erroneous perception already discussed – and which we deal with in greater detail at a later point – generate feedback that renders the process problematic and slow. Problems in the circulation of information can slow things down even more. What to do? Betts (1978, 1982, 2007) speaks of the "elusiveness of solutions."

Reforms are not without effect, but it is necessary to start out from the inevitability of certain disasters and from the unpredictability of many surprises. It is possible, then, to introduce a certain number of countermeasures, but it is necessary to be aware that none of these totally resolves the problems in question and that, on the contrary, each one has major drawbacks. Amongst the measures that Betts discusses are the following:

(1) *assume the worst*: even if there are no clear signs of a threat, act as if there were. The problem is that the prolonged absence of negative events tends to weaken attention. Routinization corrodes perception; every day in which an expected threat does not materialize attention toward the reality of dangers diminishes;

(2) *multiple advocacy*: errors in the identification of dangers are often attributed to the inattention of decision makers toward points of view that they do not share and to the difficulty of access to higher levels of the hierarchy on the part of dissident analysts who present unusual points of view. One remedy for this is to make available specific spaces to openly debate different theories and opinions, including those that are unusual and that are apparently supported by fewer data and proofs. It should be pointed out, however, that an excessive increase in the number of points of view and opinions could have the opposite effect; that is, it could increase the level of ambiguity, leading to an impasse in decision making;

(3) *devil's advocacy*: to make the process of *multiple advocacy* more effective it is possible to institutionalize dissent. One assigns to someone the task of formulating even paradoxical interpretations to put to the test the validity of the points of view that have emerged and to prevent phenomena of groupthink. This solution too has its weak points. If this role is routinized and thereby ritualized, it has a low impact; but if it is not ritualized, there is no guarantee that it will operate when necessary. Moreover, the *cry-wolf phenomenon*, illustrated in more detail in Section 1.2, could increase with the risk that the dissenting voice is not listened to when the situation becomes really dangerous.

Perrow (2007) put forward another version of the pessimistic position. Referring to a range of different contexts, he draws attention to the inevitable inadequacy of our efforts to protect ourselves from major disasters. This inadequacy is to be traced back to the limits of formal organizations in facing up to such disasters. Organizations are instruments that are by their very nature recalcitrant toward the very objectives for which they have been specifically designed. Various types of failures of an organizational kind – in management and in the regulation of systems – make organizations very ineffective in preventing and/or limiting natural disasters or disasters arising from terrorism. What is involved is a form of myopia tied to the characteristics of formal organizations and a structural dimension that is little open to modification. As we shall see further on, many factors operating at the individual, organizational, and interorganizational level make it more difficult to correctly identify warning signs. In some cases, the myopia is intrinsic to the organizational system in question, for example in organizations characterized by close connections and complex interactions (like nuclear power plants [Perrow 1999]). In these situations, failures in forecasting are inevitable in that the technical properties of the system make the observer myopic. The solution to the problem of myopia, maintains Perrow, lies in improving these technologies and in structurally modifying their workings.

In conclusion, according to the theories on failures in predicting, no matter what efforts are made, failures will still continue to take place; indeed, failures are not only inevitable but also natural. Solutions to improve foresight, like those discussed earlier, reveal a range of structural problems inherent to the achievement of a higher level of security by way of radical change. Reforms affected following disastrous events to prevent them from happening again accentuate existing problems and introduce new ones. Changes in the processes of handling and evaluating information will never be able to completely eliminate ambiguity and ambivalence. More rational information systems will never be able to compensate for the bias, idiosyncratic perception, and time limits to which decision makers are subjected. It follows that mistakes are inevitable in that paradoxes cannot be resolved even though improvements to reduce organizational dysfunctions, however limited, are possible.

Those who cover top positions in organizational structures should concentrate, not so much on furnishing responses as on posing the right questions so as to render uncertainty visible – at least to the extent that this is possible – and to give the right weight to strategic decisions. All the elements that facilitate dissent and increase access to the upper levels of a hierarchy and all the elements that increase positive skepticism about the solutions and decisions to be adopted must be reinforced and protected organizationally. At the same time, however, it is always necessary to remain aware of the partial character and the limits of all solutions.

2.4 Financial crises: black, white, or gray swan?

"Why did academic economists fail to foresee the crisis?" was the question which, at the peak of the crisis, Queen Elizabeth II asked the economists of the London School of Economics. In this section, I describe how the debate over the subprime mortgage financial crisis that began in 2007 divided between those who considered it a black swan, and those, instead, who believe the crisis could be foreseen (white swan). Finally, I consider a third possibility: that of a gray swan.

On October 4, 2008, in the middle of the financial crisis, the eighty-two-year-old ex-president of the Federal Reserve, Alan Greenspan, was called as a witness by the House Committee on Government Oversight and Government Reform.[4] After asking Greenspan several questions, the chairman, Henry Waxman, summarized things in this way: "In other words, you found that your view of the world, your ideology, was not right. It was not working." "Precisely," replied Greenspan. "That's precisely the reason why I was shocked, because I had been going on for forty years or more with very considerable evidence that it was working exceptionally well." As president of the Federal Reserve, Greenspan had, in good company with Washington and Wall Street, fostered the financialization of the global economy. Only in 1996 he did, with some worry, express the doubt that the stock market might collapse because of its "irrational exuberance."[5]

---

[4] House of Representatives Committee on Oversight and Government Reform, *The Financial Crisis and the Role of Federal Regulators*, 110th Cong., 2nd sess., preliminary transcript, 37.

[5] Greenspan, together with a large part of world finance's economic system, supported the theory/ideology of *rational markets*, based on the hypothesis of market efficiency. This hypothesis was first formulated in 1960 at the University of Chicago, with reference to the United States' stock market. According to this theory, financial markets (like other economic activities) possessed a *wisdom* that was superior to that of individuals, companies, or governments. It followed that any type of regulation meant reduced efficiency. Obviously, the financial crisis has led to the frequent and forceful questioning of this conviction.

The dominant economic theory was unable to predict the crisis, even though some economists – prestigious, but in the minority – had identified warning signs, one of the first being Raghuram Rajan (2005) and thereafter Shiller, Stiglitz, Roubini, and Krugman.

This is failure of foresight of social and economic theory is also reflected in its inability to predict the duration and the development of the crisis. It is, of course, extremely difficult to predict the bursting of a financial bubble. It is necessary to predict (a) the precise moment that the bubble will burst, (b) the place of origin, and (c) the trigger factors. In these situations, the accuracy of the prediction is essential, as it is in cases of natural catastrophes and terrorist attacks.

Opinion is divided over whether the crisis was predictable or not. Some believe it was a matter of a *predictable surprise*, in other words, of an event that was unexpected but, on the whole, predictable. If it was not predicted, then someone must be responsible for it. Others hold to the line that it was a bolt from the blue, a completely unpredictable event, or predictable only post hoc. The first position can be called "white swan" and the second, a "black swan," using the metaphor described in Section 2.3.

(1) Believers in the black swan position affirm that, because of a series of interacting factors of various kinds (individual, organizational, political), events of this type are impossible to detect and to stop. Complex systems that have artificially suppressed volatility tend to become extremely vulnerable while, at the same time, exhibiting no visible risks. They appear calm and exhibit minimal variations while accumulating growing risk beneath the visible surface. Despite the attempts by political and economic leaders to stabilize the system by inhibiting its fluctuations, the result tended to be the opposite. Palmer and Mahler (2010), using Perrow's (1999) accident theory system, argue that the complexity and coupling of the financial system caused the failure. The financial sector was highly complex and tightly coupled in the years leading up to the mortgage meltdown. In these conditions of high complexity, the meltdown was hard to prevent: it was an accident waiting to happen. These types of artificially coupled systems tend therefore to be prone to black swan situations. In a complex world, a crisis is difficult to predict. Much can be done to avoid unforeseen events and minimize damage, but not everything can be eliminated. At most, symptoms can be indicated, as meteorologists do with hurricanes or geologists with earthquakes (and it is interesting to

note that observations derived from the fields of ecology and epidemiology have recently been applied to financial networks). Given that it is very difficult to predict these events, a certain caution is required in imputing responsibility and guilt to the decision makers, assuming that they possess divinatory capabilities. At the same time, it is fundamental that these events become a source of learning, allowing to modify – even radically if necessary – the situations of weakness and criticality that made them possible, in the hope of reducing the probability that similar events will happen again in the future.

A variant on the black swan theory, the neo-institutional view, states that the agents were *unwitting* causes of the failure. The failures originated in the characteristics of the institutions that were created, in the ideologies and beliefs, in the cognitive frames, that were the source of the behavior that turned out to be disastrous for the economic elites themselves, for all the investors and for the public in general. The individual choices (of bankers, the government, of house owners) that collectively led to financial collapse were rational responses to an imperfect global financial order in which there were strong incentives to take risks. It was a matter to a certain extent of a *collapse that conforms to the norms*, rather than misconduct (except in some cases, and significant ones at that).

(2) However, according to Raghuram Rajan (2010), the truth lies elsewhere. Useful models were available to explain what was happening, just as there were numerous models capable of analyzing the lack of liquidity and the related repercussions on financial institutions. In accordance with this position, the so-called white swan, the events linked to the financial crisis were to a large extent predictable and avoidable, despite evident difficulties. It was a *predictable surprise* in that there was a preceding awareness of all the information required to anticipate the events and their consequences. In 2005, *The Economist* was already cautioning that the world increase in housing prices would be the biggest bubble ever and warned its readers to prepare for great economic suffering when the bubble eventually burst.[6] In August of that same year, Rajan, at the time chief economist for the International Monetary Fund, in a paper presented to the Federal Reserve Bank of

---

[6] "The Global housing boom. In come the waves. The worldwide rise in house prices is the biggest bubble in history. Prepare for the economic pain when it pops," *The Economist*, June 16, 2005.

Kansas City Economic Symposium, showed how financial evolution had rendered the world more vulnerable and at risk. On the one hand, the financial system more successfully exploited the ability to assume risk thanks to a wider allocation of these risks; on the other hand, the system assumed more risk than before. The system of remuneration based on incentives was one of the factors that, amongst other things, had made the financial system more vulnerable: "the changes in the financial sector have altered managerial incentives, which in turn have altered the nature of risks undertaken by the system, with some potential distortion" (Rajan 2005, p. 315). This is what led to the creation of pernicious incentives capable of inducing companies, banks, and financial institutions to increasingly assume more risk: in particular, those so-called tail risks linked to extremes that have a very low probability of verification but which can have disastrous consequences. The grouping behavior of the investors, moreover, encouraged imitation, copying investment choices in goods that were often overvalued, thus increasing the destabilization of the system. These two elements, rewards based on incentives and grouping behavior, together with restricted interest rates, constituted, in Rajan's view, a predictably high-risk mix for the financial system.

Alarm bells were ringing, therefore. If no suitable action was taken, this was due to the inability of organizational leadership to confront such events and to the self-serving interests of several well-organized subjects. Complexity and coupling, states Perrow (2010), certainly played a role in the financial crisis, but largely because the complexity masked the malfeasance that traders engaged in, and the coupling enabled failures caused by this malfeasance to propagate through the system.

Those who believe in this particular concept hold that it is the job of the entrepreneurial, organizational, and/or political leadership to identify and avoid these surprises, precisely because they are in fact predictable. This was the conclusion of the National Commission on the Causes of the Financial Crisis in the United States (NCCFC 2011), the parliamentary commission launched by the US Congress and the president to investigate the cause of the most devastating financial crisis since the times of the Great Depression in 1929. The commission concluded that:

[t]he crisis was the result of human action, not of Mother Nature or computer models gone haywire. The captains of finance and the public stewards

of our financial system ignored warnings and failed to question, understand, and manage evolving risks within a system essential to the well-being of the American public. Theirs was a big miss, not a stumble ... Despite the expressed view of many on Wall Street and in Washington that the crisis could not have been foreseen or avoided, there were warning signs. The tragedy was that they were ignored or discounted. (NCCFC 2011, p. xvii)

A predictable surprise, therefore: a white swan. The commission reported that (a) widespread failures in financial regulation and supervision proved devastating to the stability of the nation's financial markets; (b) dramatic failures of corporate governance and risk management at many systemically important financial institutions were a key cause of this crisis; (c) a combination of excessive borrowing, risky investments, and lack of transparency put the financial system on a collision course with crisis; (d) the government was ill prepared for the crisis, and its inconsistent response added to the uncertainty and panic in the financial markets; and (e) there was a systemic breakdown in accountability and ethics. These conclusions, continue the report,

[m]ust be viewed in the context of human nature and individual and societal responsibility. First, to pin this crisis on mortal flaws like greed and hubris would be simplistic. It was the failure to account for human weakness that is relevant to this crisis. Second, we clearly believe the crisis was a result of human mistakes, misjudgements, and misdeeds that resulted in systemic failures for which our nation has paid dearly. As you read this report, you will see that specific firms and individuals acted irresponsibly. Yet a crisis of this magnitude cannot be the work of a few bad actors, and such was not the case here. At the same time, the breadth of this crisis does not mean that "everyone is at fault"; many firms and individuals did not participate in the excesses that spawned disaster. We do place special responsibility with the public leaders charged with protecting our financial system, those entrusted to run our regulatory agencies, and the chief executives of companies whose failures drove us to crisis. These individuals sought and accepted positions of significant responsibility and obligation. Tone at the top does matter and, in this instance, we were let down. No one said "no." (NCCFC 2011, p. xxiii)

Economists analyzed the policies of economic and financial regulation and deregulation. They could understand the motives and interests by which US politicians pushed the private sector into financing projects for accessible housing. Others, meanwhile, deregulated private finance, resulting in increasing reckless competition and the consequent increase in incentives, for bankers and managers, to run greater and evermore complex financial risks. The economists did not broadcast what they knew and did not raise their voices to point out the risks that were being taken. Perhaps, commented Rajan (2010), the motive was ideological: they were absolutely convinced that markets were efficient, that those involved with them rational, and that the high prices were justified by economic dynamics. It seems all too clear that one of the causes of the financial crisis was the unjustified faith in rational expectations, in market efficiency, and in modern financial techniques. This faith was *encouraged* by high financial rewards for the managers and for those who should have been responsible for control and regulation. Not all economists were blinded by this ideology. Some sent out warnings regarding the level of house prices and mortgage debt. But the myth of the rational market and the conviction that the level of prices was sound were very widespread (Fox 2009).

The financial crisis was created by a mix of deregulatory policies involving the credit market, begun in the 1980s and carried forward by both the Republican and the Democratic governments, and by incentive policies in the mortgage market. It was a crisis determined by mistaken political decisions, such as that of easy credit: "To ignore the role played by politicians, the government, and quasi-government agencies is to ignore the elephant in the room" (Rajan 2010, p. 42). Income inequality had grown steadily partly because of unequal access to quality education. To counterbalance this tendency, the political system exerted pressures on the banking and financial system in order to give middle- and low-income people access to mortgage credit. These pressures distorted the loan sector, encouraging the property bubble, even though the original intention was to reduce inequality.

Such criticalities are *fault lines*, says Rajan. Similar to the fractures in the earth's surface caused by the contact and collision of tectonic plates, they are fault lines that are still present in the political and economic system. It is necessary to reform the economic and political systems to remove these criticalities; otherwise, it will not be long before another crisis rears its ugly head. The simple punishment and removal of the guilty (a necessity in most cases) do not eliminate the underlying conditions of risk. Squaring the circle is no easy task, in terms of maintaining an innovative dynamic finance as a lever for economic development but without assuming exaggerated risks with possible systemic consequences. To do this, concludes Rajan, good economics and good politics are needed.

(3) Apart from the distinction between events classified as black swans, featuring radical uncertainty, and those classified as white swans, more easily predictable, Taleb (2007) identifies events as "gray swans"– that is, predictable within limits. On the one hand, economic historians have clearly pointed out how, over time, a type of *collective repression* occurs in regard to episodes of crisis and the damage associated with them. Reinhart and Rogoff (2009), in their book *This Time Is Different,* highlight how no lessons have been learned from the historical experience of crisis. Since the end of the Second World War in 1945, there have in fact been eighteen financial crises, five of them systematic, involving up to sixty-five countries. Based on the existing literature, Reinhart and Rogoff (2009) developed a prototype of the sequencing of crises, which starts with financial liberalization, is followed by a banking crisis, then a currency crash, and ends with a default on debt (see also Section 4.2). But, despite this awareness, there was no adequate learning process or responsiveness. In sum, a sort of *myopia of learning* (March and Levinthal 1993). One of the characteristics, in fact, of financial bubbles is that they cancel historical precedents from people's minds, which gives rise to the expression *disaster myopia*, that is, the inability to predict disasters (Cassidy 2009).

But if the recent financial crisis was a gray swan, why were the alarm signals inadequate and why did they go unheeded? To answer this question, it is first necessary to investigate the individual, organizational, and institutional mechanisms that rendered controllers deaf and myopic – those controllers who should have acted as *whistleblowers,* performing the role of watchdog in relation to the reliability of companies and financial institutions. In the next chapter, a multilevel frame for analyzing organizational myopia is presented; it then is applied to the case of one of the most important and least investigated *gatekeepers*: the auditing companies.

3 | *The mechanisms of organizational myopia*

3.1 The various levels of myopia

To assess whether events such as those described in previous chapters are predictable surprises or inevitable failures of organizational intelligence, I introduce a model of analysis that investigates different levels of myopia. In organizational theory (Scott and Davis 2007) it is customary to distinguish between three levels of analysis: (1) the *socio-psychological level*, focusing on cognitive elements, on the behavior of people and on the web of interpersonal relations in which members of an organization are embedded; (2) the *organizational level*, focusing on the structures, processes, and mechanisms that affect the workings of the organization itself; and (3) the *ecological level*, focusing on the characteristics of the organization seen as a collective entity operating within a wider system of relations. In an analogous manner, in this book we identify three different levels at which the manifestation of myopia can be analyzed[1]: the individual level, the level of the single organization and the level of the network or organizational field within which single organizations operate. This distinction, without doubt arbitrary, is purely analytic in nature. In real life, the different levels operate simultaneously and are interconnected. The distinction in levels is designed to take account of and represent the broad complexity of the phenomenon in question and the various ways in which it manifests itself.

---

[1] Other scholars distinguish similar levels of analysis. Diane Vaughan (1999) identifies a cognitive level, an organizational level, and an environmental level with reference to the phenomenon of organizational deviance and the dark side of organizations. Allison and Zelikow (1999), apropos of the 1962 Cuban missile crisis, identify three different units of analysis: governmental action as choice, governmental action as organizational output, and governmental action as political result. Lastly, Snook (2000), analyzing a case of friendly fire that occurred in Iraq in 1994, distinguishes three levels of failure: individual, group, and organizational.

Level I: Individual

At the individual level, it is possible to distinguish two modes in which myopia expresses itself: intentional and unintentional. Intentional myopia has to do with states of denial (S. Cohen 2001), that is, with the deliberate refusal to pay attention to warning signs and threats, as happened in the case of the political and health institutions in the state of New York in the face of the threat of AIDS (Perrow and Guillén 1990).

Intentional myopia, however, is not always negative. As Elster (2000) points out, in certain situations the intentional limitation of choices and some forms of preventative obligation can enhance the quality of a decision and in some cases even render a particular decision practicable. In these situations, *less is more*; that is, the limitation of the options can constitute an advantage. Restriction is a kind of positive myopia: agents impose restrictions upon themselves in consideration of the advantages that they expect to derive from ignoring certain courses of action. The typical example of such preventive strategy is that of Ulysses (Elster 1979), who wants his companions to tie him to the mast of the ship and block their ears so they cannot hear and he alone can listen to the song of the Sirens without becoming victim to their seduction. The deliberate adoption of constraints allows individuals to pursue certain objectives in situations of weakness of the will in the face of passions and desires. One particularly important modern case of preventative obligation is that of a government that entrusts the control of monetary policy to a central bank. This choice weakens the political force of the government, which is aware that the common good could be put at risk if it maintains control over monetary policy, and for this reason, it delegates power to independent actors.

Unintentional myopia, instead, consists in a set of mechanisms and processes that limit the capacity of an individual to take fully rational decisions (limited rationality), to realize actions in accordance with his/her own intentions (human fallibility and errors) and to foresee events over the short and long term. Let us now examine some forms of cognitive distortion and of limits to rationality that lead to myopia at the individual level. What follows is not intended to be an exhaustive account of all individual-level mechanisms of myopia, but a survey of those mechanisms that are most recurrent and important in organizations.

The problem of rationality

The theory of rational choice – developed by the mathematician Von Neumann and the economist Morgenstern in 1947 – represents a normative perspective for the analysis of risky behavior. Rational behavior is defined as behavior in which subjects choose the alternative to which they attribute the highest degree of expected utility. The theory of subjective expected utility at the basis of neoclassical economics postulates that choices are effected (a) among a limited set of alternatives, (b) with a subjectively known distribution of the probabilities of the outcomes of each choice, and (c) in such a way as to maximize the expected value of the function of utility (Savage 1954). The principle of rationality is usually understood as an approximation, based on the conviction or the hope that deviations from rationality take place rarely when the stakes are high or tend to disappear totally in market conditions. According to the theory, the choice of *homo oeconomicus* optimizes the utility expected from its realization. In other words, the individual bets on the possible consequences of his or her choices and optimizes the expected result.

Herbert Simon (1947) forcefully calls these assumptions into question. He maintains that in real life, people do not make decisions in the way the theory of rationality suggests.[2] The capacity of the human mind to formulate and resolve complex problems is very limited. The problems that it is necessary to resolve in order to achieve an objectively rational behavior in the real world or even only a reasonable approximation of such a rationality are extremely complex. Some of the limitations on rationality are related to (a) the capacity to acquire information and the costs associated with this quest, (b) the number of alternatives that can be taken into consideration, (c) the evaluation of the consequences of such alternatives, and (d) the knowledge of future events. This set of limits prevents decision makers from taking optimal decisions as assumed in the rational model (Simon 1957; March and Simon 1993). Rather than talk of absolute rationality, then, it is necessary to talk of limited rationality. What is involved is *satisfaction* more than maximization (Simon 1957). Individuals settle on a level of satisfaction, examine the alternatives available, and select the first option

---

[2] There are a large number of criticisms of the theory of rational choice, the treatment of which falls outside the scope of this book. Here we refer only to the objections of North (1990) to the effect that the theory of rational choice lacks a consideration of the role of institutions.

that allows them to reach the level of satisfaction they aspire to with a reasonable degree of probability. The model of limited rationality views individuals in their attempt to take rational decisions, but it recognizes that decision makers do not dispose of important components of information without which they cannot be completely rational. A realistic theory of decision making and individual myopia must take account of the limits of our cognitive structure (capacity to calculate, memory, etc.) and of the environment (quantity of information, quality of information, time available, etc.).

Jon Elster's (1979, 2000) rendition of the rational choice theory is one of the most popular in the social sciences. In accordance with the classic theory of rationality, there is no connection between *external* reality (for example, constraints) and *internal* reality (for example, preferences). Elster, on the other hand, points out that adjustment processes can take place in relation to these realities. An actor can intentionally increase certain specific constraints – like Ulysses, who has himself tied to the ship's mast. Alternatively, preferences can be modified based on concrete situations. For example, a person can stop desiring that which he or she cannot reach, like the fox in the fable by Aesop, who, not being able to get to the grapes, decides that they are sour. On the other hand, the person can begin desiring something that he or she can never obtain.

Adam Smith was one of the first to consider the relevance of emotion to individual choice. In *The Theory of Moral Sentiments* (1759 [2002]), he maintains that human decisions and behavior are driven by an internal struggle between the emotions, such as fear, anger, and love (which Smith called "the passions"), and reason – the impartial spectator. Smith sees human behavior as controlled by the passions but believes that people can avoid being guided in this way by observing their own behavior from the perspective of an outsider: the impartial spectator. As Ashraf, Camerer, and Loewenstein (2005, p. 132) state, "in social situations, the impartial spectator plays the role of a conscience, dispassionately weighing the conflicting needs of different persons." In Smith's view, man's daily life is chiefly the result of a struggle between the emotional desire for immediate fulfillment (following the passions) and the practical need for a long-term plan (as an impartial spectator would do). Smith (1759 [2002], p. 222) considers the passions as largely myopic regarding inter-temporal choice and self-control:

The pleasure which we are to enjoy ten years hence interests us so little in comparison with that which we may enjoy today, the passion which the first excites, is naturally so weak in comparison with that violent emotion which the second is apt to give occasion to, that the one could never be any balance to the other, unless it was supported by the sense of propriety, by the consciousness that we merited the esteem and approbation of everybody, by acting in the one way, and that we became the proper objects of their contempt and derision by behaving in the other.

In contrast, "The spectator does not feel the solicitations of our present appetites. To him the pleasure which we are to enjoy a week hence, or a year hence, is just as interesting as that which we are to enjoy this moment" (1759 [2002], p. 221). It follows, continues Smith, that our behavior appears to the spectator wholly absurd and wrong when we sacrifice the present for the future. The impartial spectator acts, therefore, in a non-myopic way, with greater foresight, preferring to abstain from immediate pleasure in order to gain greater pleasure and future earnings. The world, maintains Smith, is not therefore inhabited by dispassionate agents but rather by real human beings (Ashraf et al. 2005).

Elster (2000) underlines how the effects of passion and emotions can produce a discrepancy between intention and behavior in various ways, for example, by (a) distorting our cognitions and generating false beliefs about the consequences of certain decisions; (b) obscuring such consequences, that is, suppressing the awareness of them; (c) inducing a weakness of will, as when we prefer options with worse consequences over options with better consequences; and (d) inducing myopia, modifying the weight of the decision in respect of the various consequences. Emotions can give rise to manifestations of wishful thinking (i.e., believing in what one desires)[3] and self-deception. In situations in which what is at issue are events that elude our control emotions can impact on the evaluation of the probability of such events occurring and/or on the evaluation of the credibility of the affirmations that describe them (Frijda 1986). Damasio (1994), on the other hand, advances a positive vision of the role of emotions, arguing that rather than leading to myopia, emotions can help us to take

---

[3] According to Camerer and Lovallo (1999), wishful thinking may also explain phenomena such as the high number of failures among new companies, the spread of short-term speculation in financial markets, and so on.

into account the long-term consequences of our behaviors. Gigerenzer (2007) endorses this positive characterization of emotions, affirming that our intelligence is prevalently unconscious, based on processes extraneous to logic and made up of gut feelings, far removed from the canons of rationality. Yet, this does not imply that these processes are devoid of regularity. In a decidedly audacious manner, Gigerenzer refers to this theory of his as "the new land of rationality."

As North (2005) writes, the most important problems that we have to confront have their origin in the fact that human beings act in economic, political, and social theaters in which the actors have imperfect information and knowledge and in which reactions to the actions of other actors are just as imperfect. The principle of rationality is not wrong in itself, but it does not guarantee human beings a secure guide in the choices they make, especially in uncertain contexts and in situations that are crucial for the process of change. North (2005) argues that the assumption of rationality is not able to adequately account for the relationship between the external environment and the human mind.[4] Behavioral economics has advanced a number of criticisms of the model of rational choice popular in neoclassical economics (Kahneman and Tversky 1979, 1998; Tversky and Kahneman 1973; 1974; Sunstein 2000). In particular, it shows how individual reasoning do not conform to some of the assumptions of the normative theories of rational choice, and that human reasoning systematically deviates from what is expected of a rational actor with adequate information. Kahneman and Tversky (1979; Tversky and Kahneman 1973, 1974) identify a few systematic biases that influence human judgment and the decision-making process. In particular, they focus on the cognitive shortcuts – heuristics – that individuals adopt to simplify the decision-making task. These cognitive strategies furnish people with a simple way to deal with complex problems; however, according to some, this might undermine the accuracy of the choice.

Two different paradigms exist regarding the effectiveness of heuristics. The first of these points out that heuristics can be inappropriate in many situations, or steer a person to incorrect evaluations

---

[4] North (2005) maintains that even a rational action may show itself to be inadequate when one seeks to explain long-term, complex problems such as economic development or non-ergodic (in continual movement) or highly unpredictable phenomena.

and decisions, in that they lead to numerous biases (some of which are illustrated later). Kahneman, Slovic, and Tversky (1982) show, for example, how people, even if they wish to act in a rational manner, suffer from systematic distortions that lead them to select suboptimal courses of action.[5] However, when the decision makers are conscious of these systematic distortions, they can correct the decisional process and reduce myopia. The second paradigm, advanced by the *fast-and-frugal heuristics* research program (Gigerenzer, Hertwig, and Pachur 2011), argues instead that, in contrast to general belief, complex problems do not require complex calculations. Relying on computational models (computer simulations) and experiments, scholars show that in certain decision-making tasks, *more is less*: in other words, having less information, less evidence, can paradoxically favor better decisions. Fast-and-frugal heuristics are effective because they simply exploit the informational structure of the environment in which the decision making takes place, using an ecological type of rationality (the result of the evolutionary adaptation of human behavior) rather than a logical type. Simon (1999) states that this program represents a revolution in the cognitive sciences and in the study of decisions. The *homo heuristicus* can make use of heuristics not because they require less effort, at the cost of less accuracy, but because they are *accurate*, in the sense that they allow both greater precision and greater adherence to the environment of the decision, in the sense of the ability to exploit contextual factors.

Other critiques of the classical paradigm of rational choice have been formulated by experimental economics (Varian 1992; Gigerenzer and Selten 2001), by the managerial sciences (Bazerman 2006) and more recently by the neurosciences, in particular, by neuroeconomics (Camerer 2005, 2007; Rangel, Camerer, and Montague 2008).[6]

---

[5] One example of systematic distortion regards the estimation of the *probability of improbable events*, in which, oftentimes, people choose a course of action that leads to worse results than those that might be achieved with other actions. For instance, people prefer to take part in a lottery with a bigger prize and a very small probability of winning it instead of choosing a lottery with a smaller prize and a much bigger chance to win it.

[6] Neuroeconomics studies how the human brain interacts with the external environment and how minds interact in groups to determine economic behavior. Camerer (2007) maintains that neuroeconomics is a field of application of behavioral economics, oriented towards using neural data to produce a mathematically and neurally systemic approach to the

As far as the neurosciences are concerned,[7] this field of study points out many of the defects of the neoclassical model, and it charges it with having neglected the role of nonconscious, automatic, and emotive processes in the decision-making act – that is, processes that cannot really be defined as conscious deliberations. In accordance with this theoretical approach, the importance of these processes in decision making involves an evolution from the figure of *homo oeco-nomicus* to that of *homo neurobiologicus* (Kenning and Plassmann 2005).

The neurosciences applied to decision making underline the distinction between cognitive (or rational) processes and affective processes, those connected to emotions and emotional responses. Human decisions are created from the interaction between controlled processes and automatic processes. Both types of process take place in our cognitive-analytical system (that is, the system that makes structured, reflective thought possible) and in the affective or limbic system. This latter is present both in humans and in animals and governs intuitive response and automatic processes; these are developed to confront evolutionary challenges, are faster than conscious ones, and occur without effort.

Experiments in brain imaging[8] indicate that when we make decisions in conditions of uncertainty, a natural occurrence for those who must decide in complex systems, there is a conflict between instinct and emotion on one hand and rational choice on the other. Since automatic processes occur continuously, the controlled (cognitive) processes required for rational decisions must take into account and avoid the automatic ones. This renders rational behavior difficult in many situations.

---

micro-fundamentals of the economy. One radical position in relation to the neurosciences is that of Churchland (1989), who maintains that the conception that we commonly have of psychological phenomena constructs a radically false theory – a theory so inadequate that, once the neurosciences reach a fully developed phase, both its principles and ontology will finish up being supplanted rather than being progressively reduced.

[7] Neuroscience is emerging as one of the most important fields of research for the study of decision-making processes. It is a constantly growing field of research. For reasons of space, I am not able to deal with it here in the detail that it deserves.

[8] This is the use of neuroimaging technology capable of measuring cerebral metabolism in order to analyze and study the relationship between the activity of specific cerebral areas and specific cerebral functions.

With regard to the choice of acquiring goods, for example, many of our decisions are not so much the product of a self-conscious calculation as the result of an instinctive and affective reaction in the face of what we codify as potential gain or loss. The assumption on the basis of which people act according to their intentions and after a very careful evaluation of their own system of desires, opportunities and beliefs is based on conceptions of a cognitive type by now bypassed by the results of research in the neurosciences. The decision-making processes' underlying actions are generated by very complex neuronal activity, and deliberate reasoning arrives only at a later point when the decision-making process has already come to a conclusion. Rather than determining choices, deliberate reasoning serves to explain to the subject his own motives, furnishing reasons for decisions ex post (Knutson et al. 2007).

There are cases in which the framing of a given decision-making problem, notwithstanding an equal level of informational content, radically changes the response given, as we shall see further on. Cohen, March, and Olsen (1972) and March and Olsen (1976) have further brought into question the model of rational choice by developing the concept of organized anarchy and the decision-making model of the garbage can. When decision-making processes are characterized by problems related to the formation of preferences (because of a lack of criteria for decision, the uncertainty of technologies or a lack of clarity in relation to the connections between the measures to take and the decisions that follow on from them) or by fluidity with regard to participation in the decision-making process (with different players entering and exiting from the scene), decisions appear more like cases of organized anarchy than the outcomes of rational choice. The metaphor of the garbage can points to the apparently chaotic nature of the decision-making process, representing it as though the participants in it threw the various types of problems and solutions involved into a garbage can. This metaphor reinforces the idea of the organized anarchy of the process, underlining the random aspect of the decisions in many organizations, an image that starkly contrasts with the representation of the rational decision as theorized by Von Neumann and Morgenstern (1947) and Savage (1954).

Distorted interpretations
Interpreting, not deciding, is the distinctive characteristic of humankind, argue March and Olsen (1983). A wide range of psychological

factors influence the decision-making process, affecting information acquisition as well as the identification and perception of threats. Here I briefly examine some of the cognitive *traps* at the basis of human inference that act as obstacles to and distort the identification of warning signs, thus leading to individual myopia:

- The phenomenon of *positive illusion* leads people to view the world and the future in a more positive manner than is justified by the facts. It also diminishes one's capacity to read unfavorable signs. Unrealistic optimism constitutes a bias in evaluation and judgment. It induces people to believe that their future will be better than that of other people (Taylor 1989).
- The phenomenon of *filtering* is a form of selective perception. What we lend attention to depends on what we expect to see. Our expectations color reality (Snook 2000; Weick and Sutcliffe 2007) and often influence in a decisive manner our perception of events and our consequent actions. If something does not fit, we tend to distort reality to make it correspond to our mental model rather than call the model itself into question.
- *Confirmation bias* is a type of cognitive error, closely tied to the mechanism just discussed. Based on a particular type of selective thought, people tend to lend attention to what confirms their own beliefs and to ignore, or underestimate, the importance of what contradicts these beliefs (Evans 1989; Reason 1990). This is an error of inductive inference based on which one tends to search for proofs that confirm one's point of view, eliminating dissenting voices and information not consistent with one's own expectations. Becoming in certain ways immune to contradiction, our opinions and convictions can become rigid with the passing of time, requiring an ever greater quantity of disconfirming evidence to put them in doubt. It is possible for there to emerge phenomena of selective memory that lead people to opportunistically forget uncomfortable facts that are not consistent with their overall vision.
- *Wishful thinking* consists in adapting one's perception to expectations. For instance, it induces people to perceive some desired, but highly improbable event or remote future situation as if it were quite possible and as if it could come about from one moment to the next. Facts, events, perceptions, written documents, and so on are interpreted more according to what one wants than according to the actual evidence.

- *Egocentrism*, instead, induces a person to interpret information to his or her own advantage. Situations are interpreted according to the role covered by the person in respect of the event in question. Individuals, in their own account of events, tend to attribute an excessive importance to the role they cover. This tendency is closely related to the phenomenon of *fundamental attribution error* (Ross 1977), a systematic deformation in people's way of interpreting the behavior of others, on account of which they have a tendency to underestimate the influence of the situation in question and to overestimate the characteristics of its protagonist. When judging others, we tend to attach less importance to the context and prefer to dedicate ourselves to classifying people often in moral terms. The consequence is that people think that they themselves and the organization in which they happen to be operating are more central than they really are within the broader overall system.
- The *self-serving bias* is the tendency for individuals to attribute their own successes to internal factors while putting the blame for failures on external factors.
- *Discounting the future* (i.e., not considering the future important) makes people tend to prefer short-term options to medium-to-long-term options (as discussed previously). This is a serious problem for political leaderships and any investments that involve a limited but guaranteed cost in the present to ensure the realization of advantages in the future or, to put it in terms that are more relevant to the themes of this book, to exchange certain costs over the short term for possible containment of damage in the future. Some of these issues were dealt with in relation to the problem of common resources in Section 1.4. The Federal Reserve System (the central banking system of the United States, also known as Fed) refused to burst the stock market and credit bubble in the years that preceded the 2007 financial crisis, with a political choice that can be partly explained on the basis of a mechanism of discounting the future. The Fed did not want to be attacked for having caused an economic crisis, thus they decided not to bear the certain but limited cost of an economic crisis back then, discounting the major, albeit not certain, cost of the future financial crisis. In other words, the Fed preferred to take the risk of a major financial crisis instead of trying to prevent it by triggering a limited economic crisis.
- *Omission bias* and maintenance of the *status quo*. Closely related to the phenomenon of discounting the future is the widespread

tendency to not provoke damages, based on which people are more inclined to make errors of omission, due to inaction, than errors of commission that cause damage, however slight. Actions that cause definite – be it limited – damage but that could, on the other hand, prevent much graver damage in the future tend to be avoided (Ritov and Baron 1990). As a result, people fail to make intelligent choices that could prevent foreseeable consequences.

- *Unintentional blindness* (Mack and Rock 1998; Simons and Levin 2003) is a form of limited visual awareness. People have a broad tendency to not observe with attention what they are directly looking at when they are focusing on something else. For example, an airline pilot that is carrying out preflight checks might not notice that another airplane is on the runway even though it is clearly visible.
- *Change blindness* (Simons and Levin 1997; Simons and Rensink 2005) is another form of limited visual awareness. It consists in the failure to recognize in an effective manner the changes in an object or in a scene, even when they are quite evident and the person in question is not distracted by other stimuli. This occurs in particular if the changes occur slowly and gradually, like in the case of the Easter Island vegetation discussed in Chapter 1.

People tend to hold to positive illusions. They are inclined to interpret events in an egocentric manner and to underestimate risks. Positive illusions help people to realize difficult tasks and to confront uncontrollable and adverse events, but at the same time they can reduce the quality of the decisions they take (Dunning, Heath, and Suls 2005). For example, certain events that took place before the 9/11 terrorist attacks were interpreted as indicators of political success instead of as signs of deficiencies in the defense system: the arrest of the people responsible for the 1993 bomb attack against the World Trade Center, the explosion in the federal government office in Oklahoma City in 1995 and the conspiracy against Manila Airlines in the same year; the rapid identification of Bin Laden and his network as the perpetrators of the bombings of the US embassies in Kenya and Tanzania, and the FBI's rapid identification of al Qaeda as responsible for the attack against the American aircraft carrier the USS *Cole* in 2000. These events, instead of being viewed as policy failures, were considered to be successes, with obvious consequences in terms of a fall in attention and concern. People who voiced fears of possible terrorist attacks on

US soil on the part of al Qaeda were dismissed as Jeremiahs. Skepticism towards the threats of unpredictable events was reinforced.

Generally, people do not evaluate options in a long-term perspective, tending instead to focus on the short term. They prefer the risk of running up against substantial but improbable losses in the future as opposed to accepting definite losses of a limited scale in the present. The case of security checks at airport check-ins is an example. If they were not obligatory, we would probably not accept so readily a (certain) loss of time (fifteen minutes or so) to prevent the risk of a (highly improbable) catastrophe. In cases like these, we are victims of *errors of omission* (Ritov and Baron 1990) that are tied to an innate human tendency to maintain the status quo (W.F. Samuelson and Zeckhauser 1988).

The phenomenon whereby in circumstances in which the benefits of an action are vague and removed in time, people are very reluctant to accept certain and immediate losses, together with the optimistic illusion that prevents us from imagining imminent catastrophes, represents one of the innate cognitive barriers that impedes leaders from having a clear vision of risks and from taking countermeasures against predictable surprises.

In short, positive illusions, egocentrism, a limited attention to the future, errors of omission, the desire to maintain the status quo, and so on are all elements involved in the question of predictable surprises. These errors operate in unison. And in addition to these factors of an individual character are other factors of a different nature – organizational, political, and interorganizational – that interact with them. Because it is impossible to change human nature – no matter how much one tries – many of the biases discussed earlier will inevitably affect individual judgment. It is therefore necessary to work above all on organizational and contextual structures to design organizations that limit the scope of these errors and channel them in a positive direction.

The importance of framing

The identification of problems and threats is a process mediated by the construction of frames. This operation of perception does not consist just in the establishment of a correspondence between a given problem and its identification on the part of the actor in question. The frames to which we refer are like lenses that make it possible to see some things

	Managerial/operational role		Engineering/technical role
Attempt to classify	Foam strikes have happened before – space shuttles have come back safely in the past		We are not sure what happened: this is an uncertain event
Routine	Review rationale from past events (provides confirmatory evidence)		Collect data to minimize uncertainty
Response	Proceed with operations unless there is clear evidence of a problem; demand proof	Conflicting	Proceed with technical inquiry within given constraints; silence after multiple tries

Figure 3.1 Two frames of reference
Source: Milliken, Lant, and Bridwell-Mitchell 2005

but that at the same time make it difficult to see others. When people adopt one type of frame, they reduce their capacity to make use of others, thereby generating rigidity. This reduces the possibility of identifying weak warning signs not captured by the frame in use. Different frames can enter into conflict with each other. In the case of NASA, in particular in relation to the problem of protective material detaching from the surface of the space shuttle *Columbia* during its launch, the engineers and managers in question viewed the same problem in different ways precisely on account of the different frames of reference they were using. These differences lie in the modes of classification, the routines, and, as a result, the responses they generated (Milliken, Lant, and Bridwell-Mitchell 2005). In some cases, stark contrasts emerged between the managers and the engineers, as the scheme presented in Figure 3.1 suggests.

Individuals' sensitivity to framing effects, as Kahneman (2003) argues, contradicts a fundamental principle of invariance. The frame within which a decision-making problem is viewed decisively influences the response that is given to it. The importance of framing in the identification of a threat is easily exemplified. In the case of the 9/11 terrorist attacks, the information on the participation of Islamic extremists in pilot training courses was passed over and was judged as irrelevant by the US defense system. Because they did not have as a frame the use of airplanes as a weapon, the information in question was not interpreted in an adequate manner.

Festinger (1957) discovers that in situations in which people behave in ways that are inconsistent with their beliefs, a psychological tension and sensation of unease would arise. In his theory of *cognitive dissonance*, he argues that individuals would engage in various forms of cognitive restructuration in order to eliminate or reduce this psychological tension. Somehow, counterintuitively, very often people change their beliefs to fit their actual behavior, rather than the other way around. To reduce dissonance, they will discard or eliminate information and elements that do not fit the interpretative framework they have adopted.

When a situation is erroneously interpreted, and, at the same time, there is a conviction that this interpretation is correct, the conditions come about for a widening of the gap between what is perceived and what is actually taking place. Once a person has formulated a fixed idea about an event or its circumstances, he or she shows a marked inclination to interpret every other piece of information in question in such a way as to confirm or reinforce his or her own understanding of the facts. This phenomenon is also referred to as *confirmation bias*. It consists in the difficulty that each one of us has in considering his or her own interpretations as hypotheses to be put to the test (Wason 1960; Einhorn and Hogarth 1978).

Perrow (1999) describes the case of a naval accident that occurred in 1978, attributable to the phenomenon of the *sloping plane of confirmation*. Focus of his attention was an error made by the captain of a Coast Guard training ship *Cuyahuga* in Chesapeake Bay (United States). One night, the captain saw two warning lights signaling the presence of another ship. In actual fact, however, there were three lights. What the captain saw made him think that the ship in question was heading away from him whereas it was approaching him. This was a case of an incorrect interpretation in which the gap between what was perceived and what actually took place grew ever wider. Two other elements of information were available to the captain: the image on the radar of what appeared to him to be a third smaller craft and a further item of data (this too originating from the radar) indicating that his own ship and this smaller craft were rapidly crossing paths. The captain, instead of interpreting this latter piece of information in a correct manner, concluded that, since the other craft was much smaller, his own ship would rapidly draw past it. The new information deriving from the radar was interpreted badly, and instead of counteracting the captain's original conviction about the lights that he had seen, it ended up reinforcing it. The ship's first officer had understood all along what was really happening but, not being in direct contact with the captain, he was not in a position to recognize that his superior's picture of the world contrasted with reality, and hence, he did not intervene. Subsequently, when the captain observed that his own ship was about to overtake the smaller craft, he realized that in so doing, he would prevent it from entering into the Potomac River. At that point, he ordered an immediate change of route to allow the fishing boat to enter the port without difficulty. It was in the course of this sudden maneuver that the ship ran up against the prow of a large ship heading in the opposite direction. Eleven people lost their lives in the disaster.

A series of experiments on how people manage risk and uncertainty carried out, once again, by Tversky and Kahneman (1981; Kahneman 2002), leads to the formulation of the notorious *prospect theory*, in which they argue that the adoption of a positive frame (perceiving results as gains) as opposed to a negative one (seeing results as losses) influences the choices decision makers make. People tend to privilege more risky choices when using negative frames and to be more prudent in making choices when using positive ones. Another example of framing is offered by Lindenberg's (2000) work, in which he identifies two classes of behavior: automatic behaviors, which do not require attention, and controlled ones, which do. In the second type of behavior, attention on the part of the actor is important but, being selective in nature, it may happen that it overlooks some aspects of the problem to concentrate on others. According to this theory, people's attention is influenced by the primary objectives pertaining to a given action; these are seen as activating particular frames that in turn give rise to certain beliefs and principles. In addition to these primary objectives, however, there also exist a range of secondary objectives, which in some circumstances can become more important than the primary ones. For example, in certain forms of self-deception it is possible to observe that a secondary objective is more important than a primary one. Let us image, for example, that in the purchase of a certain good the price-quality relationship is the primary objective and the design the secondary one. It can happen that the secondary objective significantly influences the frame in such a way as to become a deciding factor even at the expense of the achievement of the primary objective (the price-quality relationship). Lindenberg's argument is actually much broader and deeper than this, but for the purposes of our model, it is sufficient to underline the importance of framing in directing attention towards certain elements that can influence the decision-making process.

The perception of risk and danger

Contrary to what used to be argued by many scholars some years ago, the perception of risk is at times more important than its actual magnitude in purely quantitative terms. The subjective dimension of the experience leads people to construct scales of risk that are different from those that can be defined in an objective manner (where risk is the probability of an event taking place multiplied by the magnitude of its consequences). The literature on the perception of risk strongly challenges the idea that rational analysis has of risk (Kahneman and Tversky 1979). It shows how individuals react to danger in a wide variety of ways, often dependent on the way in which the risk in question is framed and presented (Slovic 2000).[9] The psychometric paradigm of the perception of risk (Slovic, Fischhoff, and Lichtenstein 1977, 1982, 1984) emphasizes the preferences expressed by individuals in relation to risks. In accordance with this paradigm, risks are subjectively defined by individuals who can be influenced by a wide variety of psychological, social, institutional, and cultural factors. Many of these factors and their interrelationships can be quantified and modeled in such a way as to give an account of the responses of individuals to the risks they encounter (Slovic 2001). The subjective perception of risk, then, is more important than the objective evaluation of it. It turns out in fact that risks with a low probability but very substantial consequences are perceived as more threatening and more probable than those with insignificant consequences (Von Winterfeldt, John, and Borcherding 1981). Other scholars (Pidgeon, Kasperson, and Slovic 2003) introduce the concept of social amplification, which points to the relationship between perception and communication. This latter element assumes

---

[9] These positions are severely criticized by Douglas and Wildavsky (1982). They argue that individual attitude to risk should be viewed in terms of broader cultural frames and of the information and forms of communication that correspond to them.

an important role in the social amplification of risks and so influences the perception of them. In contrast to the psychological approaches to risk, the cultural approaches (Douglas and Wildavsky 1982) affirm that individual perception and people's response to risks can be understood only in relation to the cultural background of the people in question and not through individual cognition. Risk is interpreted as a socially constructed phenomenon. Because of this, the different ways in which societies or specific social groups construct risks and dangers depend on the forms of social organization that characterize them.

Our analysis of the *Columbia* space shuttle disaster demonstrates the great dangers involved in the process of labeling events. The NASA managers defined the detachment of the foam coating from the surface of the shuttle as an *in-family* as opposed to *out-family* event. They were not alarmed by the images of the launch that pictured – however unclearly – the foam material peeling off the shuttle. Labeling an event as in-family requires that it is reportable, and in order for it to be reportable, people have to have an appropriate language; that is, they have to have at their disposal the vocabulary that will enable them to define it. These very same words, however, can limit what is seen and hence what is reported (Weick 2005a). The labels at the disposal of a particular group color what its members perceive, leading them to tend to overestimate the number of in-family events that occur (Weick 2005a). This phenomenon reduces the possibility of defining penetrating frameworks for unexpected events and limits the recognition of threats.

A number of psychologists have documented the effects of the pressure of time on individual cognition and performance. Zakay (1993) demonstrates how the perception of temporal pressures leads to inferior performances, whereas Wright (1974) shows that managers do not use information in a suitable manner when they operate in conditions of urgency. Simon (1992) argues that motivational pressures influence attention in a way that often leads to an inadequate treatment of information. This research confirms that when an individual operates under pressure, his or her attention focuses on a particular target or function and cannot easily be directed away from it.

The analysis of a range of mechanisms that at an individual level lead to myopia helps to explain many of the failures of rationality and provides one set of reasons why people make certain decisions that can appear wrong or be labeled as errors ex post. One of the limits of the explanations that concentrate only on this level, however, is the tendency to isolate the decision maker from the broader context within which decisions are actually taken, leaving in the background the organizational and interorganizational dynamics that instead constitute the spaces within which what can and cannot be decided is determined.

Level II: Organizational

In the previous section, we saw that some of the failures in decision making in organizations are in part due to failures in the cognitive processes of individual decision makers. Other obstacles to effective decision making go beyond the human mind. In this section, I explore the barriers that manifest themselves at the organizational level. At this point, then, organizations and their modes of operating become the principal object of the analysis. In what follows, I try to explain organizational behavior in terms of the objectives, structures, cultures, modes of coordination, constraints, and practices that the individual members of organizations have in common.

At the organizational level, myopia can be explained in terms of a range of models of inference. If an organization produces an output of a certain kind in a given moment, this result derives from the structures that constitute it, the procedures it uses, and the repertoires of knowledge and action that characterize it. In this regard, March and Simon (1993) identify two different logics of action: a logic of consequences and a logic of appropriateness:

The first, analytic rationality, is a logic of consequences. Actions are chosen by evaluating their probable consequences for the preference of the actor. The logic of consequences is linked to conceptions of anticipations, analysis, and calculation. It operates principally through selective, heuristic search among alternatives, evaluating them for their satisfactoriness as they are found. The second logic of action, a matching of rules to situation, rests on a logic of appropriateness. Actions are chosen by recognizing a situation as being of a familiar, frequently encountered type, and matching the recognized situation to a set of rules. ... The logic of appropriateness is linked to conceptions of experience, roles, intuition, and expert knowledge. It deals with calculation mainly as a means of retrieving experience preserved in the organization's files or individual memories. (March and Simon 1993, p. 8)

The logic of consequences is based on analytic rationality. Actions are chosen by individuals based on their preferences and their evaluation of the probable consequences of such actions on themselves. The logic of appropriateness, instead, is based on the appropriateness of the rules to specific situations. Individuals make choices by making reference to a situation recognized as familiar, already encountered, and typical and by linking it up to a specific set of rules. The distinction between the two different logics lies at the basis of the differences between the individual level and the organizational level. At an organizational level, in fact, preferences and interests are seen as a social construction that comes about within specific organizational contexts. Thus, preferences and interests have in respect of organizations an endogenous as opposed to exogenous origin. As Keohane (1988) maintains, institutions do not merely reflect the preferences and power of the units of which they are made up; rather, they themselves form those preferences and interests. Organizational routines are central to explaining the workings of organizations, and they cannot be seen just in terms of rational strategic calculation. Routines and the organizational logic that underpins them are an independent variable that comes about within a complex interaction of relations between the subunits that make up an organization. Organizational routines are characterized by a logic of appropriateness and not by a logic of consequences.[10]

At the organizational level, myopia is favored by the inadequacy of the way in which organizations analyze threats, integrate information, create incentives for action, and learn from experiences. The collection and elaboration of information is never just a problem of single individuals – notwithstanding the importance of the organizational

---

[10] Scholars who emphasize efficiency see organizations as aggregations of interests within which problems of cooperation and collective action are not important. For this reason, they tend to pay greater attention to principal-agent relationships (March 1994) as a key to understanding organizational behavior. Instead, scholars who emphasize culture recognize the importance of this relationship but nonetheless tend to see interests as a social construction dependent on the setting in which a given organization operates. Organizational choices in relation to interests are made more according to appropriateness than based on the consequences. Organizations are considered as recalcitrant instruments in the realization of objectives – reluctant players in respect of the ends for which they have been deliberately designed (Perrow 1986; Perrow and Guillén 1990).

roles they might cover – but also an organizational problem. It is a collective problem of the institutional entity in which the process itself takes place. March (1978) emphasizes the coexistence in the decision-making process of multiple rationalities[11] that call into play various organizational elements and dynamics. In situations of *problematic preferences, unclear technology* and *fluid participation* (part-time participants) in the decision-making process, the process itself tends to be a model of organized anarchy structured like a garbage can in which problems, solutions, and participants pass through one choice option to another in such a way that the nature of the choice, the time required to make it, and the problems that it resolves depend on the complex interaction of the various elements involved (M.D. Cohen, March, and Olsen 1972; March and Olsen 1976).

As we saw in Chapter 2, Perrow (2007) argues that, no matter what efforts are made, formal organizations have structural limits that make them very inefficient in predicting, preventing, and containing the various types of unexpected events that occur (e.g., natural and man-made disasters). *Organizational failures* take place constantly and are very widespread. They can become dangerous in unpredictable situations and competitive environments. Both individuals and management fail to realize the tasks expected of them for various reasons: human errors, cognitive failures, and failures in organizational planning. Alternatively, they fail because the difficulty of the tasks exceeds their capacity to face up to them. Organizations are difficult to run and they do not always do what they are supposed to do, observes Perrow (2007). Moreover, they manifest various contrasting interests both internally and externally. Alongside organizational failures, there are also managerial failures, for example, when top management deliberately makes choices that can damage the company, the people that work in it, the clients, and/or the public and society in general. These failures or instances of misconduct (Vaughan 1999), notes Perrow (2007), can be traced back to the fact that top management pursues personal interests even to the detriment of the interests of the company. Speaking of cultural changes turns out to be fairly unconvincing

---

[11] March identifies seven different forms of rationality that compete amongst themselves in decision-making contexts: limited rationality, contextual rationality, game rationality, process rationality, adaptive rationality, selective rationality, and a posteriori irrationality.

because such changes do not significantly modify the dimension of power or the organizational structure.

The organizational dimension, then, is of considerable importance in understanding myopia. There are many factors and mechanisms that go beyond the individual dimension and that lead to organizational myopia. Let us examine the most important ones in detail.

Failures in analysis

Failures in analysis occur when organizations fail to identify and make use of information available in relation to emerging threats. These failures in analysis are due to factors such as the following:

- *Selective attention* that leads key actors in organizations to focus their attention on certain problems, thus allowing other problems to develop without being seen. Selective attention manifests itself when decision makers ignore certain strong evidence because it does not correspond to their beliefs.
- The *noise* caused by a multiplicity of information, warning signs, and data that confuses leaders and prevents them from appreciating the importance of certain threats, for example, when contrasting information directs attention towards other problems and other threats. The problem of *false alarms* is connected to this issue. False alarms reduce the capacity of an organization to react to warning signs, causing it to fail to recognize a true threat when it presents itself.
- *Information overload*, which increases confusion, induces people to ignore areas and problems with low priority and leads them to fail to identify emerging threats or to identify them too late. An overload of information can occur either because of an insufficient quantity of resources for the pile of information to be analyzed or because of the specter of the potential threats increasing rapidly without an adequate compensation in resources being accorded to the people who have to confront them.

Failures in coordination and integration

One of the problems that organizations have to constantly confront and resolve is coordination. The problem of coordination is a classical theme in the field of organizational studies (Thompson 1967). As organizations grow in size, they become vertically diversified and develop hierarchical levels of status. At the same time, as organizations adopt new tasks and functions, horizontal differentiation increases. To realize complex tasks, organizations divide activities into parts, assigning them to individuals and/or organizational units. The individual organization members and/or units then have to integrate the tasks with their own efforts.

For coordinated action to be possible, highly differentiated organizations (or organizational units) require equally high levels of integration (Lawrence and Lorsch 1967). This process is impeded by two factors: on the one hand, the diversity of the individual members of the organization (each with his or her own convictions, interests, idiosyncrasies, etc.) and, on the other hand, the need to preserve and develop this very diversity so as to be able to confront the complexity of the environment in which the organization operates. Differentiation does not signify solely segmentation and specialized knowledge; it also implies different attitudes and orientations (Snook 2000).

The fragmentation of organizational structures, especially when they are not suitable for a particular mission, can create serious problems of cooperation and coordination (Parker and Stern 2005). Wilensky (1967) argues persuasively that failures of intelligence are partially induced by a range of organizational elements of a structural nature such as hierarchy, centralization and specialization. Bureaucratic-organizational factors can create and exacerbate problems that are chronic and corrosive of information processes, policy making, and policy implementation (Parker and Stern 2005). Bureaucratic conflicts can create pathologies that lead to political failures, while intraorganizational rivalries can degenerate into the construction of fiefdoms, with clearly negative impacts on the sharing of knowledge and information and on the realization of objectives. This is what happened, for example, in the case of the *Columbia* space shuttle disaster. When the engineers became aware of the problem of possible damage during the launch phase and asked for further images without following the established procedures, they were reprimanded by the NASA administration for an act that was considered to be a manifestation of insubordination and not a desire to guarantee optimal margins of safety. Finally, a further barrier to cooperation is represented by the routines and standard operating procedures typical of every organization. These routines are, on the one hand, necessary for the normal working of the organization, but, on the other hand, they can constitute powerful barriers to the perception of new problems.

A typical cause of failure in organizational coordination consists in the existence of distinct *silos* of knowledge and information within organizations (Bazerman and Watkins 2004). The bureaucratic form of organization (Weber 1922), structured in a functional-hierarchical manner, is a powerful obstacle to intra-organizational coordination (Galbraith 2002). In order to achieve results in the context of high levels of differentiation – necessary to create the set of bodies of knowledge that is fundamental for any organization – it is essential for there to be high levels of integration capable of synthesizing the knowledge present in the various organizational units (Lawrence and Lorsch 1967). As Snook (2000, p. 213) indicates, "a series of critical coordination failures combines to decrease the reliability of the system and increase the likelihood of an accident."

Heath and Staudenmayer (2000) point out how individuals, when they design organizations and organizational processes, or when they participate in them, fail to understand the importance of coordinated action. In so doing they manifest what the two authors refer to as *coordination neglect*: the failure to effectively integrate and distribute tasks undertaken by different members of an organization. "When individuals design organizational processes or when they participate in them, they frequently fail to understand that coordination is important and they fail to take steps to minimize the difficulty of coordination. To summarize this hypothesis, we say that individuals exhibit coordination neglect" (Heath and Staudenmayer 2000, p. 157). The more complex a task is, the more it is divided among organizational units through specialization. Organizations tend to focus on the task assigned, being encouraged to do so by pay systems. They pay more attention to individual performance and less to the task's integration into the broader work system. "In many examples of component focus, managers seem to focus on technology rather on the broader issue of organization" (Heath and Staudenmayer 2000, p. 168). Communication is crucial for integration and coordination, because communication failures produce integration failures. The role of multiple failures in the coordination of different organizations is highlighted by Snook's (2000) analysis of a friendly fire incident in Iraq.

A number of problems in coordination lead to organizational myopia. This is the case with phenomena like (Heath and Staudenmayer 2000) *partition focus*, which consists in the tendency of people to neglect coordination because they focus more on the division of tasks than on their integration, and *component focus*, which consists instead in the tendency of people to concentrate more on the tasks for which they are responsible than on interaction with the other parts of the process in which they are involved, thereby neglecting the interrelations and the interactions between the various components of the process. *Inadequate communication* makes the overall phenomenon of coordination neglect worse. Communication tends to be inadequate because of a multiplicity of psychological processes. For an individual, it becomes difficult to fully consider the perspective of other individuals when they seek to communicate. Finally, the existence of *specialist bodies of knowledge and specific languages* makes communication within complex organizations and between organizations problematic, giving rise to processes of structural secrecy (Vaughan 1996). The four mechanisms cited (partition focus, component focus, inadequate communication, and specialist bodies of knowledge and languages) impede coordination in the integration of the various parts and open the door to the unexpected in that they slow down the identification of signs of weakness and the effective recognition of threats.

According to Roberts, Madsen, and Desai (2005, p. 81), "organizational problems and failures occur when organizations fail to take cognizance of organizational interfaces or *the space between.* ... Organizations encounter problems because people concerned with them failed to comprehend the complex interactions among different organizational subunits that contribute to disaster." The expression "space between" indicates the importance of relationships among the different entities under study (Bradbury and Lichtenstein 2000).

In the case of the 9/11 terrorist attacks, for example, the achievement of cooperation was impeded by a series of factors including rivalry and competition between the agencies involved, the fragmentation of the decision-making process and the difficulty of reconstructing a unitary point of view (other important factors are discussed in the next section). Further organizational factors made it difficult to actively take note of the threats and to understand the information at issue. The FBI was structured in such a way as to protect information and not to share it, and that constituted a strong cultural bias regarding the problem of coordination. Being based more on a reactive as opposed to proactive approach to policing, the organization had as its principal objective that of gathering reliable evidence to present in the context of trials. Thus, it had powerful reasons not to share information, in order to prevent defense counsels – in the event that they became aware of it – from drawing advantage from it in the course of courtroom proceedings. The FBI was not organized, then, to collect and distribute information. Moreover, cultural limits and limits in objectives made such an exercise even more problematic. Finally, in addition to all these obstacles, there were also constraints of a procedural and legal kind on the acquisition of information, like the restrictions pertaining to the defense of the rights of individuals, designed to prevent intimidation and abuse.

Failures in control

A further factor that leads to organizational myopia is the problem of the *diffusion of responsibilities*. This has been analyzed at length by social scientists engaged in the study of cooperation within groups and organizations (Olson 1965; Latané and Darley 1970; Hackman 2004). Its root causes are both cognitive and motivational. Refusing to assume responsibility for a problem or a task is something quite common when the problem or the task is perceived as difficult or intractable. The diffusion of responsibilities in groups may be exacerbated by the problem of the missing hero: a situation everyone, though recognizing the existence of a problem, refuses to deal with, in order to avoid having to sustain the costs and risks associated with a search for a solution (Schelling 1960; Platt 1973). In the case of the 9/11 terrorist attacks the commission of inquiry pointed out that the various agencies involved operated like a set of specialists in a hospital: as described in Chapter 1, each one ordered tests, looked for symptoms, prescribed solutions, but without there being any coordination of the team (NCTA 2004). An important aspect of the problem in question relates to the activity of control and the mechanisms of allocating responsibilities. A lack of control is encountered more readily (a) in border areas, where responsibilities are not clearly defined, or (b) in areas where there is an overlap of control and two or more people control the same process.

Even when two or more people (or organizational units) control different processes, but where the confines of the processes are not well delineated, there can come into existence areas in relation to which it is not clear where responsibility lies. In cases like this, each controller may think that the responsibility for the control of a particular area lies with someone else, with the result that, in the end, no one controls it. In the situation of overlapping control, on the other hand, two or more operators control the same process, producing a situation of redundancy. In this case, appropriate modes of relating and communicating may not be defined. If this is so, it may happen that each one of the operators neglects to effect a control, thinking that his or her colleague has already made it, with the result that here, too, the mechanism of control turns out to be a failure.

In conclusion, the confusion of operators is provoked by the fact that the responsibility for control is not correctly specified. At the organizational level, this is what occurs when two or more organizations are involved in the same process or in closely related processes. Social psychologists refer to this situation as the *diffusion of responsibility* (Latané and Darley 1970; Brown 1986): if everyone is responsible, in fact no one is. There thus comes into being a process instantiating the *fallacy of social redundancy* (Snook 2000), in which the increase in the number of controllers does not improve the activity of control but rather exposes it to potential *holes*.

Failures in deciding

Janis (1982) draws attention to the importance of the phenomenon known as *groupthink*. This typically occurs when a small homogenous group seeks to reach a decision under pressure. In situations in which small groups made up of from six to twelve people operate in a highly cohesive manner, this cohesion produces a strong psychological push towards a form of consensus that tends to suppress dissent and the consideration of alternatives. Group thinking leads to an incomplete evaluation of alternatives, a failure to examine the risks involved in the choices that are made, and a failure to propose alternatives. Stress and the need for confirmation can suffocate alternative hypotheses, doubts, and objections, giving rise to an uncritical thought that reaches premature conclusions with the possibility of provoking catastrophic consequences. The phenomenon of group thinking and the incapacity to evaluate reality are characterized by a range of specific features: a shared illusion of invulnerability, an excessive faith in the morality of the group, the rationalization and the collective discrediting of warning signs, the stereotyped perception of external groups or the enemy as irrational and inadequate, the self-censure of dissidents and the consequent illusion of unanimity. Groups can manifest various cognitive properties depending on how communication within them is organized. Differences in performance between two groups may depend on differences in the social organization of distributed cognitions more than on differences in the cognitive characteristics of the particular individuals in them. An instance of confirmation bias at the level of the group such as group thinking is not founded, then, on individual confirmation biases but rather has its own autonomous nature. The individuals in a group could converge on a shared interpretation different from and far removed from any particular individual interpretation within the group and even in contrast with their own individual confirmation biases.

Other scholars (M.D. Cohen et al. 1972; March 1988) propose the decision-making model of the garbage can – already discussed in this chapter – according to which organizations, far from basing decisions on a model of Weberian rationality or of limited rationality (Simon 1947), take decisions based on poorly defined preferences, operate with technologies that are not clear and use frameworks of participation in decision-making processes that are fluid, open and characterized by highly differentiated levels of participation. In accordance with this model, solutions, far from being a response to problems, are independent of them.

Organizing and the failure of the imagination

"Imagination is not a gift usually associated with bureaucracies ... It is therefore crucial to find a way of routinizing, even bureaucratizing, the exercise of imagination. Doing so requires more than finding an expert who can imagine that aircraft could be used as weapons" (NCTA 2004, p. 344).

The *9/11 Commission Report* (NCTA 2004) affirms that the basic cause of the failure to foresee the 2001 terrorist attacks was the inefficacy of the bureaucracy of the organizations responsible for the internal defense of the United States. At the same time, however, it maintains that it is necessary in some way to render routine the exercise of imagination, certainly without relinquishing command to some expert with special powers of clairvoyance but nonetheless without falling into the traps of bureaucracy. How is it possible to effect such a balance between organization and imagination?

The *9/11 Commission Report* (NCTA 2004) draws attention to a fundamental limit on the part of the organizational system for the defense of the United States that impeded it from seeing ex ante what appeared predictable ex post: the limitation in imagination and myopia in forecasting what would take place in the future. Weick (2005a) argues that organizing can limit imagination in three ways: through the restriction of (1) perception, (2) conjecture, and (3) mindfulness.

These three limits constitute organizational dilemmas in that they are organizational inevitabilities inextricably connected to the growth of a formal organization, that is, necessary evils for the effective working of the organization. Regarding the first dilemma, "organizing restricts perception because requirements for coordination necessitate generalizing. Generalizing can suppress both recognition of anomalous details and imaginative development of their meaning" (Weick 2005a, p. 431). Thus, organizing brings with it generalizing and the subsumption of heterogeneous particulars under generic categories. In this way, formal organizations necessarily entail abstraction (Tsoukas and Vladimirou 2001). In the passage from the particular to the generalization, there takes place a reduction in the possibility of reading the potential implications of weak warning signs and of analyzing apparently insignificant details (like the fact that a number of Islamic extremists were attending pilot training courses) which, if placed in relation with other information, could give rise to a very meaningful overall picture.

In this regard, Weick (2005a) introduces into the vocabulary of organizational design a new term, invented by Baron and Misovich (1999): the *share ability constraint*. This term indicates that, if people want to share their cognitive structures, it is necessary for these structures to take on a particular form. With the growth in social complexity, people pass from a knowledge based on perception to a knowledge based on categories. This passage from perception to categorization is determined by the need for organizational coordination. But this brings with it a cost: intellectual and emotive distancing in collecting details through direct perception. People tend to remember the name of the things they have seen rather than the qualities that they have observed or felt. This turns out to be problematic when significant details are located outside the connotation of names, for in this case, people will not note them. The progression from perception to formalized abstraction diminishes the identification and collection of details that are vital for the imagination. A first organizational dilemma thus emerges: an increase in coordination is, on the one hand, a necessity induced by the growth of a formal organizational structure but, on the other hand, a limit and obstacle to the perception of events and to imagination.

The second dilemma relates to the relationship between the norms of rationality and the restriction of abductive reasoning[12] based on inference. Inferences are conjectures about reality that need to be validated by an experimental proof (Peirce 1931–1935; Eco and Sebeock 1983), and they may lead to the creation of a new idea. Abductive reasoning refers to reasoning that forms and evaluates hypotheses in order to make sense of puzzling facts (Thagard and Shelley 1997): it has to do with the formulation of conjectures starting out from apparently insignificant and non-connected data and leads one to reconstruct meaningful connections (Ginzburg 1990). One forms provisional theories and then waits for the lapse of time and the greater degree of knowledge necessary for them to eventually spring forth. Examples of this type of reasoning are medical diagnoses and archaeological reconstruction. The relationship between abductive reasoning and organization is problematic. Organizing tends to determine norms of rationality to promote order, predictability, and the reduction of uncertainty (Thompson 1967). On the one hand, these norms of rationality are necessary for the government of complex formal organizational structures, but, on the other, they reduce abductive reasoning, which is an important instrument for imagination.

The third organizational dilemma in relation to imagination relates to restraints on mindfulness. Mindfulness, understood as the full awareness of discriminatory detail, "involves the combination of ongoing scrutiny of existing expectations, continuous refinement and differentiation of expectations based on newer experiences, willingness and capability to invent new expectations that make sense of unprecedented events, a more nuanced appreciation of context and the

---

[12] Abductive reasoning (from the Latin *abducere*, "to lead from") constitutes, according to Peirce (1931–1935), the *first stage* of scientific inquiries and of any interpretive processes. Abductive reasoning is a strategy of solving problems and discovering relevant premises. It consists in the process of adopting an explanatory hypothesis and covers two operations: the selection and the formation of plausible hypotheses. As a process of finding premises, it is the basis of the interpretive reconstruction of causes and intentions, as well as of inventive construction of theories. The other inferential processes are deduction and induction. Deduction is a process of reasoning in which conclusions follow necessarily from the premises presented. Induction, instead, is the process of inferring general laws from particular instances.

way to deal with it, and identification of new dimensions of context that improve foresight and current functioning" (Weick and Sutcliffe 2007, p. 33). Mindfulness makes it possible to capture more details and to synthesize them in richer conjectures. It also represents a pre-requisite for imagination, which in its turn is a powerful antidote to organizational myopia. High Reliability Organizations (HROs), which I discuss at greater length in Section 5.1, operate according to the characteristics of mindfulness. HROs maintain a reliable performance in spite of being constantly exposed to the unexpected. They have a great incentive to contain the unexpected because when they fail to do so the results can be catastrophic. For this reason, the definition of what is dangerous is continually reviewed. HROs give attention to failures, even little ones, more than to successes. They are constantly concerned with constructing a sense for the unexpected, and they attach more value to competency than to hierarchy.

Mindless organizations, on the other hand, give attention to successes even when what are involved are in actual fact non-successes (as in the case of the FBI's arrests after the 1993 bombing of the World Trade Center and other subsequent events). They tend to create simplistic frameworks of events, and they are based on a rigid hierarchy. In such contexts, an act of imagination is often interpreted as an act of insubordination (Weick 2005a). This is what happened in the case of the *Columbia* disaster when a certain number of engineers asked for further images of the loss of material from the surface of the shuttle to verify for possible damage, violating existing NASA procedures and rules. The organization reprimanded the engineers for not having respected the procedures and then failed to put in place corrective action that may have prevented the disaster.

To conclude, then, organization and imagination seem to be in contradiction. Pursuing the former would seem to entail reducing the latter. Some organizations, however, have developed models and methods to co-manage both requirements. And it is to these that it is necessary to look in order to be able to reduce organizational myopia. Organizations succumb to crises because their top management, basing itself on past successes, lives in a world circumscribed by its own cognitive structures. Listening to dissent, that is, to the people who express doubts or point out dangers and problems, helps to understand that there are different visions of the world and that one's own beliefs and perceptions could be wrong. But this is easier said than done, and hierarchical organizational structures do not help. Lyman Porter and Karlene Roberts (1976) show how top managers do not listen to their subordinates with attention. People in hierarchical structures speak or seek to speak with people who stand in a higher position in the hierarchical chain rather than with people who stand in a lower position. They send a larger number of messages to people who stand in a higher position than they do to people who stand in a lower position. They give greater attention to messages and communications originating from their superiors than to those deriving from their subordinates, seeking to establish and consolidate relations with the former.

One particularly important problem relates to the matter – already cited earlier – of sharing information. Posner (2006), referring to the US defense system, writes that intelligence lies in the resolution of a stubborn dilemma. On the one hand, data need to be widely distributed and shared in the system, but, on the other hand, the more data are as economic widespread, the more acute is the danger of a disastrous breach in the system of security. Centralization resolves some problems in relation to the sharing of information, but it reduces its availability and quality. Decentralization, on the other hand, encourages initiative and facilitates adaptation to environmental changes, but it blocks the flow of information. This dilemma was a significant problem in the United States defense organization before the 9/11 terrorist attacks and stood at the basis of many of the holes in the information network of various agencies.

Level III: The interorganizational field

No organization, least of all a medium-sized to large one, manages to carry out complex activities by itself. Every organization needs to interact, make exchanges, and cooperate with a range of other organizations. Organizations do not operate in a vacuum but rather are embedded within a context made up of other organizations of different kinds and with different scopes. Homeland security, for example, is a complex and fragmented area of governmental activity, in which a growing number of problems and cases do not find an adequate response in the traditional operational structures. Such an organizational entity cannot be seen as a single, unitary actor but rather needs to be viewed as being made up of a large number of distinct

organizational actors – as operating, in other words, at an interorganizational level. Organizations are modeled by the contexts in which
they are formed (Aldrich and Ruef 2006). The organizational environment of any particular organization can be conceived as a network of
other organizations (Nohria 1992). Every organization forms a node
in a network of nodes that constitutes an organizational (DiMaggio
and Powell 1983; Powell and DiMaggio 1991; Davis and Powell
1992; Fligstein 2001) and juridical (Edelman and Stryker 2005) field
made up of a mass of norms, rituals, symbols, and social behaviors. All
these elements together form a recognized sphere of institutional life,
and they are involved in various ways in the activities of the various
bodies – regulators, controlling agencies, stakeholders, key suppliers,
competitors, technology producers, and so on – that contribute to the
working of the level of the organizational context.

These networks restrict the actions that individual organizations
can undertake and in their turn are modeled by them (Nohria 1992).
Their defining characteristics are the organizational network itself,
the connections between components in it and the modes of differentiation and integration of the various actors involved in the operation
of the system. By differentiation at the interorganizational level, we
mean hierarchical – both vertical and horizontal – differentiation and
differentiation between functional areas, between organizations, and
between organizational units within space. Integration, on the other
hand, consists in the degree of coordination (or, more broadly, the
degree of interaction) among distinct organizational entities. Failures
to regulate the various subjects (Perrow 2007) make organizational
systems extremely vulnerable. At the interorganizational level, processes of coordination and integration are crucial issues. Where there
are high levels of differentiation, it is necessary to have high levels
of integration (Lawrence and Lorsch 1967). Differentiation does not
just entail segmentation and specialized knowledge but also different
attitudes and orientations (Snook 2000). Organizations in a complex
system can easily differ in the way in which their members think and
work (Lawrence and Lorsch 1967).[13] In the first place, they may differ

[13] Lawrence and Lorsch discuss problems of differentiation and integration in
an intraorganizational context and in the relationship between organizations
and the external environment. Their model is of particular use in dealing with
analogous problems at the interorganizational level (Lawrence and Lorsch
1967).

in terms of their orientation towards goals, generating conflicts in relation to priorities, and, as a result, producing coordination problems. A
second potential difference lies in their members' orientation towards
time, towards the speed with which they do things (differences, for
example – so far as the air transport system is concerned – that arise
between the people who are responsible for regulations and controls
and the people who furnish services). Finally, a third difference lies in
interpersonal orientation, that is, in the way in which the members of
one organization interrelate with those of other organizations in terms
of organizational structures, cultures, overall preestablished organizational hierarchies and specific currently existing hierarchies. In this
case, extensively hierarchized organizations, on the one hand, and, on
the other hand, organizations accommodating more autonomous
professional operators may encounter difficulties in relating and
coordinating with each other. In making use of different languages
and in adopting very distinct modes of behavior, they run the risk of
giving rise to potentially ambiguous communications. This can create
difficulties and cause delays in coordinating the mutual adjustment
that is necessary for the formation of reciprocal interdependence
that derives from processes based on closely interconnected activities
(Thompson 1967).

As many scholars observe, interdependence creates uncertainty for
every organization when the stakeholders in question have the means
and the motivation to take decisions that might not reflect the interests of the organization (Lawrence and Lorsch 1967; Thompson 1967;
Pfeffer and Salancik 1978; Milliken 1987). A large number of problems come into being for organizations when they fail to be cognizant
of organizational interfaces or to understand the complex interactions
among different organizations or organizational subunits.

Achieving an effective balance between coordination, specialization,
autonomy, and control is a problem confronting both organizational
theory and the practice of management and risk management. At the
interorganizational level, an increase in the number of the organizations involved in a network and in the size and degree of specialization of each one tends to be accompanied by an increase in the degree
of structural secrecy characterizing them (Vaughan 1996). The consequence is that it is very difficult for a *controlling* organization to
effectively monitor the organization under its control. This is because
the specialized nature of the knowledge inhering to the individual

organizations and the organizational complexity characterizing them make them incomprehensible and therefore not amenable to control. If the controlling organization does not have within it the knowledge relating to the particular organization under control, it runs the risk of conducting merely perfunctory, formal, and nonsubstantial controls founded on a cognitive and informational base generated exclusively by the organization being controlled. In this way, an important function such as that of control risks being emptied of significance.

The NCTA (2004) identified a large number of organizational flaws in the relations between the organizations responsible for security (the FBI and the CIA). The particular problems identified included problems of coordination, problems of integration, blocks in communications, and a lack of exchange and sharing of information, among others. These problems of an interorganizational character weakened the defense system, reducing its capacity to prevent attacks. Such conclusions are consistent with what had been found by Turner and Pidgeon (1997) and Vaughan (1996) years before in relation to other situations. The *9/11 Commission Report* (NCTA 2004) stresses that a number of opportunities were lost in respect of information that could have been (but was not) examined more closely and that contained important warning signs for the defense system. An efficient sharing of information between the CIA and the FBI, and among these two agencies and the FAA, would have significantly improved homeland security conditions. A number of scholars (Ingram 2002; Greve 2005a) have carried out a specific analysis of the problems and the failures of the transfer of information among the organizations in question. They collocate the particular case within a broader class of phenomena referred to in terms of interorganizational learning. So far as the case of the 9/11 terrorist attacks is concerned, on a number of occasions, a more effective collaboration within and among agencies would have led to significant results. Agents in the CIA were in possession of important information on some of the nineteen suicide terrorists, but they did not share this with the FBI because they did not think they were authorized to do so.

Interorganizational learning is something that is quite common between companies. It takes place, for example, in the form of the spread of innovative technology and management practices (Strang and Soule 1998) and is manifest in the high level of similarity between organizations not just in the same sector but also in different sectors

(DiMaggio and Powell 1983). If interorganizational learning is so widespread in private companies, why is it neglected – as is so evident in the case of the 9/11 terrorist attacks – in public sector organizations? Greve (2005b) explains this inconsistency in terms of the fact that government agencies have a government mandate that specifically defines their role and that seeks to avoid duplications and overlaps as much as possible. Thus, government agencies are all different from one another and are not in competition amongst themselves. In theory, these characteristics of non-overlap and non-competition should represent an incentive for interorganizational learning, there not being any dynamics of a conflicting nature. But in actual fact, however, the division of activities and the nonoverlap are never realized in an exact manner. Areas of overlap and redundancy are always present. On the other hand, it is necessary to recognize that public agencies confront problems that are fundamentally different from those of companies and that this is even more true of agencies that have to deal with security, as the case of the 9/11 terrorist attacks illustrates. The consequence of this is that interorganizational learning comes about in ways that are different from those in private companies.

So far as the 9/11 case is concerned, the raw data necessary to predict and prevent the disaster was available, but the organizations in question failed to transform it into information that had sense, that is, into evidence capable of lending support to decisions and action. The limited amount of attention given to the information was also due to the fact that for some of the agencies involved, concern for problems of terrorism was very low. For example, the FAA was certainly more worried about delays in air traffic than any terrorist threat. This lack of attention has been evaluated as an error but only ex post, that is, with hindsight bias; ex ante it might very well not have been an error. Without a careful analysis of the cost-benefit relationship involved in the specific case, it is simplistic to affirm that the priorities of the FAA were right or wrong. In this respect, Bardach (1998, 2005) affirms that government agencies find it easier to work together if they are able to see clearly and immediately the benefits resulting from collaboration. This consideration has a number of important implications for institutional design.

The governmental or bureaucratic politics approach argues that policy outcomes are the result of the interests and preferences of the various bureaucracies in competition with each other (Stern and Verbeek 1998; Allison and Zelikow 1999; Parker and Stern 2005).

This perspective underlines the extremely politicized nature of organizational life and the impact that in-house interests, rivalries and intra- and inter-agency competition can have on decision-making processes and on the evaluation of information and threats. The approach in question focuses on the interaction between a multiplicity of agencies and organizations in a pluralistic politico-administrative environment (Allison and Zelikow 1999; Parker and Stern 2005). Referring to the reorganization of the national Norwegian defense system, Lægreid and Serigstad (2006) point to how the process of reform was not only a process of defining decision making but also a complex process of defining, interpreting, and developing a sense of unity among the various organizational actors in the process.

The problem of terrorism, for example, is encompassed within the mandates of a large number of agencies and organizations. In the United States, these are the Department of State, the Department of Defense, the Transport Department, the Justice Department, the CIA, the FBI, the FAA, the Immigration Services Department, and the local police. It is extremely difficult for all these agencies and organizations – which in their turn divide into innumerable units and subunits – to share information and coordinate their analysis of threats and their responses to them. Moreover, they are characterized by cultural and procedural differences and by political rivalries that can have a further impact on the sharing of information and on the definition and implementation of policies (Vertzberger 1990; Preston and Hart 1999; Parker and Stern 2005). All this makes the process of decision making extremely fragmented and results in a very limited sharing of priorities.

At an interorganizational level, problems can arise in relation to the agenda setting of the decision makers of the various organizations in an organizational field (Meyer and Rowan 1977). A first problem consists in the fact that the agendas of decision makers fill up with a multiplicity of different items. This situation reduces the level of their attention not least because of the fact that policymakers tend to work on objectives in a selective and sequential manner rather than simultaneously (Simon 1947; March 1994). A second problem concerns framing, a factor already examined in relation to the individual level. This expresses itself in a failure on the part of many actors to reconstruct a unitary and shared picture of the problem and the threat in question. This reconstruction is made difficult because of problems of coordination and sharing of information. Finally, questions with a high political priority can divert attention towards problems of a short-term nature, the contours of which are better defined, the media interest in relation to which is keener and in respect of which the interests of decision makers are more involved.

The attentiveness of responses to threats depends on how the individuals involved perceive, feel, and act. Individuals are activated and at the same time constrained by the complex institutional structures in which they are embedded (Giddens 1984; Stern 1999) and by the interests at stake. Garret and Sobel (2002) have conducted a study on disasters in the United States that the Federal Emergency Management Agency (FEMA) officially recognized as such, and on the sum of financial aid allocated. They claim that the decisions of presidents to declare disasters and to allocate funds are determined by the political interests of the presidents in question and the members of the committee that controls FEMA. Presidents give preference to states that are politically important for their election and reelection. Garret and Sobel conclude that over half of the aid for disasters in the United States is determined more by political considerations than by the magnitude of the disasters themselves. According to Perrow (2007), the failure to intervene in the case of Hurricane Katrina in Louisiana depended precisely on the fact that that state was not politically important for the presidency of the time.

The problem of special interest groups and veto players

At the level of the interorganizational field, a particularly important role is performed by those players who by way of their action or failure to act can block or impede both processes of change and the taking of decisions in response to threats. Special interest groups are groups that pursue specific interests even to the detriment of collective interests. They thereby pursue gains for themselves even though these may be much smaller than the social costs that their actions produce (Bazerman and Watkins 2004).

Activation in the face of threats or weak warning signs can be contrasted by veto players[14] present in the system. These players have

---

[14] With the term *veto player* reference is made to the individual and collective decision makers whose agreement is necessary for a change in the status quo to take place (Tsebelis 2002). The more veto players there are in an organizational system, the more difficult it is to change the status quo.

little difficulty in opposing change and the taking of decisions that are costly for them. As March and Olsen (1989) argue, attempts at reorganization that ignore networks of power and interests are destined to fail or, at any rate, to turn out to be inconsequential. Unfortunately, it is not enough to sideline incompetent actors. Referring to the United Kingdom, Power (2007) shows how the recent history of the regulation of risks points to a new emphasis on the governance of organizations that analyze risks including regulators and private companies.

The problem of specialization and coordination

A large number of problems act as an obstacle to an efficient coordination among the various organizations involved in specific areas of interest. It is difficult to coordinate different agencies, not least because they tend to resist being regulated in their turn by other agencies (J.Q. Wilson 1989). In reference to the field of national security, for example, coordination is further complicated by the vertical nature of policy making, with policies being organized for specific purposes and articulated in a functional-hierarchical manner with weak mechanisms of coordination (Kettl 2003). One critical factor that relates to coordination between various organizations and agencies is referred to as *negative coordination* (Mayntz and Sharpf 1975). This occurs where, for a given organization, the desire to coordinate is stronger than the desire to be coordinated. In this context, a central place is assumed by the question of how to construct concrete responses to problems that are not routine, that is, questions for which there is not a repertory of standard responses.

Lægreid and Serigstad (2006), referring to national security, distinguish three approaches to coordination, which correspond to three different models of organization. The first model is of a *top-down* hierarchical nature. It assumes that the driving force of an organization originates at the top and is directed towards the bottom. This implies strong political control. The idea of top-down coordination is based on the assumption that in order for effective coordination to take place an organization needs to have already identified at its head office the people who will take responsibility for the coordination and that the relations among the various lower-level and parallel organizations are very clear and characterized by well-defined and shared objectives. In other words, it is assumed that the existence of a hierarchy will facilitate the implementation of policy. In highly uncertain and changing circumstances, this hierarchical organizational model may reveal marked limits in its efficiency. A second organizational model, the *network model*, is often more appropriate. In unstable environments requiring flexibility, rapid decisions, and continuous changes, it is necessary to decentralize authority and to place less emphasis on formal structures. This need arises because it is vitally important for information to circulate within the organization and because this flow can easily be obstructed by rigid organizational structures of a hierarchical type. The focus of this approach, then, is to create systems that are at one and the same time versatile and flexible. Attention is not directed towards establishing a strong command and centralized control but towards building a better way to collect and process information. Finally, a third model, known as the *agency model*, integrates strong supervision and the systematic regulation of semi-independent agencies with a principle of separate responsibility on the part of each agency. This model represents a hybrid between the hierarchical model and the network model, on the one hand, assigning ultimate power to a hierarchical leadership with functions of regulation and control, and, on the other hand, ceding semi-autonomy and a degree of responsibility to the organizations that operate in the field. Lægreid and Serigstad (2006) conclude that there is no single right way to organize national security. Organizational structures without doubt play a significant role in the overall calculation, but many critical issues both at the theoretical and the empirical level remain unresolved. In terms of structural design, there is no immutable solution. The task of achieving an effective balance between an appropriate form of political control of a vertical kind and the coordination of the various policy areas at a horizontal level is a dilemma that transforms over time and that needs to be constantly managed rather than resolved once and for all.

Through the levels

The three levels of analysis that I have presented come together to form a unitary conceptual approach. Each successive step in the passage from the individual level to the organizational level to the inter-organizational level entails not a confutation of the previous level but rather an integration of it. Every level stresses a set of specific dimensions and problems that contribute to explaining certain dynamics, while others remain either in the background or invisible. The passage from one level to the subsequent level contributes to taking an account of what remains to be explained from the former, thereby unveiling a multiplicity of organizational rationalities and logics of action.

In our description of the case of the 9/11 terrorist attacks, we have drawn attention to the existence of various levels of failure that rendered myopic the organizational makeup of the US defense system. The large number of threats in relation to possible attacks and the information on the pilot training courses being undertaken by Islamic extremists were not taken into consideration because they did not enter into an adequate mental framework. Moreover, the information in question circulated with extreme difficulty because of a complex and fragmented organizational system characterized by inadequate levels of coordination and integration. A range of specific organizational deficiencies made it difficult to forecast the attacks: problems of cooperation among agencies, jealousy over information, an organization of projects that was not conducive to an in-depth examination of warning signs and threats not specifically relating to the particular projects that the various organizational units had already undertaken, bureaucratic conflicts, and other pathologies discussed previously. Similar dynamics were present in the space shuttle disasters. The individual myopia evident in the failure to give adequate consideration to the state of the O-rings in the case of *Challenger* and the damage *Columbia* underwent during its launch depended on the flawed nature of specific procedures for the evaluation of risk that limited classifying problems as in-family (problems that are known and not worrying) and out-family (the opposite). The power conflicts between the various internal organizational units within NASA had the effect that the damage to *Columbia* was not subjected – as should have happened – to careful examination. Similarly, the erroneous evaluation of the state of the O-rings before the launch of *Challenger* was provoked by problems of coordination and responsibility between NASA and its suppliers in relation to security.

Addressing the famous case of the Cuban missile crisis, Allison and Zelikow (1999) describe the decision-making process that characterized the events (above all from the point of view of the United States) by way of an analysis that unfolds in terms of three levels: that of the rational actor, the organizational level, and the political level. In 1959, Fidel Castro ousted the then dictator Fulgencio Batista from power and nationalized the sugar industry controlled by US. This decision greatly irritated the Americans because the island had always been considered part of their sphere of influence. The retaliatory measures that the Americans took induced Castro to form an alliance with the Soviet bloc. In October 1962, President Kennedy was informed of the installation of a number of Soviet bases on the island and the presence of atomic missiles pointing towards US soil. A meeting of the executive committee of the National Council of Defense was immediately convoked. Its members identified seven alternative courses of action that might resolve the problem: (1) not do anything, (2) take diplomatic action, (3) negotiate with Castro, (4) propose an exchange of the Soviet installations in Cuba and the US installations in Italy and Turkey, (5) invade Cuba, (6) make an air strike, and (7) effect a naval blockade. Every solution had its pros and cons. In the end, the decision went in favor of a naval blockade, which satisfied both Kennedy and his military and diplomatic advisers. The naval blockade became operational on October 24, 1962, a few days after the news arrived from the Kremlin that the Soviet Union would remove the bases. At first sight, Kennedy's decision seems a perfect instantiation of the model of the rational decision: analysis of the situation, evaluation of the options, evaluation of the pros and cons of each practicable option, and the choice of the best solution from the point of view of the costs and benefits. The result obtained – the removal of the Soviet bases – seems to confirm this hypothesis. In actual fact, however, a more careful analysis of what really happened does not confirm this ideal version of the decision-making process. To the contrary, it appears that this version is very much conditioned by hindsight bias: given that the result of the decision was positive, the decision itself must also have been positive. As we have seen, seven solutions to the problem in question were taken into consideration, but the procedure used to evaluate them corresponded much more to the notion of limited rationality proposed by Simon's (1947) and to the decision-making mechanisms revealed by March (1994) than to any process based on absolute rationality. In the frantic days that preceded the decision to impose a naval blockade, the evaluation of the various options was based essentially on the criterion of satisfying the president, and amongst the various options taken into consideration at the beginning that of a naval blockade did not feature. After having discarded the other options, the search for a solution was taken up again, and it was only at this point that there emerged the hypothesis of a naval blockade. The various options that were advanced in the course of the crisis were not invented by the members of the group of decision makers at the moment of the crisis itself; rather, what was involved were possible future initiatives that had been elaborated beforehand by the various organizations responsible for national defense. Every solution had been prepared by a specific organization (the army, the navy, etc.) in accordance with the capacity and interests of the organization itself. Model I (rational choice) generates various hypotheses as to why the Soviet Union had decided to install nuclear missiles in Cuba (for example, to defend the island or to expand its own power) as well as the various possible options to take in response. Model II (organizational behavior), on the other hand, focuses attention on what concrete action the government and the US defense organizations were or were not able to take. The logic inherent to the workings of organizations furnishes new hypotheses to explain the facts that took place, the real options at issue, and the nature of the decision-making processes involved. The interpretation of an organizational kind shows how the various solutions proposed were determined by the particular characteristics inhering to the organizations that elaborated them. Organizations – in the account offered by Allison and Zelikow – are instruments that are not particularly intelligent in facing up to unexpected events and that are averse to responding adequately to problems not foreseen in the programs that they have developed previously. Finally, Model III (the political model) reinterprets the choice of the naval blockade, showing how the political leaders in question were influenced by the roles that they covered and by their responsibilities in those contexts. This level takes us to the heart of decision-making mechanisms, characterized by negotiated decision-making processes. To understand and explain the decision-making process at this level, it is necessary to understand the different elements involved: the actors at play, their aims, their power and degree of influence over the final decision, the current rules of the game, and the space for action. The various interpretations in competition among themselves reflect the tendency of each model to produce different responses to the same question (Allison and Zelikow 1999). Interpretation of a political kind makes it possible to understand how the *political* operators in given contexts have negotiated amongst themselves to identify various solutions.

As with the three models used by Allison and Zelikow to analyze the case of the Cuban missile crisis, so the three levels that we have discussed (individual, organizational, and interorganizational) furnish different sets of evidence for the analysis of given situations. The three levels, moreover, are much more than just three different visual perspectives or approaches. On the contrary, each one is a conceptual framework that consists in a set of assumptions and categories that crucially influence what the analyst finds. On the one hand, each of the three models produces different explanations of a given event. On the other hand, each one contributes together with the others to offering a deeper and more complete explanation of the same event.

3.2 Myopia of the gatekeepers

In discussions of the financial crisis that started in 2007, a recurrent question has been why warning signs were not heeded by a series of organization gatekeepers – such as rating agencies and auditing companies – who should have been controllers of the financial and economic reliability of companies, banks and financial institutions. To answer this question, it is first necessary to investigate the individual, organizational, and institutional mechanisms that rendered controllers deaf and myopic – those controllers who should have acted as whistle-blowers, performing the role of watchdog in relation to the reliability of companies and financial institutions. Much has been written about rating agencies,[15] but less attention has been paid to the role of the auditing companies. Here, I apply our multilevel frame to analyze the case of these important and least investigated gatekeepers.

---

[15] The National Commission on the causes of the Financial and Economic Crisis in the US (NCCFC) concludes that "the failures of credit rating agencies were essential cogs in the wheel of financial destruction. The three credit rating agencies (Moody's, Fitch, and Standard & Poor's) were key enablers of the financial meltdown. The mortgage-related securities at the heart of the crisis could not have been marketed and sold without their seal of approval. Investors relied on them, often blindly. In some cases, they were obligated to use them, or regulatory capital standards were hinged on them. This crisis could not have happened without the rating agencies. Their ratings helped the market soar and their downgrades through 2007 and 2008 wreaked havoc across markets and firms ... From 2000 to 2007 Moody's rated nearly 45,000 mortgage-related securities as triple-A. This compares with six private-sector companies in the United States that carried this coveted rating in early 2010. In 2006 alone, Moody's put its triple-A stamp of approval on 39 mortgage-related securities every working day. The results were disastrous: 83 per cent of the mortgage securities rated triple-A that year ultimately were downgraded" (NCCFC 2011, p. xxv).

Why did auditing companies not reveal criticalities in the accounting and financial situations of banks such as Barclays, Bear Stearns, Fannie Mae, Freddie Mac, Lehman Brothers, the Royal Bank of Scotland, and many of the other main players in the financial crisis of the summer of 2007? Why did the auditing companies not predict the imminent crisis and the failure of numerous companies such as Enron, Parmalat, WorldCom, Adelphia, Bristol-Myers Squibb, Global Crossing, Tyco, and many others? Was it a matter of involuntary errors of evaluation by controllers or organizational deviance? These failures raised more than one doubt concerning these organizations' reliability, transparency, and evaluative ability.

In the next few sections, I use the multilevel frame presented in the previous pages to analyze the auditing companies' failure of control.

The auditing companies and the failure of control

Auditing companies check the regularity and correctness of company accounting, certifying the reliability of the accounts and balance sheets of various companies. The auditing procedures focus mainly on checking the completeness, accuracy, and validity of the various economic transactions that are gathered in the balance sheet (Power 1997). In this way, they partly contribute to smoothing out the informational asymmetries existing among managers, shareholders, and creditors. The profession of the auditor developed and auditing companies proliferated following the separation of the property of the company from its control, due precisely to the need to control the effective management of the company. In addition to the original task of reducing problems of *agency* between principal (shareholder) and agent of the principal (company's managers), there is the need to balance out the informational asymmetry existing between the demand and supply of capital, certifying the truthfulness of the accounting data. The auditors and the auditing firm thus become for all intents and purposes the custodians of *corporate governance*.

These *gatekeepers*[16] have two different roles that in practice overlap. The first is to be professional (and/or professional organizations)

---

[16] The term was invented by Lewin (1947) with reference to those who can both facilitate and impede information flow (W.W. Burke 2005). The term *gatekeeper* refers to specific organizations and/or professions that carry out some form of

capable of preventing things from going wrong, a sort of private police force that stops companies from having access to capital from the market if their accounts are not in order. The second role is very similar to that of other organizations (such as the SEC, the Central European Bank, the International Monetary Fund) and that is to be *guardians of trust* (Shapiro 1987) or *reputational intermediaries* (Gourevitch 2002). Central to the character of this second role is the concept of *reputational capital* (Mutti 2010), in the sense that deviant behavior in favor of a client would be anti-economic, since it would damage the image of the entire company. But this is more a position of principle than the result of empirical verification. For similar reasons relating to the necessity of having a solid reputation to operate in these fields, strong barriers exist in the sector to the entry of new firms, and the tendency to oligopoly that derives from this[17] limits the number of firms to which companies turn to. Auditing companies are private agencies that carry out a function in the public interest, the value of which transcends the confines of the organizations involved and often has a relevant impact on the state of capital markets.[18]

In the following sections, using the multilevel micro-meso-macro frame, I highlight two organizational aspects that undermined auditing companies' capacity of control: (1) the first pertains to the *object* of the auditing activity; (2) the second aspect pertains to the *structure of relationship* between the auditing company and the company being audited. Regarding the first of these aspects, these organizations (like rating agencies, supervisory authorities, etc.) can make mistakes because they claim to, or are forced to, express evaluations concerning something that is not certifiable, which depends on situations of

---

external, independent control. Examples of this, apart from auditing and rating agencies, include financial analysts, investment banks, and legal and business firms.

[17] In the sector of rating agencies, for example, just three companies (Standard & Poor's, Moody's and Fitch) hold 96 percent of the overall market.

[18] In the sentence against Arthur Young & Co, Chief Justice of the Supreme Court Warren Burger stated (1984) that independent auditors assume a public responsibility that goes beyond any specific relationship with the client. This supervisory *public watchdog* position requires that the agency maintain total independence from the client and complete faith in its public obligation. The function of auditing, according to the US Court, is linked to the production of reliable corporate information that must be considered a *public good* in that it makes it possible to form rational economic decisions that are fundamental for economic growth.

radical uncertainty, such as predictions about a crisis or developments of entire productive sectors, ultra-complex financial products, SWFs (Sovereign Wealth Funds), and so on. These are situations, therefore, that by definition cannot be reduced to calculated risk, not even through sophisticated mathematical models. There is an expectations gap (Power 1997) between what the regulators and controllers state they can do and what can in fact realistically be done.

Regarding the second aspect, there are individual and organizational factors that sometimes render the activity of auditing problematic. Starting from the 1970s, auditing companies also began to develop non-auditing activities (consultancy, services, etc.) significantly. These activities have reached the point where they amount to 70 percent of the companies' earnings, creating serious problems to the independence of the auditors. If an auditing company provides auditing and consultancy services to a business, and makes substantial earnings from the non-auditing activity, the auditor will find itself in a position in which its autonomy of judgment is reduced. In fact, any negative judgment it makes could affect the acquisition of its consultancy services.

Furthermore, auditing companies have acted as lobbies in order to block processes of reform aimed at limiting the potential conflict of interest inherent in the structure of these relationships. All this creates certain problems in the activity of auditing that are worth analyzing. Some of these problems are still present today, as the financial crisis has shown, and risk undermining the ability of these organizations to be reliable gatekeepers (Coffee 2006): organizations, in other words, capable of raising and lowering *the gates* that regulate the flow of information.[19]

Even though the analysis revolves around the auditing companies and their relationships with client companies in a context of widespread ownership, many of the conclusions reached are still valid for other gatekeepers such as rating agencies. Organizational studies have prevalently placed (too much?) emphasis on the processes of organizations' adaptation to external pressure. Less attention has been paid to the fact that organizations can be politically proactive rather than

---

[19] The analysis focuses on auditing companies in the specific context of *widespread ownership companies* (with many shareholders, as in the United States, United Kingdom, and Japan) even though, as will be seen, there are elements in common with the *centralized ownership* model more prevalent throughout Europe.

reactive, creating or favoring the creation of norms to their own advantage (Perrow 2002; Moore et al. 2006). Some specific organizations, for example, can encourage and, in some cases, determine legislative and normative changes to their own exclusive advantage or block the activation of standards that, although in the collective interest, might reduce margins of action and potential earnings.

The problem of failure of controls is not a new theme, but it has become increasingly important following the recent financial crisis. Power (1997) points out how control practices, rather than preventing abuse, more usually have a legitimating function with reference to decisional organs: the controls are rationalized inspection rituals focused more on form than on substance. If, on the one hand, there has been an *explosion of controls*, with a great deployment of resources invested in this field and with a constant increase in the number of people involved in control activities, on the other hand, a certain ineffectiveness is noticeable in the action of control itself (Sikka 2009).

As will be explained later in more detail, auditing companies carry out a central function to guarantee market trust; this function goes beyond the legal confines of single organizations and of the specific commercial activities they are engaged in and establishes them, to a certain extent, as providers of public goods. Precisely because of this, attention to distortional dynamics and effective regulation becomes a necessity of public relevance.

The various levels of failure: micro-meso-macro

The auditing field is divided into three distinct groups of actors: (1) the state and the agencies that regulate and control financial markets, (2) the auditing companies (the main ones being Deloitte & Touche, Ernst & Young, KPMG, PricewaterhouseCoopers) and professional auditors, and (3) the companies subject to auditing.

The causes of failure have been many, some well-known and others less visible. I examine these factors through a multilevel frame aimed at highlighting the links between the macro, meso, and micro levels:

(1) the micro level, the *individual*, pertains to bias and error in the decision-making processes of auditors operating in a context of radical uncertainty;

(2) the meso level, *organizational*, refers to the profound organizational and strategic changes which have taken place in the composition of the portfolio of activity since the 1990s. These changes have seen the role of consultancy activity and other various services to companies becoming dominant with respect to simple auditing, with significant repercussions on the activity of auditing; and

(3) the macro level, *interorganizational* and *organizational field*, refers to the dynamics relating to high concentration and the situation of oligopoly, to the complex attempts at reform and regulation by the responsible bodies (the SEC in the United States) and the action of lobbying in order to impede possible processes of reform.

In this section, I analyze the various levels of failure and criticalities, which in many cases are still present in the auditing system.

Individual level – micro

As we have seen, the individual level refers to biases, heuristics, mistakes in decision-making processes and violations. At the individual level, the myopia of the controllers is influenced on one side by the specific characteristics of the activity of certification in contexts of radical uncertainty and on the other by processes and mechanisms that foster a series of biases, even involuntary ones, in evaluation.

Bazerman, Morgan, and Loewenstein (1997) maintain that in this regard the failures in the activity of auditing are rarely the result of collusion between the auditors and their clients. The failures are rather the natural product of the relationship between the auditor and the client, which depends on the institutional structure in force, according to which "it is psychologically impossible for auditors to maintain their objectivity; cases of audit failure are inevitable, even with the most honest auditors" (Bazerman et al. 1997, p. 90). If it is a matter of intentional bias, this may be corrected with the threat of legal sanctions. The problem, however, pertains rather to so-called unintentional bias, that is, bias of which the operators are not wholly aware and which can lead them to make errors of judgment and evaluation. The principal mechanisms that can distort the independence of the evaluation process are (a) self-serving bias and wishful thinking, (b) familiarity, (c) discounting the future, and (d) escalation of commitment.

(a) As seen in Section 3.1, *self-serving bias* (Messick and Sentis 1979; Babcock and Loewenstein 1997) leads, in the evaluation of a specific situation, to the interpretation of information in a way that is convenient to the person who is evaluating the situation. The definition of what is right is therefore strongly influenced by the role that the auditor has with respect to the event under judgment. The problem arises when an auditor has an interest in considering the data being evaluated from a certain perspective, with the consequence that it becomes difficult to give an impartial or independent evaluation. *Wishful thinking*, on the other hand, consists of adapting perception to expectation and desire. Facts, events, perceptions, written documents, and so on are all interpreted in the light of what they are wanted to be rather than according to the evidence. This becomes particularly relevant if an auditor's critical evaluation of the economic status of a company may have a negative influence on the business relationship between the auditing firm and the client company.

(b) The mechanism of *familiarity* influences the decisional process in uncertain situations (Bazerman, Loewenstein, and Moore 2002) – for example, if an auditor is involved in a situation in which his decisions could give rise to potentially negative consequences for the client, or for other unknown subjects (investors, for example). Based on this dilemma, the auditor might approve a doubtful evaluation in order to minimize damage due to familiarity with the person or organization. The longer the relationship with the client lasts, the more likely it is that this bias in judgment will make itself felt. The pitfalls of familiarity are sometimes reticular in character, as Mizruchi and Stearns (2001), amongst others, point out with reference to credit concessions in the banking world. When an executive, in a situation of uncertainty following a request for credit, turns to a colleague for information and reassurance, if a strong bond exists between them then this reassurance tends to be based on affection rather than information (familiarity of acquaintance). The opposite tends to be the case if the bond is a weak one (low familiarity of acquaintance), when informational and cognitive elements will usually prevail over sentiment.

(c) The mechanism of *discounting the future* brings individuals to prefer short-term to mid- or long-term options, especially if the latter are uncertain.

This list of mechanisms highlights the difficulty of interpreting information without bias. Bias may evolve into conscious corruption if the result of the actions becomes very evident. For example, an auditor's bias may, over time, bring about a series of small and apparently insignificant adaptations to small imperfections in a client's financial practices, for example, by overlooking minor irregularities. At a certain point, correcting this bias might make it necessary to admit previous errors, and so things become rather difficult for an auditor: the result is that it is easier for the latter to go on with the adaptations in the hope that the errors will not be discovered and that the problem will be solved sooner or later.

(d) This leads to the *escalation of commitment* mechanism, which can make the problem extremely difficult to correct (Bazerman et al. 2002). One example of this mechanism is the case involving the Italian multinational dairy and food corporation Parmalat. Overwhelmed by a massive financial collapse at the end of 2003, the company was forced to declare bankruptcy. The Parmalat crash was the biggest scandal of bankruptcy fraud and market manipulation perpetrated by a private company in Europe. Although discovered only towards the end of 2003, it was later shown that the company's financial difficulties were already detectable in the early 1990s. The hole left by the company was about 14 billion euros.

The sentence of the Milan Court (December 18, 2008, judgment filed May 5, 2009) highlights how, during the 1996–1997 assessment of the company's balance sheet, the auditors became aware of certain irregularities and that part of the debt had been concealed. When they asked Fausto Tonna (at that time Parmalat's financial director) for an explanation, they found that he did not deny the evidence, but he asked them to *let the matter slide* for the moment, since he claimed it would only take the company three or four years to offset the debt. As time passed, the auditors, having already accepted the original compromise, found themselves with their hands tied: all they could do was sit still and try to cover their backs as best they could (Milan Court sentence, December 18, 2008). The missing debt went from 300 billion lira in the 1996–1997 balance sheet to 740 billion lira the following year. This, then, is a condition of *cognitive path dependency*, with decisions made previously influencing those made later in a sort of progressive *lock-in* from which it is difficult to escape.

The distinction between conscious corruption and unconscious bias is important in that the two elements respond to different incentives and work in different ways. They can also work together, as certain cases demonstrate. In the Parmalat case, for example, a fictitious company, Bonlat, was set up in the Cayman Islands by Tonna and Grant Thornton auditors, with the specific purpose of concealing the enormous losses. "The auditing of this company was always entrusted to Grant Thornton, so that nobody else would look into it" (Milan Court sentence, December 18, 2008, p. 239).

It is also important to underline that the operators' awareness of these biases can be a potential antidote to their manifestation, in that it makes it possible to control them, partially reducing their effect.

Bias in the decision-making process and the analysis of interests at an individual level need to be reconstructed and understood within a more complex picture of a social and organizational kind. Granovetter (1985) maintains that social (and organizational) action is always socially situated and cannot be explained solely based on individual motivations or psychological mechanisms. The objectives and strategies of economic actors depend both on their position in the organizational structure, which shapes interests and identity, and on their conception of reality, which in turn is influenced by the culture of their group of reference (Fligstein 1990). This brings us to the following level of analysis.

Organizational level – meso
Since their origins, auditing companies and the accounting profession have undergone many types of changes, both economic and legal. One factor in particular relating to these changes is especially important, and that is the increase in consultancy services and their impact on the culture of professional business. Since the early 1990s, the income derived from consultancy services, compared with that derived from accounting services, has seen a considerable increase. In the space of a decade, from 1990 to 1999, earnings due to consultancy activity doubled with respect to income derived from auditing. The comingling of consultancy and auditing activity was already a matter of discussion at the end of the 1970s, given that it seemed a critical point in relation to the transparency and impartiality of the auditing companies' evaluations. Stevens (1981) points out how the Big Eight, as it was then, by providing consultancy services, were thus involved in the commercial affairs of their clients. This financial and professional involvement with the client was incompatible with the responsibility and independence of an accounting inspection. In 2000, some researchers warned the

SEC that the rapid growth in consultancy activity that had developed during the 1990s within the five biggest auditing companies had made the conduction of impartial financial audits substantially impossible. The intertwining of (partisan) consultancy activity with that of (impartial and uncommitted) auditing made the latter potentially problematic. The profits of the auditing companies increasingly derived from consultancy activity, which meant that handing out negative opinions in the role of auditors would threaten the continuity of their contracts for consultancy. The Enron and Arthur Andersen collapses were the natural consequence of this type of intermeshing. It was a question of *predictable surprise*, avoidable if preventive action had been taken (Bazerman and Watkins 2004).

The 1990s was the period in which most auditing companies learned how to use their role as auditor to sell consultancy services – services that were originally unrelated to their own area of work (Carey 1970). Thus, the auditing companies' business relationship with their clients became increasingly closer, both in terms of consultancy activity and of initiatives involving co-marketing, finance, and joint ventures. During the 1990s, these companies, realizing that greater potential profits lay in the marketing of services to their clients, profoundly altered their business model, transforming auditors into sales people. Stealing a client from a competitor was certainly a far more difficult maneuver than was selling new services to existing clients. The idea of professional distance and separation from the client began to be increasingly considered an obsolete and outdated practice. Incentive systems for partners developed alongside this tendency. Towards the end of the 1990s, at Ernst & Young, accounting division partners were requested to promote consultancy services to client companies for which they handled the activity of auditing. In cases of refusal or lack of success, there was a 10 percent reduction in income (Dugan 2002). Similar mechanisms were in place in other auditing companies. At Arthur Andersen, it was expected that the partners of the auditing division would double their earnings thanks to the sales of consultancy services. In situations like this, it is psychologically very difficult for the auditors to maintain their objectivity in professional activity: cases of failure are inevitable even for the most honest, most professional auditor. While auditing activity in the period 1993–1999 grew from 5,485 to 9,150 billion dollars, the increase in consultancy activity was dramatic: for the same period, from $6,570 to $21,466 billion (see Table 3.1).

Table 3.1. *Revenue for service lines of main auditing firms (in billion dollars)*

	1993	1994	1995	1996	1997	1998	1999
Auditing	5,485	5,823	5,762	6,195	6,738	7,812	9,150
Nonauditing[20]	6,570	7,469	9,298	11,110	13,728	18,105	21,466
Total	12,055	13,292	15,051	17,305	20,466	25,917	30,616

Source: Bazerman and Watkins (2004).

Table 3.2. *Revenue mix for service lines of main auditing firms*

	1993	1994	1995	1996	1997	1998	1999
Auditing	45%	44%	38%	36%	33%	30%	30%
Nonauditing	54%	56%	62%	64%	67%	70%	70%

Source: Bazerman and Watkins (2004).

Sikka (2009) presents less systematic but more recent data that confirms the same trend. This indicates a strategic alteration in the commercial nature of auditing companies, with an increasing dependence on non-auditing resources and with potential repercussions on the independence of auditing activity (see Table 3.2). In the 1980s, PriceWaterhouse was the first company to radically modify its business. Revenue relating to consultancy represented 6.8 percent in 1980, increasing to 13.3 percent in 1985. The company mission was changing: the company was transforming itself into a *full-service business advisory firm* (Allen and McDermott 1993). In the mid-1980s, Deloitte & Touche CEO Michael Cook declared that one of the company's objectives was to change its image from a company of professionals that did business to a company that commercialized professional services (Stevens 1981). This led to a profound strategic and cultural change in line with a *financial conception of control*[21] (Fligstein 1990),

[20] Tax services, management consultancy, information technology, and other non-auditing services.
[21] According to Fligstein (1990), from 1880 to the end of the twentieth century, in the US economy, there were four successive conceptions of company control, four different modalities and perspectives through which managers and entrepreneurs exercised control within the company and towards the

which favored not only diversification but also brought with it a concept of the business in purely financial terms, with the productive unit being evaluated on the basis of its ability to generate short-term revenue. These changes had profound implications for remuneration and career systems. Partners who were not able to achieve market objectives were forced to resign, thus abandoning the previous tradition of partnership as tenure. New criteria were established for promotion to partnership based on marketing and commercial ability rather than technical skill and knowledge. The tension between the various consultancy and auditing areas of the auditing firm began to become critical, finishing in long drawn out legal cases, as in the Arthur Andersen example. Here, the consultancy division separated from its mother company to become Accenture, one of the most famous and important consultancy firms in the world.

The disparity in earnings between professionals involved in auditing and those working in the consultancy sector influenced the cultural transformation of the auditing profession, increasingly focused on commercial factors and with a waning professional image when compared to that of consultancy. This led to forms of cross-selling, with auditors being encouraged to *promote* consultancy services; based on their sales results, they were significantly rewarded with incentives and bonuses. The culture of accounting, as the partners of the companies themselves admitted, was changing rapidly: the commercial interests of consultancy were becoming more important than were those interests relating to the sphere of auditing.

Enron, for example, was an excellent client for Arthur Andersen, who in 2001 earned $25 million for certification activity and $27 million for consultancy work. As criminal investigations brought to light, the partners of Arthur Andersen estimated that they would soon be earning $100 million from Enron as a client. With this expectation in mind, Arthur Andersen, instead of reporting the deeds and misdeeds committed by Enron, preferred to hush things up. One hundred fifty-nine Andersen personnel took part in Enron business meetings and were involved in making decisions regarding company strategy.

external: (1) direct control of the competitors, dominant until the end of the nineteenth century; (2) control centred around the product in the early years of the twentieth century; (3) control through marketing, common from the 1920s to the decade after the Second World War; and (4) widespread financial control from the middle of the 1950s and thereafter.

This generated a symbiotic relationship that made it very difficult for the Andersen company to go against Enron's requests. A process of *normalization of deviance* (Vaughan 1996) was thus fostered, persuading the auditors to consider small nonconformities as irrelevant, in a progressive spiral which led to a company completely out of control being certified as in order. In the end, violation became the norm, following the mechanism of escalation discussed earlier. Similar conclusions were reached by the judges of the Milan Court in the Parmalat sentence (Milan Court, Parmalat Sentence, 2008, p. 243):

the systematic compliance with the policies of falsification established by the Parmalat Group (anterior to the years 2002/2003 and for which Italaudit SpA answers today) was the evident instrument for the preservation of a multiple number of auditing positions, for which there was corresponding agreement and which resulted at the end of the year in real effective payment of the sums agreed upon.

It should, however, be stated that there are no empirical studies that demonstrate that every auditing company, while certifying a firm that provides it with a significant percentage of income for consultancy services, invariably *sweetens* the result of the audit. It is also true that it is not easy for a firm to fire an auditing company, since it is obliged to justify its reasons (to the Commissione Nazionale per la Società e la Borsa [CONSOB] in Italy and to the SEC in the United States). It is equally true that a firm may try to *seduce* the auditing company by offering highly remunerative consultancy contracts – contracts (allowed by law or as an exception thereto) which would certainly be put at risk by a negative outcome of the evaluation.

The real conflict lies not so much in the actual earnings that an auditing company derives from its consultancy activity as in the prospect of future income. Even though a client doesn't pay the auditor a great deal for its consultancy services, this could change significantly if the auditor demonstrates a capacity to be understanding and reasonable.

Interorganizational level – macro

Every organization is *embedded* in a network of relationships with other organizations and its development depends on this interorganizational context. The organizational and legal field to which the organization belongs contributes to the definition and limitation of courses of action, while organizational specialization increases the level of *structural secrecy* (Vaughan 1996), thus making it difficult for the controlling organization to carry out credit checks on the controlled organizations. Certain interorganizational-level factors are relevant in explaining the changes that have occurred and their impact on the problem of auditor independence: (1) the reduced threat of legal disputes, (2) the failure of discipline in the profession and of professional self-regulation, (3) the significant increase in market concentration, and (4) lobbying activities in order to block the reform of the auditing sector.

Let us now examine each factor.

(1) Since the 1990s, there was a progressive reduction in the deterrence capacity of legal disputes, in parallel with the reduction in the SEC's operative capacity to prosecute violations of standards by auditing companies. It was a change fostered by a political climate less favorable towards regulation and control. In the mid-1990s, auditing company lobbies worked to reduce the effect of class action activity through the promulgation of a law (the 1995 Securities Litigation Reform Act) that reduced exposure to prosecution and responsibility for auditing companies in case of fraud (Coffee 2006).

(2) Alongside this decrease in external controls and sanctions, there was also a decrease in cases of self-discipline in the profession by professional associations. The US auditing profession and firms in the 1990s stood free from all sanctions and controls and continued their rapid transformation into a rather different creature. As will be seen later, attempts were made in those years to regulate the sector in order to avoid this blatant conflict of interests, but such initiatives were seen as threats by companies in the sector and therefore produced no result. The auditing companies vigorously opposed any proposal to separate their auditing activity and consultancy services.

(3) A further change involved the progressive process of concentration within the auditing field. The necessity of having a preexisting reputational capital created barriers that precluded new competitors from entering the sector, or at least made it difficult for them. Whereas in the 1990s, eight companies (the so-called Big Eight) carried out 90 percent of accounts auditing (Stevens 1981, 1991), by the 1990s this had dropped to six companies and, a few years later, to five. After the Enron-linked collapse of Arthur Andersen in 2002, four dominating companies remained in the field, with Pricewaterhouse-Coopers, KPMG, Ernst & Young, and Deloitte & Touche monopolizing the scene

and constituting a sort of *private certification* of financial markets. This huge centralization of private power certainly creates a problem in terms of impartiality. Competitors in such a concentrated market can in fact collude in a number of different ways – for example, by not competing with one another for reputation capital.

(4) Attempts at reform in the auditing field have always been impeded by lobbies that have successfully blocked any serious manoeuvre to regulate the system. In June 2000, the SEC drew up a project aimed at reinforcing the independence of the certification sector through limiting personal and financial relationships between auditors and their client companies and making consultancy work separate. Parliamentary pressure exerted by the lobbies thwarted the endeavor, producing a softer version that only requested client companies to declare how much they paid for auditing services and how much for consultancy (Mayer 2002). These new rules did nothing to prevent the Enron scandal and neither did they help solve the problem of the auditing companies' independence. Until the Sarbanes-Oxley Act in 2002, auditing companies in the United States were not subject to any regime of supervision.[22] Other reform attempts aimed at establishing a

---

[22] The Sarbanes-Oxley Act (SOA) was the US Congress's response to the wave of financial scandals that started at the end of 2001. The SOA was designed with the aim of improving corporate governance and guaranteeing the transparency of accounting records, including the possibility of criminal prosecution. The act included a prohibition on firms providing both consultancy and auditing activity for the same company and on providing consultancy for a company in which a top manager had previously worked for the auditing firm. Penalties were increased to up to twenty-five years for accounting fraud and the obligation to pay back bonuses in case of fraud guilt. More than bringing about a truly structural reform, the law placed a great deal of trust in the deterrence value of severe penalties as the best remedy for preventing financial scandals. In fact, although it legislated for the separation of consultancy and auditing activities, this could also be gotten around in certain situations (through other advisory or tax-planning services) with the approval of the Audit Committee. In addition, the act impeded investment banks from harassing analysts who expressed negative opinions on a client of the bank; introduced a sort of antifraud decalogue; redefined the responsibility of the SEC; and established the Public Company Accounting Oversight Board (PCAOB), a supervising body for the balance sheets of listed companies. Expert opinion regarding the effectiveness of this reform is divided. Some observer believed it was one of the most significant government acts in the economic field since the New Deal. Others (Bazerman et al. 2002) see it as a missed opportunity, since it did not eliminate structural conflicts of interest, leaving a series of unresolved aspects that could lead to new financial scandals and disasters.

Table 3.3. *Auditing company financing*

Year	Arthur Andersen	Deloitte & Touche	Ernst & Young	KPMG	Pricewaterhouse-Coopers°
1997	$ 2,380,000	$ 785,000	$ 1,380,000	$ 600,000	$ 900,000
1998	1,985,000	360,000	1,420,000	420,000	960,000
1999	1,840,000	890,000	1,200,000	850,000	1,220,000
2000	2,480,000	2,524,000	1,200,000	1,340,000	1,425,000
2001	1,540,000	580,000	1,320,000	1,175,000	1,240,000
2002	–	1,027,000	2,343,860	1,430,000	3,160,000
2003	–	660,000	1,980,000	925,000	1,680,000

° The 1997 total is the sum of the financing relating to Pricewaterhouse and Coopers & Lybrand, which before this were two separate companies.
Source: Office of Public Records, http://sopr.senate.gov.

series of controls were pursued by Arthur Levitt, SEC president from 1993 to 2001, but without success.

The lobbies won the parliamentary battle (thanks to significant contributions to both parties in Congress, as evident from Table 3.3), maintaining that their success was based on *reputation* and that this could not be put at risk without rendering their evaluations irrelevant. According to their argument, the market was already functioning in such a way that any auditing company that was not impartial in its evaluations would be forced out the market. In addition, they adduced reasons based on a vision of the market in which there should be no regulatory interference.[23]

Auditing companies and the financial crisis

The financial crisis highlighted certain questions regarding the role and effectiveness in the evaluation of risks of international financial institutions (the International Monetary Fund, World Bank, Basel 1 and 2), the main market regulators (rating agencies, auditing companies, financial analysts, etc.) and control systems and risk management within companies and banks. Many questions were raised regarding the real efficacy and value of auditing practices. The auditing

[23] It is interesting to note that Enron chief Kenneth Lay was himself actively involved in 2000 in opposing any attempt to reform the system and to bring in stricter regulations for auditing companies.

companies themselves have been penalized by this myopia, with a significant reduction in their balance sheets of more than $230 million. The silence of the auditors (Sikka 2009) is made evident by the fact that these companies gave positive responses without reservation (in 2008 for the activity carried out in 2007) to a host of banks and financial companies (see Table 3.4) which played an important role in the financial crisis just a few months, or even weeks, after receiving reports of reliable accounting records from the auditors.

Episodes like this encourage a radical reflection on the role, value, and independence of auditors and confirm the strong doubts regarding the real effectiveness of the Sarbanes-Oxley Act's reforms in terms of eliminating, or reducing to any great extent, the risks of collusion and conflicts of interest that form the basis of the auditor-client relationship. Providing consultancy services, even with constraints and an established rotation of auditors, the auditing firms continue to carry out quasi-management activity and cannot be fully objective in evaluating the outcome of the transactions that they themselves have helped create.

The private sector of auditing cannot in this way be independent from the companies that it evaluates. This criticality was not adequately addressed by post-Enron reforms such as the Sarbanes-Oxley Act, weakening the auditing firms' ability to contribute to the availability of reliable information concerning the companies' systems. In addition to this criticality relating to the *form* of the auditor-client relationship, there is another relating to the objective of auditing. The intensification of financial capitalism has raised serious questions regarding the basic knowledge possessed by the auditor (Sikka 2009). Auditing firms developed in an industrial economy, basing their evaluations on tangible goods that could be examined, counted, and measured. In an economy based instead on complex financial instruments (such as derivatives), with value depending on future events and fluctuations that can reach millions of dollars, are auditing firms really capable of adequately evaluating the situation? The events of the recent financial crisis do not inspire a great deal of faith in their reliability.

Conclusion

The analysis of the main criticalities in the auditing system – namely the structure of relationships between the controlling and controlled

Table 3.4. *The main banks and financial companies involved in the crisis had been evaluated positively by auditing firms in 2008 for activity in 2007*

Company	Country	Auditing firm	Date of auditing report	Monetary compensation (in millions in terms of local currency)	
				Auditing	Other services
Abbey National	UK	D & T	03-04-2008	£2.8	£2.1
Alliance & Leicester	UK	D & T	02-19-2008	£0.8	£0.8
Barclays	UK	PwC	03-07-2008	£29	£15
Bear Stearns	USA	D & T	01-28-2008	$23.4	$4.9
Bradford and Bingley	UK	KPMG	02-12-2008	£0.6	£0.8
Carlyle Capital Corporation	Guernsey	PwC	02-27-2008	N/A	N/A
Citigroup	USA	KPMG	02-22-2008	$81.7	$6.4
Dexia	France/Belgium	PwC + Mazars & Guérard	03-28-2008	€10.12	€1.48
Fannie Mae	USA	D & T	02-26-2008	$49.3	–
Fortis	Netherlands	KPMG + PwC	03-06-2008	€20	€17
Freddie Mac	USA	PwC	02-27-2008	$73.4	–
Glitnir	Iceland	PwC	01-31-2008	ISK146	ISK218
HBOS	UK	KPMG	02-26-2008	£9.0	£2.4
Hypo Real Estate	Germany	KPMG	03-25-2008	€5.4	€5.7
Indymac	USA	KPMG	02-28-2008	$5.7	$0.5
ING	Netherlands	E & Y	03-17-2008	€6.8	€7
Kaupthing Bank	Iceland	KPMG	01-30-2008	ISK421	ISK74

Table 3.4. (*cont.*)

Company	Country	Auditing firm	Date of auditing report	Monetary compensation (in millions in terms of local currency)	
				Auditing	*Other services*
Landsbanki	Iceland	PwC	01–28–2008	ISK259	ISK46
Lehman Brothers	USA	E & Y	01–28–2008	$27.8	$3.5
Lloyds TSB	UK	PwC	02–21–2008	£13.1	£1.5
Northern Rock	UK	PwC	02–27–2008	£1.3	£0.7
Royal Bank of Scotland	UK	D & T	02–27–2008	£17	£14.4
TCF Financial Corp	USA	KPMG	02–14–2008	$0.97	$0.05
Thornburg Mortgage	USA	KPMG	02–27–2008	$2.1	$0.4
UBS	Switzerland	E & Y	03–06–2008	CHF61.7	CHF13.4
US Bancorp	USA	E & Y	02–20–2008	$7.5	$9.6
Wachovia	USA	KPMG	02–25–2008	$29.2	$4.1
Washington Mutual	USA	D & T	02–28–2008	$10.7	$4.3

Note: D & T = Deloitte & Touche; E & Y = Ernst & Young; PwC = Pricewaterhouse-Coopers.
Source: Sikka (2009).

organizations, and the radical uncertainty that characterizes the object of the auditing activity – leads to the conclusion that its failure does not lie in the incapacity or corruption of the auditor and that deviant behavior cannot only be avoided by the motivation to preserve the reputational capital of the auditing companies. In companies, opportunistic behavior and decisions contrary to ethical norms can spring, not so much because of a compromise between ethics and profit, or a cynical neglect of collective interests, but rather because of environmental pressures and mechanisms that foster an individual decisional process which is defective both from a moral and rational point of view.

What happened in the 1990s and the recent financial crisis represent the natural product of the client-auditor relationship. The nexus of interests that is such a strong feature in the relationship between controller and controlled has, following the development of consultancy activity, generated a conflict of interests[24]– one which has deeply invalidated auditing activity, favoring decisional bias and the systematic disregard of control norms, such as, for example, in the case of the prohibition on protracting auditing responsibilities beyond a certain limit.[25] This problem was not completely eliminated by the Sarbanes-Oxley Act.

Individual-level biases in decision-making processes, evaluation, and interest analysis need to be reconstructed and understood within a broader organizational picture. Table 3.5 provides a summary of the criticalities and mechanisms operating at different levels. The biases and decisional mechanisms analyzed are in fact fostered by organizational-level factors, like the change in the nature of auditing companies from suppliers of auditing to commercial suppliers of services to companies. The auditing activity thus loses part of its centrality in

---

[24] A conflict of interest is legally defined as a situation in which a general interest is threatened by a private interest in relation to a real or apparent incompatibility between duties pertaining to the private sphere and those that pertain to the public arena.

[25] The problem of conflict of interest regards not only the auditing companies but also all the gatekeepers, such as rating agencies, banks, business lawyers, and so on. As concerns rating agencies, for example, Paul Volcker, ex-president of the Federal Reserve, has stated that they certainly contributed to the failure of the system and there was as yet no plan for reforming them. And this was due to the fact, he went on to say, that nobody had found another economically sustainable way to pay them for their work.

Table 3.5. *Summary of the various critical factors and mechanisms at different levels*

Levels	Critical factors and mechanisms
Individual	– Self-serving bias – Wishful thinking – Familiarity – Discounting the future – Escalation of commitment
Organizational	– Growth in consultancy services – Dependence on nonauditing resources – Reduction in the centrality of auditing in the economic structure of the company – Role transformation of the profession of accountant (more marketing oriented)
Interorganizational, Organizational field	– Decline in the threat of legal disputes regarding checks – Reduction in professional self-discipline by companies – Increasing oligopolistic concentration – Lobbying to block reform of the system

the overall structure of the company at the expense of the consultancy activity. The auditor is heavily involved in the commercial activity of the consultancy service, with bonuses and incentives aimed at stimulating commitment in this area. These factors at an organizational level develop within the transformation of the organizational field, which has witnessed the progressive concentration of the sector into an oligopolistic entity, the reduction in forms of control and professional self-discipline and the practice of constantly exerting pressure on parliamentary groups in order to block any plan involving standards that could put future earnings at risk.

The analysis carried out, even though focused on the context of auditing companies operating with a distributed property structure, makes it possible to highlight the various levels of failure in the auditing system and also provides useful points of reflection for the financial sector as a whole. As Coffee (2006, p. 374) states, "The government of the professions by the professions tends to produce mainly government for the professions." The recent financial crisis has brought to the fore not only the failure of the market as a self-regulating system but also the failure of the public system of control and regulation. The supervising authorities also failed in their primary task because they received little help from the gatekeepers, such as the rating and auditing firms, compromised as they were by evident situations of conflict of interest.

Thus there remains a need to inquire how, notwithstanding their evident failures, the controllers and regulators continue to operate without their reputations ever having been questioned (Mutti 2010), especially in a situation in which, following the crisis, new institutional rules and strategies are being sought aimed at making sure a similar crisis never happens again. Such strategies seem however to be valid more for the symbolic value of their emotional and cognitive reassurance rather than for any real effectiveness regarding the actions deployed in the field.

The auditing system, as a producer of public goods that transcends the techno-legal confines of the subjects involved and of the commercial relationships that created them, requires structural changes, as well as continuous scrutiny and evaluation. The discussion on how to identify more efficient and reliable forms of regulation and control, in particular in a situation of increasing *financialization* of the economy (Epstein 2005; Dore 2008; G.F. Davis 2009), should consider that we are operating in an area characterized by radical structural uncertainty – which is extremely difficult to reduce.

4 | *Anticipating risk: the problem of learning*

4.1 Learning from failures, errors, and problems

The term *organizational learning* designates a process of change in cognition and action, a process both ingrained in organizations and influenced by them (Crossan, Lane, and White 1999; Vera and Crossan 2004). The dimensions of cognition and action are therefore closely connected (Edmondson 2002). Organizational learning includes processes that take place at an individual, group and organizational level (Boh et al. 2007; Crossan et al. 1999; Easterby-Smith, Crossan, and Nicolini 2000); it is not, however, simply an accumulation of individual learning. For learning to be considered organizational, individual cognition and action must be shared between people and incorporated into institutionalized routines, rules, and procedures (Argyris and Schön 1996; Berends, Boersma, and Weggeman 2003).

According to a cognitive perspective of learning that focuses on the treatment of information (Klimecki and Lassleben 1998), learning involves the acquisition, distribution, storage, retrieval, and interpretation of information for decision making (Huber 1991; Walsh and Ungson 1991). Levitt and March (1988, p. 318) affirm that organizations learn "by encoding inferences from history into routines that guide behavior." Organizational learning happens when new options for action are recognized (Huber 1991); it is a particular type of learning that takes place in key individuals in organizations – individuals whose learning is connected to the consequent organizational change. In accordance with this approach, learning is a cognitive process that only individuals can undertake, and organizational learning is simply a metaphor. Simon (1991), for example, states that learning takes place within the individual mind. It follows that an organization can learn either through its members or by bringing in new members who possess knowledge that the organization did not previously possess.

Other authors maintain that organizations can learn because they possess abilities identical or equivalent to those of individuals, abilities that make it possible for them to learn (Duncan and Weiss 1979; Gahmberg 1980; Hedberg 1981; Levitt and March 1988). In this sense, organizations are treated as if they were individuals. Organizations themselves learn, in ways that are independent of what individual members learn. Organizational learning is a result of organizational, not individual, processes.

Organizational learning is a socially constructed process (Daft and Huber 1987; Dixon 1992). In terms of the learning process, learning appears to be discontinuous, and subject to frequent interruptions (March and Olsen 1975; Engestrom, Kerouso, and Kajamaa 2007), rather than occur in a linear way, as was initially maintained (Huber 1991; Dixon 1994; Nonaka 1994).

"Do human societies learn? If so, how do they do it; and if not, why not?" Sheila Jasanoff (2005) asks herself. Learning from a disaster is a complex, ambiguous process – conditioned by culture, yet not easily forced into a univocal, totalizing narrative. Jasanoff reconducts the different forms of inquiry about disasters to a specific *civic epistemology*: the styles and the modalities of public inquiry and accountability, the strategies for allocating responsibilities and achieving objectivity. With this useful concept, Jasanoff signifies the public ways of knowing, "constituted, displayed, and reaffirmed within the decision-making processes of states, including those aimed at the management of risk and prevention of harm" (Jasanoff 2005, p. 211). Civic epistemology refers "to the mix of ways in which knowledge is produced, presented, tested, verified and put to use in public arenas" (Jasanoff 2005, p. 226). Seen in this light, civic epistemology is a constitutive element of the political culture of risks: "the particularity of national civic epistemologies lies, in part, in the boundary that each framework constructs between factual and moral causes or, put differently, between responsibility and blame" (Jasanoff 2005, p. 212).

The relevance of learning from error has a long history. According to Popper (1984 [1994]) it was the pre-Socratic philosopher Xenophanes, born probably in 571 BC who developed a theory of truth founded on the integration of the idea of objective truth with that of human fallibility – a line of thought that continued through Socrates, Montaigne, Erasmus, Voltaire, Hume, Lessing, and Kant. But it was only towards the middle of the 1900s with philosophers

such as Popper and Bachelard that the idea of error as solely negative changed and it began to be considered instead as an occasion for
learning. Popper (1963, 1984 [1994]), beginning with the observation
that no methodological process exists that makes it possible to avoid
error, upholds the necessity for a new *ethic* of error, one that is valid
not only for the natural sciences. This new ethic is based on two principles: acceptance of the idea that avoiding every error is impossible,
even though it remains our task to try to avoid it whenever possible,
and the need to move from a position that tends to conceal error to an
approach which encompasses the idea of learning from error, identifying it, and correcting it with the help of others. These positive instiga-
tions run into more than one difficulty however when transposed into
an organizational context.

Many authors (Rasmussen 1990; Sagan 1993; Vaughan 1996;
Turner and Pidgeon 1997; Perrow 1999; Choularton 2001; Busby
2006; Elliott and Smith 2006; Mahler 2009) underline the difficulty
of learning from accidents and errors and ask what action must be
taken in order to prevent the risk that the same errors occur again.
According to others, learning is, in the first place, guided by failures
(Wong and Weiner 1981; March 1994; Lipshitz and Barak 1995;
Argyris and Schön 1996; Zakay, Ellis, and Shevalsky 1998; Ron,
Lipshitz, and Popper 2006). For Luhmann (2000), the fundamental
premise for learning is that the organization can distinguish between
success and failure and that organizational learning occurs when
there is the attempt to solve known problems, to analyze and reflect
on sources of failure and error, and to draw conclusions regarding
cause and effect (Mahler 2009). Argyris and Schön (1996) maintain
that organizational learning, as with the individual, is concerned initially with the identification and successive correction of error: learning occurs when error – defined as a misalignment between intention
and consequence – is detected, corrected, and removed. Identification
of error therefore constitutes the first step in the process of learning. Argyris and Schön (1996) distinguish two forms of learning:
(1) *single-loop learning*, based on an extremely simple feedback
mechanism that includes the detection of error and its correction, in
the maintenance of existing organizational norms; (2) *double-loop
learning*, aimed at changing existing norms and assumptions responsible for the generation of erroneous behavior; this form, modifying
the underlying premises to behavior and attempting to reduce the

repetition of error, interrupts the course of routine practice and promotes organizational learning.

If there is a certain amount of agreement on the fact that learning from error is fundamental for organizational learning, on the other hand, failure does not always produce learning and change. In fact, the tension induced in the organizational system by failure, may foster the persistence of unsuitable behavior rather than transform it (Staw 1976, 1981). Moreover, when change is induced by failure, there seems to be a tendency towards limited modifications or improvements in procedure rather than radical innovation (Manns and March 1978; March and Olsen 1989). March (1988) underlines how successful organizations tend to not change their strategy, independently from its relative value.

Choularton (2001, p. 62) argues that in the case of accidents "while superficial learning is common, more fundamental lessons are harder to learn." Busby (2006, p. 1391) affirms that "organizing around risks of catastrophic failure critically involves processes of systemic reform whose efficacy is limited by conditions that organizing itself tends to produce." Referring to NASA space shuttle accidents, Mahler shows how "organizational learning was compromised because information needed to identify hazardous conditions and analyze the causes was misdirected, filtered, misinterpreted, and ignored" (2009, p. 163). *Structural secrecy* (Vaughan 1996) produces an information deficit that is not caused by the intentional strategies of individuals but by other factors associated with organizational structure. Especially in large organizations, information regarding weak signs and near-misses (accidents that almost took place) is not collated and elaborated precisely because there is a lack of formal reporting systems. Yet, there are also situations in which signs of danger are intentionally hidden.

Turner and Pidgeon (1997), referring to Wilensky's (1967) concepts of *failure of intelligence* and *failure of foresight*, underline the inability of the members of an organization to recognize and become aware of the danger signs which transpire before an accident occurs. Some authors use the term *organizational intelligence* to refer to the capacity of an organization to obtain and elaborate clear and reliable information that supports the process of being aware of what is going on. The information should be interpreted in the same way by operators belonging to different professional communities. However, this usually does not happen, and the same event is considered in different ways by different communities that work in the same organization.

With regard to the problems relating to learning, the two most important theories about accidents – the Normal Accidents Theory (NAT) and the High Reliability Theory (HRT) – follow two different approaches. The NAT (Perrow 1999; Sagan 1993) is essentially pessimistic in tone, emphasizing the limits of learning, while the HRT (Roberts 1990, 1993; Rochlin 1993; LaPorte and Consolini 1994; Weick and Sutcliffe 2007) is more optimistic. According to the NAT, the obstacles to learning are many and include the inaccuracy and incompleteness of information about events, the high level of ambiguity of feedback, the politicization of internal environments (in which the identification of the causes of the accident are aimed at protecting the interests of the most powerful actors), and the sectoralization of complex organizational systems, which discourages the sharing of information (Sagan 1993). Perrow's analysis highlights that, notwithstanding the dangers inherent in the technology and socio-technical systems examined, ignoring warning signs is not unusual and that the learning process is often absent (Perrow 1999).

According to the HRT (which is looked at more closely in Chapter 5), in contrast, learning from error can improve existing managerial practices and increase safety conditions even within the context of complex, high-risk organizations. Organizational learning from error can constitute a crucial factor for the improvement of learning in general (Sitkin 1992; Vince and Saleem 2004) and for the increase in organizational reliability and resilience. Learning from the fact that "minor errors can foreshadow problems and failures on a larger and more serious scale" (LaPorte and Consolini 1994, p. 27), it is possible to strive to recognize and avoid major disasters. Weick and Sutcliffe (2007) state that HROs (High Reliability Organizations; see Section 5.1) encourage the reporting of errors, use near-misses as an opportunity for learning, and are wary of the potential passivity generated by success, of self-complacency, of the temptation to reduce safety margins, and of the trend towards automation. One of the five principles of HROs is preoccupation with the possibility of failure and for every organization the discovery of errors and criticalities is a fundamental objective, because even the most insignificant error can give rise to a dangerous threat to the survival of both people and the organization (Roberts 1990; Zhao and Olivera 2006). HROs put a lot of work therefore into discovering errors, near-misses and criticalities that can be indicators of far more serious problems and risks in the system. However,

[t]o detect a failure is one thing. To report it is another. Research shows that people need to feel safe to report incidents or they will ignore them or cover them up. Managerial practices such as encouraging people to ask questions and rewarding people who report errors and mistakes strengthen an organization wide culture that values reporting. (Weick and Sutcliffe 2007, p. 50)

To obtain this sort of result, however, it is fundamental that operators are not punished for their warnings, even when this involves errors that they have committed themselves. As Schulman observes (1993a, 1993b), highly reliable organizations do not punish their members when they try to do the right thing. Punishment would render learning and organizational improvement difficult to realize. HROs favor the creation of *safe areas* (Grabowski, George, and Roberts 1997) through the construction of anonymous warning systems and brainstorming and go beyond simple interpretations related to placing blame on operators (Haunschild and Sullivan 2002; Kim, Hongseok, and Swaminathan 2006).

Apart from errors, there exists another type of failure within organizations: problems. While an error is understood as a misalignment between what is planned and the result obtained, a *problem* is a difficulty connected to the ability of the operator to carry out a specific task. As with errors, problems represent an important source of information for the identification of systemic criticalities, and this means that it is necessary to take them into consideration in terms of organizational learning. Tucker and Edmondson (2003) observed the behavior of twenty-six nurses working in nine hospitals. The aim of the research was to understand the way in which organizations learn, or do not learn, from failure. The researchers individuated two different ways of responding to problems: (1) *first-level problem solving*, in other words, the activation of immediate reparative solutions, and (2) *second-level problem solving*, that is, the adoption of long-term solutions aimed at eliminating the underlying conditions that generated the detected problem. In particular, first-level problem solving is employed when the operator improvises strategies in order to overcome the immediate difficulty and favor the completion of the assigned task. In this case, even when the solution seems at first to be successful, the causes that may contribute to causing similar problems in the future are not removed. Paradoxically, first-level problem solving turns out to be counterproductive, because it impedes the reporting of problems and the promotion of organizational learning. Personnel, deriving temporary benefit from the immediate solution, rarely inform their superiors, generating a vicious circle that blocks the process aimed at eliminating the causes of the problem. This strategy conceals the existence of the problem and thus hinders change.

Second-level problem solving, on the other hand, is employed when operators not only provide a temporary fix for the problem but also activate action designed to remove the basic factors that caused the problem in the first place. This process includes reporting the criticality to those in charge, sharing evaluations regarding the cause of the problem, implementing practicable changes, and the verifying their success. However, the activation of a higher level of problem solving often runs into difficulty, in particular because of three aspects closely connected to the process of first-level problem solving, these being excessive emphasis on individual vigilance, attention to efficiency, and decisional autonomy. These elements induce personnel to assume responsibility for resolving problems when they arise and create barriers to organizational development. They encourage independence, pushing operators to work individually on their own specific task without evaluating the presence of common underlying processes. This independence can have pernicious effects, because it leaves the operators to solve the question on their own, limiting interaction and reducing the possibility of favoring occasions for improvement.

When a problem arises, the operator tries to activate a first-level problem-solving process in order to be able to go on with the assigned task. The greater the effort employed to handle the situation in the moment, the less success there will be in the attempt to pass to second-level problem solving. Obstacles to the problem's definitive solution are not effectively removed, contributing to conflict, burnout, and personal dissatisfaction.

4.2 Myopia of learning and rare events

When what Bazerman and Watkins (2004) call a *predictable surprise* takes place, as, for example, with the Enron collapse, politicians and journalists tend to attribute blame and responsibility to a small number of deviant actors rather than to the conditions of the system that made abuse possible or to deficiencies in the control and regulation system (Vaughan 1999). With reference to disasters and related issues of safety, Turner and Pidgeon (1997) ask which political, institutional, cultural, and symbolic structures favor organizational myopia. The two researchers argue that the question is no longer if an organization or a society has learned or failed to learn everything possible in relation to a specific accident, but if they are convinced or not about being able to handle safety better in the future. The knowledge of an organization is the result of the connections between the intelligence of a number of individuals (Nonaka and Takeuchi 1995; Stacey 2001). Because organizations depend on individual knowledge and intelligence (Burton-Jones 1999), they must increasingly develop strategies to acquire, distribute, and share the information that individuals possess, passing from individual knowledge to organizational knowledge. Learning may therefore be modeled in terms of organizational connections formed by a network of individuals involved in influencing one another through reciprocal learning (Glynn, Lant, and Milliken 1994). In accordance with this perspective, learning takes on the configuration of a recursive process between individual and group learning. In this sense, organizational intelligence may be compared to human intelligence based on the interconnectedness of neurons.

Organizations suffer from *learning disabilities* when leaders are unable to capitalize on and codify the lessons generated by previous errors. Organizations often fail to learn from past errors because of deficiencies in the mechanisms that are required to codify and share the key lessons learned to as great an extent as possible. A series of barriers may hinder effective organizational learning from crises (D. Smith and Elliott 2007), and myopia in the identification of weak signs, in the gathering and interpretation of relevant information, is at the basis of the processes of organizational decline (Weitzel and Jonsson 1989).

Weitzel and Jonsson (1989) show that the failure to detect crisis signs can lead to the dissolution of an organization through five stages: the *first* stage is characterized by the leaders' *blindness* in identifying warning signs, such as, for example, the external and internal changes that can threaten the organization's long-term survival. The *second* stage, called *inactivity*, features the negation of change, notwithstanding signs and indicators, even very evident ones, of deterioration in performance. Data are presented in a creative way, bestowing an aspect of normality on what is not in fact normal. In the *third* stage, *error*, the organization decides to deal with the problems since it can no longer ignore the negative indicators. Further errors in the attempt to correct the critical conditions leads the organization to the *fourth* stage, *crisis*, characterized by a situation of panic spreading through the members and by erosion of the organization's social fabric. This in turn calls for change, even radical change, in the company's higher echelons, and reorganization. Should the measures applied turn out to be inadequate, the scene is set for the *fifth* and last stage, *dissolution*, in which organizational decline is irreversible and no remedial steps are possible, except to close down the organization, minimizing damage to the members and economic losses as far as possible.

March and Levinthal (1993) identify three forms of learning myopia: *temporal myopia* is the tendency to ignore the long term and focus on the short term. The second, *spatial myopia*, is the tendency to ignore the larger picture and learn from the *near neighborhood*: "Learning tends to favor effects that occur near to the learner" (March and Levinthal 1993, p. 110). In benchmarking, too, for example, managers prefer similar cases from the technological and organizational point of view rather than those that come from very different contexts. In doing this, however, they miss out on learning opportunities. The third form is *failure myopia*, the tendency to oversample success and overlook failure. All three forms of myopia compromise learning effectiveness. Research into the attribution of causality to events demonstrates that individuals are far more likely to attribute success to ability and failure to luck rather than the opposite (Miller and Ross 1975). As a result, state March and Levinthal (1993, p. 105), "persistent failure leads to a tendency to overestimate the risks of actions, and persistent success leads to a tendency to underestimate those risks."

To survive, organizations have to unlearn (Nystrom and Starbuck 2005): studying organizations that had to deal with periods of crisis, the two authors demonstrate how past learning inhibits new learning; to learn and develop new ideas and new behaviors, those of the past must be unlearned, and the reasons for their inadequacy identified.

A further learning problem following events such as disasters is the so-called control panic syndrome. In cases of low and ineffective coordination, the most common response is to centralize control, as is suggested by the project for the reorganization of the US defense system in the *9/11 Commission Report* (NCTA 2004). Certain academics state, however, that the structure of the new department and intelligence agencies should in fact be decentralized, in order to adapt to the enemy they are fighting against (Perrow 2007). Should this not be the case, the threat posed by highly decentralized terrorist networks would be met by a structure involving two new highly centralized, hierarchical agencies. To some extent, post-event control of panic may be considered a form of reorganization myopia.

Learning from rare events

Rare events are events that occur outside the everyday experience of an organization – events that are considered by those who work in and run organizations as unique, without precedent, and difficult to categorize. It should be specified that rare events as such do not really exist: they can only be defined with reference to a specific context (Lampel, Shamsie, and Shapira 2009). It depends, in other words, on the position of the observer to define what is and what is not rare. An event, for instance, may be rare for one organization and quite common for another. The category of rare events is closely linked to that of accidents, whether deliberate (such as the 9/11 terrorist attacks) or unintentional (Chernobyl, the shuttle disasters, etc.).

Precisely because of this rarity, such events pose a variety of problems in relation to organizational learning. Christianson et al. (2009) studied the case of the collapse of the roof of the Baltimore & Ohio (B&O) Railroad Museum Roundhouse onto its collections during a snowstorm in 2003. Their findings reveal that rare events:

trigger learning in three ways. First, rare events act as audits of existing response repertoires. Prior weaknesses and lack of preparation become salient targets for new learning, and behavioral potential is unmasked and converted into action. Second, rare events disrupt and can strengthen organizing routines. Interruptions provide opportunities to reorganize routines, particularly those that involve interpreting, relating, and re-structuring. These reorganized routines tend to produce quicker and more effective responses to subsequent interruptions. Third, rare events redirect organizational identity. The learning that occurs in responding to rare events – specifically around what the organization can do and how it is perceived by others – may alter how it defines itself. (Christianson et al. 2009, p. 847)

Other authors instead point out the difficulty of learning from rare events, as in the case of the financial crisis: with no experience to refer to, for example, when faced with a sudden collapse in stock market quotations or large credit contraction, many people believed that it was a matter of highly improbable events. When the economy is going well, people find it hard to imagine that things will not always continue in the same way. Referring to financial crises, Reinhart and Rogoff (2009) distinguish a specific syndrome, called *This time is different.* The essence of this syndrome is "rooted in the firmly held belief that financial crises are things that happen to other people in other countries at other times; crises do not happen to us, here and now. We are doing things better, we are smarter, we have learned from past mistakes" (Reinhart and Rogoff 2009, p. 1).

Organization leaders may pay little attention to events with low probability estimates (a) because they are difficult to predict and (b) because the costs of preventing them may be higher than the costs of the event itself. As Lampel, Shamsie, and Shapira (2009, p. 836) state, "organizations may focus on rare events because probability estimates suggest that they are likely to recur, or may ignore them because probability estimates suggest that they are unlikely to pose a threat or opportunity." It is probable however that "organizations are more likely to invest in learning the causes of rare events that are seen as likely to occur" (Lampel et al. 2009, p. 837).

Risen and Gilovich (2007) affirm that small sample characteristics of rare event results can produce erroneous inference. Levitt and March (1988) introduce the concept of *superstitious learning* to define a situation in which "the subjective experience of learning is compelling, but the connections between actions and outcomes are misspecified" (Levitt and March 1988, p. 325). In this regard, Zollo (2009, p. 894) argues "that superstitious learning is a particularly relevant problem for these types of decisions not only because causal linkages between actions and outcomes might be poorly inferred, but also, more basically, because their performance outcomes are often very difficult to assess in objective ways."

In addition, a rare event such as an accident may render organizational learning difficult in that organization leaders may try to shift blame away from themselves or to look for a scapegoat in order to avoid judicial trial and insurance costs. With reference to accidents, Perrow (1999) displays a certain amount of skepticism regarding the possibility of learning in complex organizational systems. Possibilities of improvement are remote, says Perrow, given that these organizations do not learn from accidents, because the feedback derived from the experience is ambiguous; in such systems, moreover, organizational learning is realized in a context of high politicization and low transparency, reports on events are based on the scapegoat concept, and, finally, the secrecy that surrounds them makes it difficult to learn correctly from accidents that occurred in other situations.

4.3 Incubation period and latent factors

The analysis of unforeseen events such as organizational accidents highlights how these are characterized by a period of incubation and by a series of premonitory signs. Rather than unpredictable cataclysmic events, it is a matter of organizationally constructed socio-technical events (Turner 1978; Vaughan 1996; Turner and Pidgeon 1997; Reason 1997). Risk incubation is a form of pre-accident encounter in which there is an organized suppression of risk (Turner and Pidgeon 1997) and of organizational intelligence (Wilensky 1967). By organizational intelligence here, we mean the capability of an organization to make sense of complex situations and act effectively, to interpret and act upon relevant events and signs in the environment, and to reflect and learn from experience.

Barry Turner was the first academic *to think of* the problem of understanding disaster as a socio-technical problem, with social, organizational, and technical processes interacting to produce the phenomena to be studied. Even though his book on the subject is titled *Man-Made Disasters* (Turner 1978),[1] in reality, Turner analyzes accidents in terms of their being generated by organizational action and its limited rationality (Simon 1947, 1955, 1956). Turner studies the preconditions for accidents, locating them within the organizational system and demonstrating how certain combinations of technical, social, administrative, and institutional factors can generate accidents in a systematic fashion.

---

[1] The book *Man-Made Disasters* was published in 1978, but here we refer to the new 1997 edition written with Nick F. Pidgeon, which came out after Turner's premature death in 1995.

Organization is concerned with intention and the execution of intention: "[d]isasters always represent failures of intention, and if we can come to know in more detail how such failures occur, we shall also learn important lessons which apply to the management of organizations in general" (Turner and Pidgeon 1997, p. 4). Central to this is the concept of *disaster incubation*: "[t]he man-made disaster model defines disaster incubation in terms of a discrepancy between some deteriorating but ill-structured state of affairs and the culturally 'taken for granted': or more specifically the norms, assumptions and beliefs adopted by an organization or industry for dealing with hazard and danger" (Turner and Pidgeon 1997, p. 187). The man-made disaster model highlights how organizational vulnerability arises from unintended and complex interactions, each of which would, individually, be unlikely to defeat the established safety system. The organizational culture is central in determining – or not – the vulnerability of the system, in particular with reference to its contribution to creating myopia in relation to forms of danger.

Studying first three (Turner 1976) and then another eighty-four (Turner 1978) cases of organizational accidents that occurred in Great Britain in the period between 1965 and 1975, Turner identifies a common sequential chain of events that precede and follow an accident. Accidents are not therefore unpredictable cataclysmic events: they take place after *incubation periods* – periods that vary in terms of length of time.[2] Turner highlights a sequence of events associated with the development of a disaster and this sequence can be used as a guide for the investigation of accidents and disasters. Six stages were described (Turner 1978):

1. *Notionally normal starting points*: (a) initially culturally accepted beliefs about the world and its hazards; (b) associated precautionary norms set out in laws, codes of practice, mores, and folkways.
2. *Incubation period*: the accumulation of an unnoticed set of events that are at odds with the accepted beliefs about hazards and the norms for their avoidance.
3. *Precipitating event*: brings attention to itself and transforms general perception of stage 2.

---

[2] This idea of accident incubation will be taken up by J. Reason (1990) with the perspective of latent error and pathogenic factors resident in an organization.

4. *Onset*: the immediate consequences of the collapse of cultural precautions become apparent.
5. *Rescue and salvage – first stage adjustment*: the immediate post-collapse situation is recognized in ad hoc adjustments that permit the work of rescue and salvage to be started.
6. *Full cultural readjustment*: an inquiry or assessment is carried out and beliefs and precautionary norms are adjusted to fit the newly gained understanding of the world.

With this sequence, Turner presents a dynamic perspective of the accident, which ranges from beliefs, to weak signs, to the accident itself, to cultural and normative readjustment. This is a typical movement for all organizations that generate accidents. Analyzing in detail three cases of accidents occurred in Great Britain, Turner (1976) identifies a series of recurring elements that were common to the various incidental events:

- *rigidities in perception and beliefs in organizational setting*: the accurate perception of the possibility of disaster was inhibited by cultural and institutional factors;
- *the decoy problem*: one element that contributed to the accidents is that attention dedicated to well-defined problems relating to the accident tended to distract from other problems, less defined but equally important in the genesis and dynamic of the accident: "a way of seeing is always also a way of not seeing" (Turner and Pidgeon 1997, p. 49);
- *organizational exclusivity (disregard of non-members)*: people within the organization tended to refuse help from outside, believing that they knew the risks and the work situation better than the others;
- *information difficulties*: four different situations were present: unknown information; information known but not fully appreciated; information known to someone but not combined with other information in time to be useful; and information available but ignored because inconsistent with the organization's model of understanding;
- *the involvement of "strangers" especially on complex "sites"*: this was seen as another risk factor. In fact, when access to potentially dangerous processes or to sites could be limited to competent and

suitably trained people, the possibility of generating an accident was
reduced;

- *failure to comply with regulations already in existence*: the evidence
  from the accidents highlighted the inadequacy of the regulations in
  force at the time of the accident, either because they were out of date
  or were difficult to apply to an altered technological, social, and cultural context;
- *minimizing emergent danger*: dangers were underestimated and
  the organization management found it difficult to wholly perceive
  the seriousness of certain emergent dangers. In some cases, there
  was a conflict of opinion over the dangers, or help was not asked
  for; and
- *the nature of recommendations after disaster*: one important function of the courts that held enquiries into the accidents was to produce recommendations to prevent the repetition of particular types
  of accident. These recommendations, however, were defined with
  respect to well-structured problems that were revealed by the accident rather than ill-structured problems that existed prior to the
  event.

To sum up, the man-made disaster theory sees the incubation of an
accident as a discrepancy between certain ill-structured situations that
present signs of deterioration and factors that the organization has
taken for granted (norms, assumptions, convictions) in regard to the
risks and dangers to be faced. Errors and communication difficulties
are at the base of *failure of foresight*:

The development of an incubation period prior to a disaster is facilitated
by the existence of events which are unnoticed or misunderstood because
of erroneous assumptions; because of a cultural lag which makes violations
of regulations unnoteworthy; and because of the reluctance of those individuals who discern the events to place an unfavorable interpretation upon
themselves. The development of the incubation period is further facilitated
by difficulties of communication between the various parties who may have
information which, if redistributed, could end the incubation period. (Turner
and Pidgeon 1997, p. 105)

Turner's theory of disasters is also a safety theory. Disasters are not
sudden events: they have a long incubation period, and if the relevant
information is obtained, it is possible to halt this incubation period,
avoiding the disaster.

The Latent Factors Theory

Developed by James Reason (1990), the Latent Factors Theory (LFT) was modified in his various works (Reason 1997, 2008). The basic idea is that an accident is generated by an unsafe act on the part of an operator (error or violation), but this unsafe act is fostered if not determined by a series of latent factors. These are critical factors of an organizational nature, such as gaps or leaks in defenses, weaknesses, or lacks created involuntarily by decisions taken by managers, regulators, or planners. The consequences of latent errors are long-lasting and can remain silent for long periods until a human error, interacting with this critical situation, precipitates the accident. The operators are therefore heirs of defects within the system. The combination of unsafe acts and latent factors explains the genesis of accidents.

Reason distinguishes two types of action that violate safety conditions: errors and violations. Errors are unintended, and violations are deliberate (the act, not the occasional negative consequences), even though they are not committed in order to damage a system or its customers/patients. Reason (1990, 2008) argues that error is the failure of planned actions to achieve their intended outcome. Error is a deviation between what was actually done and what should have been done.

Violations are deviations from safe operating procedures, standards, or rules. Violations may be deliberate or erroneous. In the latter case, the operator is not aware of violating a fixed regulation (as, for example, exceeding the speed limit without realizing it). Deliberate violations are more interesting, since they signal possible organizational problems. The accidents involving the Chernobyl power plant (1986) and the roll-on, roll-off ferry *Herald of Free Enterprise* (Zeebrugge, March 1987) were both caused by a series of violations. In the case of Chernobyl, the violations were rare and exceptional; in the case of the ferry, they were routine: the ferry sailed away from harbors with the bow doors open in contravention of shipping regulations. These violations, combined with a large number of other factors, lead to catastrophe.

Violations should not be confused with acts of sabotage, where both the act and the damaging outcome are intended. Violations are also encouraged by the fact that, while benefits are immediate, costs are remote from experience, and seem unlikely. It should be specified that the distinction between errors and violations is immensely difficult to measure empirically and the borders between the two unsafe acts are often uncertain.

Latent factors

Every accident is generated by a web of active errors and latent factors (Reason 1997, 2008). The former, as we have seen, are unsafe actions of various kinds that have an immediate effect and are generally associated with the activity of frontline operators, such as control room staff, train drivers, pilots, flight controllers, and so forth. Latent factors, on the other hand, are decisions or actions whose dangerous consequences may lie silent for a long time, becoming evident only when combined with provocative local factors that break through the system's defenses and determine the accident. Such factors may be planning faults, unsound managerial decisions, errors in supervision, communication problems, inefficient training, and so on.

Active errors provide the trigger for an accident, made possible by the presence of latent factors. Increasing the number of latent factors increases the likelihood that an active error will generate an accident. These latent factors are similar to the latent pathogens present in the human body. The more of them there are, the greater the possibility of contracting an illness. The greater the number of pathogenic elements (bad management decisions, core organizational processes – designing, building, maintaining, scheduling, budgeting, etc.) in an organization, the greater the likelihood that an operator will commit an error and trigger an accident.

The dynamic of accident evolution is shown in Figure 4.1. There are three interconnected levels that can generate an adverse event accident: individual level, organizational level, and interorganizational level (Catino 2010):

1. The *individual* level involves unsafe acts (slip, lapse, mistakes, and violations) performed by frontline staff.
2. The *organizational* level involves critical organizational factors that are generated by managerial strategy and processes during the time. Those factors include allocation of responsibilities, expertise distribution, division of labor, system of control and coordination, technology, communication system, procedures, training programs, and so on.

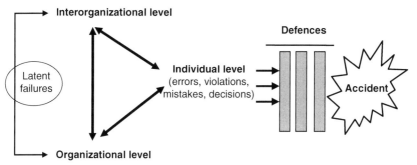

Figure 4.1 Multilevel model of accident evolution
Source: Modified from Catino (2010)

3. The *interorganizational* level involves the environment where the organization works and it refers to external organizations that can influence your organization. In this level, we can find regulators, policy makers, procedure makers, technology designers, and so on.

Reason (2008, p. 29) also states that there are two ways "in which the consequences of these upstream factors could impact adversely upon the defenses. There was an active failure pathway in which error and violation producing conditions in the workplace could, at the individual or team level, create unsafe acts. ... There [is] also a latent failure pathway that transmitted pathogens to the defenses directly." This model is of a probabilistic kind, and not deterministic, in the sense that a high number of critical situations increases the likelihood that an accident will occur.

4.4 Beyond human error: individual blame logic versus organizational function logic

Accidents and disasters in organizations are shocking events for society. These events call for an explanation. When an accident happens in an organization, there are two possible approaches to explain its origin and dynamics (Catino 2008). The first approach, called *individual blame logic* aims at finding the guilty individuals; the second, called *organizational function logic*, is more focused on organizational factors.

The individual blame logic (IBL) is an accusatory type of approach and is typical of criminal law, but it is also prominent in organizations based on a punitive culture (Avery and Ivancevich 1980). More generally, this approach fits in with the wish of society to identify a clear cause for the accident (Helsloot 2007). The organizational function logic (OFL) is an organizational and functional type of approach that intends to identify the factors within the system that favored the occurrence of the event. In this approach, once these factors are removed, hopefully similar events cannot happen again or will be less likely to happen. The two approaches are characterized by two distinct logics of inquiry, which generate different consequences.

The way in which the same accident can appear objectively different under the two logics stems from the fact that there are two processes of different *framing* at work (Dewey 1938; Shrivastava and Schneider 1984; Dodier 1995). Each one selects from the abundance of facts what is relevant for inquiry, based on the different finalities to be pursued. What is taken into examination is only what is considered *significant* in relation with the goals of the inquiry. This leads to a different way of reconstructing the truth. The concept of *cause*, together with the one of *finality*, is the element which most distinguishes the two different inquiry logics and is also the most controversial.[3] The two logics thus possess different frameworks (Goffman 1974), they operate with different paradigms (Kuhn 1962), and they have different processes of *sensemaking* (Weick 1995). The two logics achieve a different kind of accountability: the "what happened" question thus relates to a social and institutional construction of the facts, as it is possible to evince from the comparison in Table 4.1.

The Individual Blame Logic (blame culture) and its side effects

When an accident occurs, there is a tendency to immediately identify the individuals who caused it and to blame them. The underlying assumption of the IBL approach is that people make mistakes because they do not care about their tasks and activities. Its linear causal model underestimates the organizational context, and any effort to identify blame is oriented towards people on the frontline: when a

---

[3] Russell (1918) suggested the elimination of the concept of *cause* from the vocabulary since even advanced natural science, for example, physics, has acknowledged that there is no such thing as an ultimate cause.

Table 4.1. *Inquiry logics: a comparative overview*

	Individual blame logic	Organizational function logic
Aim	Identify the guilty; sanction	Understand, explain, improve
Principal question	Who caused the accident?	What factors favored the accident?
		How and why did the defense system fail?
Concept of cause	Causal linear model	Cause networks; systemic approach; latent factors
Locus of failure	Individual	Built organizationally
Form of post-accident inquiry	Judicial inquiry	Organizational analysis
Context	In the background; accidental; does not exclude individual responsibilities	Structuring action
Result	Only individual Removal of the *bad apple*	Organizational and interorganizational
Undesired effects	Inertia to change; subjective attribution of the disaster	Individual irresponsibility

guilty person is found, he or she is held responsible for the accident. In practice, that means that the "bad apple" is removed or punished. This concern over individual responsibility is based on the following beliefs (Reason 1997):

1. *Voluntarity of actions*. People are considered free agents, able to choose between safe and unsafe behaviors. Several studies demonstrate that 80–90 percent of accidents involve human actions. Because such actions are perceived as subject to voluntary control, it is assumed that accidents are caused by negligence, inattention, inaccuracy, incompetence, and so on.
2. *Responsibility is personal*. The personal model is founded on individual responsibility. Its goal is to find the individual who made a mistake.
3. *The sense of justice is strengthened*. IBL is emotionally satisfying; after a serious accident, or, worse, a disaster, the identification of blame tends to satisfy every person involved, as well as the general public.

4. *Convenience*. Conceiving of individual responsibility has many
advantages for organizations, both from a legal and an economic
perspective. It keeps the organizational structure unaltered, the
same power system and rules, identifying an individual responsible
for the accident, and determining the adequate punishment. People
who directly provoke an accident are often the frontline operators.
It is clearly easier to identify a person who is in close contact with
the system (pilot, doctor, nurse, control panel operator, train con-
ductor, etc.) as responsible of the event.

On the other hand, IBL raises a number of perverse or side effects.
First of all, the identification of a guilty individual does not change the
prevailing situation and does not improve the organization. Second,
that approach is focused on the past and makes people scared about
legal disputes and sanctions, discouraging incident reporting and
organizational learning. Finally, IBL is characterized by two particular
forms of bias: *hindsight bias* (Fischhoff 1975) and *fundamental attribution error* (Fiske and Taylor 1984; Gilbert and Malone 1995) (see
also Chapter 3). Thus, IBL does not eliminate risk factors and does not
guarantee that an analogous event will not recur with other actors. It
also makes difficult to discuss and spread information about errors. In
reference to healthcare systems, Merry and Smith (2001) declare that
working under the threat of legal prosecution promotes a climate of
fear. For these reasons, doctors tend to hide their errors and to engage
in defensive medical practices. The persistence of a blame culture, reinforced by a certain type of judicial action, becomes the main obstacle
to the creation of an effective culture of patient safety.

Learning from errors is significantly influenced by the institutional
dilemma of blame (Reason 1997; Turner and Pidgeon 1997; Catino
2008). This refers to the politics of an organization with respect
to individual accountability in case of errors, including how errors
ought to be managed and who should be blamed. This constitutes
a dilemma because organizations face a trade-off between blaming
people for unsafe acts and learning from such acts (e.g., understanding organizational factors that caused a specific event). According to
Abramson and Senyshyn (2010, p. 555), "most management studies
have framed punishment as a mode of reprisal simply intended to
correct the bad behavior of a harm doer to prevent its recurrence, but
there has been little evidence that punishment is effective in achieving

these goals." Individuals in organizations may be reluctant to report negative information, especially when this can lead to disciplinary sanctions, or result in being blamed or ridiculed because of an error (Edmondson 1996). Moreover, following Rochlin (1993), we argue that there is a cultural dimension to how organizations deal with errors. As Hutter (2005, p. 91) points out, "different views of organizations lead to various ways of seeing risk and different ways of apportioning responsibility and blame." The politics of blame (Sagan 1993) can therefore discourage operators from reporting problems and errors. This lack of incentives may reduce the validity of available information about threats and risks. Dekker (2005) observes that judicial proceedings, or their possibility, can create a climate of fear, making people reluctant to reporting errors and sharing information. This can hamper an organization's potential to learn from errors. Morrison and Milliken (2000, p. 708) believe that "when an organization is characterized by silence, this is less a product of multiple, unconnected individual choices and more a product of forces within the organization – and forces stemming from management – that systematically reinforce silence." Organizational silence blocks negative feedback and the organization's ability to detect and correct errors, and therefore prevents double-loop learning (see Section 4.1). The preceding barriers are strongly influenced by the organizational context in which learning from errors takes place, in particular the specific safety culture of an organization and the norms and rules regulating specific professions. If errors are considered mainly as an indication of professional incapacity or negligence, operators will be likely to hide them.

According to IBL, once the *guilty actors* are found and removed, it is very likely that the organizational system will continue to function with the same organizational conditions and mechanisms that lead to the error and accident. Being mainly interested in assessing individual responsibilities, the IBL creates a sense of fear of sanctions and of legal actions. In a punitive organizational environment, the individuals refuse risks and worry more about their own legal safety than the safety of the user, customer, patient, and so on. The Institute of Medicine (United States) aims to decrease errors in the health field by 50 percent in five years, but as Brennan observed in a 2000 article in the *New England Journal of Medicine*, every effort made to prevent the damage derived from a medical treatment is obstructed by the *dead weight* of a legal regime which induces the operators to secrecy and silence (Brennan 2000).

There are many reasons for imperfect learning (Turner and Pidgeon 1997). Some of them are related to the institutional dilemma of the blame, to the fact that danger and blame are constitutive characteristics of the society, elaborated to defend the chosen mechanism (Douglas 1985, 1992; Douglas and Wildavsky 1982). Merry and Smith (2001), referring to the health system, affirm that working under the threat of legal action creates an atmosphere of fear that does not lead to the best management of people in a medical system. Hutter (2005, p. 84) states:

The trend to invoke the criminal law in apportioning blame (and punishment) in the case of organizational risk encounters can have profound implications for system learning. In Britain it has effected a move from inquisitorial to accusatorial styles of accident investigation. The inquisitorial system is intended solely to determine the cause of the accident, not to apportion blame. But this has encountered more and more problems as there has been increasing pressure to invoke the criminal law. It has led, for example, to defensive strategies which restrict the flow of information ... So the accusatorial approach can pose serious problems for the flow of information.

The *demonization* of errors prevents physicians from admitting and discussing them publicly since this information could be used against them in criminal lawsuits. The legal system puts the doctor and the patient one against the other (Gawande 2002), forcing both to give an unrealistic version of the facts. Therefore, fear of legal consequences favors the fact that errors are hidden. Adopting the IBL, the organization is not able to understand its own errors. The result is organizational inertia rather than change: if one or more are hold responsible for what happens, why change things? The persistence of a blame culture, reinforced by a certain type of legal action, becomes then the first obstacle to the creation of greater safety. Figure 4.2 reports the IBL vicious circle, which often leads to organizational inertia. Since the main goal of the IBL approach is to determine individual responsibility – to find who is guilty – organization members would not report their errors, thus making organizational learning and change very difficult.

As Vaughan writes (1996, p. 392), "the benefit of explanations that locate the immediate cause of organizational failure in individual

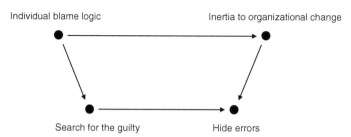

Figure 4.2 The vicious circle in the individual blame logic
Source: Catino (2008)

decision makers is that quick remedies are possible. Responsible individuals can be fired, transferred, or retired. New rules that regulate decision making can be instituted. Having made these changes, the slate is clean. Organizations can go on." Turner and Pidgeon (1997) affirm that the impact of the legal system has the power to suffocate any attempt of learning from errors. For example, during a legal inquiry, the organizational improvements could be omitted or delayed because it could constitute implicit admission of previous negligence. In this case, these improvements would show that the organization possessed elements that could have avoided the accident. Drabeck and Quarantelli (1967) supported the perfect rationality in the identification of scapegoats following disasters and the usefulness for the managers of identifying the blame at the individual level, thus avoiding structural changes of the organization. In *Totem and Taboo*, Freud (1913 [1950]) refers to an old popular tale with its roots in Hungary. A murdered girl is found in a village. Investigations identify the blacksmith as the killer, and he confesses. The elders of the village form a tribunal and condemn him to death: he will be hanged in the main square. But the evening before the execution, the *bürgomeister* realizes that the murderer is also the only blacksmith in the community, that there is no replacement readily available, and that if the sentence is carried out, the village will quickly be bereft of tools and equipment. On the other hand, the village does have two tailors, only one of whom is really necessary for the requirements of the population. Therefore, he duly chooses one of the tailors to be hanged the next day instead of the more useful blacksmith. The village continues to be well-supplied with keys and knives and, at the same time, thanks to the sacrificed substitute, has satisfied its need for justice.

Public opinion was lead to believe that the exemplary punishment of the guilty individual could serve as a future deterrent. But this is a myopic belief. In reference to the *Challenger* accident, Vaughan (1996, p. 408) affirms that "this case shows why it is so difficult, for the normative and legal system to assign the right responsibilities when the organizations have harmful results. It is well known that the division of labor in organizations obscures the responsibilities of the organizational actions." This type of analysis not only runs the risk of not producing changes, but also risks limiting itself to an extremely dangerous blame culture. It is also true, more prosaically, that when a single person is identified as responsible for the disaster, the individual responsibility is split from the responsibility of the organization, with overall significant economic and financial advantages for the system.

Organizational function logic

The OFL is based on the assumption that failure is part of the human condition, and if we cannot change the human condition, then conditions under which human beings work can be changed (Reason 1997). The organizational model views human error more as a consequence than as a cause. If the IBL leads to the identification of the person who is responsible for the event, the OFL instead leads to the identification of the latent factors and organizational criticalities that are at the origin of the accident. Remedying this can keep other accidents from happening in the future. According to Dekker (2005, p. 15), "Rather than judging people for not doing what they should have done, the new view presents tools for explaining why people did what they did. Human error becomes a starting point, not a conclusion." The OFL therefore reconducts the causal factors of an event to the whole organization. It acknowledges that accidents are the result of mistakes made by individuals, but these mistakes, however, are socially organized and systematically produced (Vaughan 1996). From this approach, accidents are derived from a connected sequence (usually rare) of defects in numerous defense systems, safeguards, barriers, and controls to protect the organization from unknown hazardous events. OFL approaches usually distinguishes the *human errors*, which activated the accident committed by the operators closest to the task, from *latent factors* understood as organizational criticalities which made the accident possible, or sometimes caused it: temporal pressures, equivocal technology with ambiguous man-machine interfaces, insufficient training, insufficient support structures, a work atmosphere that is not safety prone, unclear procedures, communication problems, and still other factors (Reason 1990, 1997). It is obvious that the human factor is the element that directly induces an accident in most cases, but the human factor is only the *first-order cause*[4] of the accident history, which is completed through the analysis of the entire sequence of events and of the latent and preexisting organizational factors.

The analysis of famous accidents like the ones occurred in Chernobyl or Bhopal shows that these disasters were not caused by the coincidence of technological failures and human errors, but by the systematic migration of the organizational behavior towards the accident under the influence of efficiency and cost reduction pressures in aggressive and competitive environments (Rasmussen 1997). The analysis of the air disaster of Linate (Catino 2010) points out how the flow of events cannot be led simply to the action of a single operator. This OFL approach highlights the limits of a model of direct causality. Focusing on the causal relationship between actions and events that lead to an accident is reductive, because it does not incorporate the indirect relationships between events and feedback effects. An example of indirect factor is the management commitment to safety: whether managers pay attention or ignore signs of danger (i.e., near-miss) does not per se cause an accident, but contribute to increase, or decrease, its likelihood. While the IBL is not likely to produce organizational changes, the OFL can be used for determining the organizational conditions of the accident and removing the latent critical factors. Above all, the OFL looks for those critical organizational conditions that, if not removed, will continue to create risk and error conditions *independently* of the people who are operating. Figure 4.3 shows the OFL virtuous circle. The goal of the OFL approach is to detect organizational latent failures that cause adverse events; therefore, organization members are more inclined to report errors and problems: this approach creates the conditions for organizational learning.

The OFL tends to substitute the question, "Who caused the accident?" with "What conditions and mechanisms have increased the

---

[4] If the goal is to assign the blame, as in the individual blame logic, the reconstruction of the causal chain often stops when someone or something is identified as being suitable for the blame.

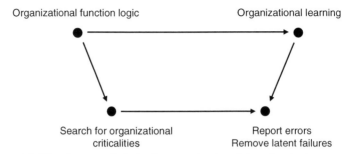

Figure 4.3 The virtuous circle in the organizational function logic
Source: Catino (2008)

possibilities of its happening?" "How and why did the defense systems
fail?" and "What can we do so that the event will not be repeated?"
(Reason 1997). As ascertained by research from the last twenty-five
years, disasters and accidents in organizations are not generated by a
single cause but by a number of interrelated events that taken singu-
larly can appear totally insignificant and not influential in the origin
of the accident. However, they enter into relationship with each cause,
and in the presence of a weak defense system, they increase the possibility that an accident will happen. As a detail, for the OFL, both an
accident and a near-miss are of equal interest, if they are morphologically similar. The near-miss in fact is weakly relevant from the legal
point of view, but crucial in the organizational function perspective.
It informs the analysts about the state of risk of a system, and the
observation of its magnitude and frequency is essential to understanding its latent critical areas. Reason (2008, p. 136) argues that "accident investigations have three related goals: explanation, prediction
and countermeasures. ... Individual factors alone have only a small
to moderate value for all three goals. Overall, workplace and organizational factors contributed the most added value. There are rapidly
diminishing returns on pursuing the more remote influences, particularly to countermeasures and risk management."

The central aim of the OFL is to learn from errors and accidents.
Based on the lessons learned from the event, it attempts to actively
generate better foresight ability in the operations of the organization (Toft and Reynolds 1994). The OFL is typical of the *generative
organization* (Westrum 1995) which in its ideal form is a thinking
and self-aware organization. It is constantly on the lookout, and

continuously reviews its own procedures. A generative organization is a highly reliable organization which never considers safety as a condition that has been definitively achieved, but as an objective which has to be pursued continuously (LaPorte and Consolini 1994; Weick, Sutcliffe, and Obstfeld 1999; Weick and Sutcliffe 2007). The aim of the organizational function logic is to make organizational learning possible and to favor organizational change, at different levels, as well as introducing a possible *clinical* dimension. Therefore, such an inquiry has pragmatic value, in the sense that the results can help the subject review the functioning logics of the organizational system, improving the knowledge the actors have of the system and of their own context of action (Friedberg 1993).

OFL is typical of organizations based on a just culture. A just culture is about protection of people who are willing to report. Within a just culture, frontline operators or others are not punished for actions, omissions or decisions taken by them that are commensurate with their experience and training. However, gross negligence, willful violations and destructive acts are not tolerated (Eurocontrol 2006). Just culture concerns the sustainability of learning from failures through the reporting of errors, adverse events, and incidents (Dekker 2007). If operators and others perceive that their reports are treated unfairly or lead to negative consequences, the willingness to report will decline. Reason (1997, p. 195) describes just culture as "an atmosphere of trust in which people are encouraged, even rewarded for providing essential safety-related information – but in which they are clear about where the line must be drawn between acceptable and unacceptable behavior." A just culture organization is aware that a culture of safety crucially requires the creation of an open, free, non-punitive environment in which people can feel safe to report adverse events and near-misses. A climate of openness can make people more willing to report and discuss errors, and learn more about the system in the process (Edmondson 1996). Conversely, a "practice of blaming create an atmosphere that tends to stigmatize people and discourage them from speaking up" (Weick and Sutcliffe 2007, p. 132). Ruitenberg (2002) cited a 50 percent drop in incident reports after the prosecution of air traffic controllers involved in a near-miss.

It is important to stress that equating blame-free systems with an absence of personal accountability is erroneous (Dekker 2007). In a just culture, staff can differentiate between acceptable and unacceptable acts (Ferguson and Fakelmann 2005). To establish a just culture it is fundamental to separate the acts that will not be punished (slips, lapses, etc.) and which must be tolerated until, reporting them, the organization can learn and improve, from those acts that, even if reported, cannot and must not be tolerated (outside the two lines, gross negligence, criminal offences). On this operation – not an easy one – depends the effectiveness of the creation of a just culture.

In the next chapter, I expand on the theme of learning from errors in the context of High Reliability Organizations, their preoccupation for failures, and the importance of detecting weak signs to avoid myopic behavior.

5 | Implications for organizational design

Disasters and accidents are a normal part of our existence, not exceptional events (L. Clarke 2006). As Hutter affirms (2010), we cannot expect to live in a risk-free society, and we have to be prepared for the unexpected. The origin of risk increasingly derives from complex socio-technical systems rather than natural phenomena, and accepting risk is part of accepting organizations (Douglas 1992).

Some events are difficult to predict, in that they occur suddenly and with no previous weak signs; other events and accidents are preceded by *incubation periods* where dangers such as small incidents, near misses, and close calls are registered, as will be seen later. Yet, management may demonstrate myopia and fail to take note of the weak signs that foreshadow these accidents. Certain organizations however seem to be particularly skilled in coping unexpected events and containing their consequences: these are called High Reliability Organizations (HROs). Reliability "means anticipation and resilience, the ability of organizations to plan for shocks as well as to absorb and rebound from them in order to provide services safely and continuously" (Roe and Schulman 2008, p. 5). The concept of reliability differs from the concept of efficiency, even though both can (and must) coexist within the same organization. HROs balance the tension between rewarding efficiency and rewarding reliability (Roberts and Bea 2001).

The problem of reliability does not refer exclusively to organizations that operate in high-risk environments but also to other organizations that operate in continuously changing environments.

5.1 High Reliability Organizations

High Reliability Organizations, thanks to the management processes that they feature, show greater ability to confront unexpected events and risk conditions with a low rate of errors (Rochlin, LaPorte, and

Roberts 1987; Roberts 1990, 1993, 2009; Schulman 1993a, 1993b; LaPorte and Consolini 1994, 1998; LaPorte 1996; Roberts and Bea 2001; Weick 1987, 1993; Weick, Sutcliffe, and Obstfeld 1999; Weick and Sutcliffe 2007; Roe and Schulman 2008).

The term *High Reliability Organization* was coined by Berkeley researchers, among whom were Karlene Roberts, Gene Rochlin, and Todd La Porte, to describe the operational characteristics and functioning mechanisms of some high-risk organizations, such as the US Navy carrier *Carl Vinson* (Rochlin, LaPorte and Roberts 1987), the Federal Aviation Administration En Route Air Traffic Control in Fremont, California (Schulman 1993a) and the commercial nuclear power plant Diablo Canyon in California (Rochlin and Von Meier 1994). These organizations operate in extremely high-risk environments but with high standards of reliability and safety. To perform effectively under these conditions, people in HROs pursue safety as a priority objective, decentralize decision making, invest heavily in training, learn from errors and weak signs, build in redundancy, and reward people who report failures (Rochlin et al. 1987; Weick 1987; LaPorte 1988; Roberts and Rousseau 1989; Roberts 1990; Schulman 1993a; Weick and Roberts 1993; Roberts, Stout, and Halpern 1994; Weick 1995; Weick et al. 1999; Bourrier 2005; Tamu and Harrison 2006; Weick and Sutcliffe 2007; Roe and Schulman 2008).

An aircraft carrier is effectively defined as "a million accidents waiting to happen" (Wilson 1986, p. 21). A navy veteran describes life on a carrier:

So you want to understand an aircraft carrier? Well, just imagine that it's a busy day, and you shrink San Francisco Airport to only one short runway and one ramp and one gate. Make planes take-off and land at the same time, at half the present time interval, rock the runway from side to side, and require that everyone who leaves in the morning returns that same day. Make sure the equipment is so close to the edge of the envelope that it's fragile. Then turn off the radar to avoid detection, impose strict controls on radios, fuel the aircraft in place with their engines running, put an enemy in the air, and scatter live bombs and rockets around. Now wet the whole thing down with sea water and oil, and man it with 20-year-olds, half of whom have never seen an airplane up-close. Oh, and by the way, try not to kill anyone. (Rochlin et al. 1987, p. 78)

Not one of the aircraft monitored on the screens by flight controllers had had a collision with other aircrafts. This was not a phenomenon to be ascribed to luck, but to the specific processes activated by the organizations to prevent accidents.

At first, HRO research focuses on a specific group of high-risk organizations that followed a variety of actions in order to achieve *nearly error-free performance*. The idea, in other words, is to concentrate on little-studied excellent performers rather than negative cases. Through the analysis of daily operations within organizations that successfully carry out high-risk activity with a low rate of errors and accidents, the researchers identify the management strategies and processes which produce increasing levels of safety in the respective organizational contexts (Rochlin et al. 1987). An HRO is one that is judged to supply a product, activity, or service that respects the level of performance required or desired and at the same time guarantees a low rate of errors or accidents (Rochlin 1993, p. 16).

As Roberts (1990, p. 160) states, "within the set of hazardous organizations there is a subset which has enjoyed a record of high safety over long periods of time. One can identify this subset by answering the question, 'how many times could this organization have failed resulting in catastrophic consequences that it did not?'" If the answer is in the order of tens of thousands of times, then the organization is *highly reliable*. A High Reliability Organization is one that has the ability to maintain a high performance level for a given function under determinate conditions and for a specific time. Reliability is the ability to manage the various working conditions with continuity and efficiency, even though these conditions may fluctuate widely and be extremely high-risk (Weick et al. 1999), because the organizations cannot reduce the external demand for services (for example, the arrival of a high number of planes at an airport, or a peak time for emergencies in an ER).

Initially, when talking about HROs, academics were referring to specific organizations such as nuclear plants (Marcus 1995; Bourrier 1996), organizations for air traffic control (LaPorte 1988), aircraft carriers (Rochlin et al. 1987), and the electric power grid (Roe and Schulman, 2008). Yet Rochlin (1993) points out how difficult it is to define the constitutive properties of HROs: high reliability tends to be an *organizational bricolage* rather than an analytically distinguishable category. When Weick, Sutcliffe, and Obstfeld (1999) refer to HROs, they use the term *specific successful cognitive processes*, rather than refer to a specific type of organization. These cognitive processes are found in the best nuclear plants, in the best and most reliable air traffic control organizations, in the best aircraft carriers, and so on. Weick (1987) defines reliability as "a dynamic non-event": *dynamic* because processes remain within acceptable limits thanks to continuous and progressive adjustments and compensations carried out by operators and a *nonevent* because safe outcomes claim little or no attention.

Examples of HROs

An aircraft carrier seems to be organized in a hierarchical manner, with command lines of authority running from the captain down to the lowest level of crew member. Most of the daily operations are carried out according to procedures and following rigid rules of discipline. Operational manuals dictate the execution of tasks and lessons learnt are quickly codified into operational procedures. But researchers discovered that in reality things were far more complex than they at first appeared failures (Rochlin et al. 1987). For example, in a situation of uncertainty such as the difficult recovery of an aircraft, the organizational structure changed rapidly. In cases like this, group members interact as a group of equals, like colleagues rather than as superiors and subordinates. Cooperation and communication become more important than do the orders emitted according to the hierarchical chain of command. Events take place suddenly and quickly and therefore cannot be managed following rigid formal procedures: members act like a team, each one watching what the other is doing, and they are in constant communication via telephone, radio, and written messages. The flow of information and communication produced makes it possible for the organization to be more *resilient* and to avoid errors.

The interesting aspect is that there is a third level of organizational structure that is activated in emergency situations, such as an aircraft on fire on the flight deck. The group has carefully rehearsed the procedures to follow in such an event, and every member has a precise role to play. So, in an emergency situation, the group reacts immediately and effectively without hierarchical direction. A multiple organizational structure such as this constitutes a profound innovation in terms of organization theory based on the opposition between formal and informal organizations and formal and real organizations.

Three different types of organizational structure coexist within the same set of operators, therefore, and are activated depending on the situation that has to be faced. In ordinary situations, procedures and hierarchy dominate and ensure the overall running of the system and efficiency. When the situation becomes a high-risk one, and decisions have to be taken quickly by frontline operators, the hierarchical and procedural model is set aside and the organization that is activated can function more effectively through cooperation, communication, and absence of hierarchy. Finally, in emergency situations, predefined ad hoc procedures are effectively activated by a group that has gone through a long period of practice and simulation training. In other words, there is no single organizational structure; rather, there is an organization that defines and redefines itself depending on the complexity of the task to be carried out. As Weick (1969) states, the correct term is not perhaps *organization* but *organizing*.

In addition, scholars discovered the presence of an ongoing research process by operators at all levels with the aim of "doing things better." Young officers continually proposed new ideas to higher ranking officers and this *interaction* between a more academic, fresher kind of thinking (from the young) and one more expert in practical terms generated a positive engagement, improving safety and the overall reliability of the system.

Studying the Diablo Canyon nuclear power plant, Schulman (1993a) identifies various operating forms of decision making. As in the case of the aircraft carrier, Diablo Canyon appeared to be an extremely hierarchical organization with a rigid line of command from the director of the plant down to operational levels. In daily practice, however, Schulman found that the plant possessed a widespread institutional culture based on the idea that in a plant of that kind, surprises were likely to be continually popping up. The result was the presence of two different sets of decision-making procedures. The first and more visible one consisted of regulations and procedures defined by tasks and operations, some of them carried out by computers, others by personnel. But these procedures could not take into account unforeseen events with unpredictable consequences. A nuclear power plant, as also Perrow (1999) shows, is a complex system in which the interactions among parts are complex and the connections among components are tight, making unpredictable events highly likely. And in Diablo Canyon, in fact, the people working there knew that not all solutions could be contained in a book of procedures and that it was necessary to be flexible in operating and have a culture oriented towards learning. Even the selection of personnel was carried out according to these criteria.

Learning took place in terms of the right ways to do things: ways that were constantly being reoriented and updated by operators aware that not all necessary skills had a place in the instruction manual. This kind of learning would not have been possible if the organization at Diablo Canyon had been starkly hierarchical. Hierarchy might work well for systems that could be decomposed into subunits, but a nuclear plant is by its very nature a holistic entity characterized by *tightly coupled* connections (Schulman 1993a). In consequence, communication and cooperation among the various units that guarantee the functioning of the plant must occur in as direct a way as possible and not through rigid bureaucratic channels. Schulman, therefore, argues that even nuclear technology could become reliable if management and operational processes are reliable. One consideration that emerges from the academics' studies of HROs is that these organizations do not constitute ad hoc types (nuclear plants rather than air traffic control) but are reliable only if organizational processes are reliable. A nuclear power plant and an aircraft carrier are certainly high-risk organizations, but in concrete reality, we can have ones that are fallible and others that are highly reliable. Everything depends on the characteristics of the functioning and the processes adopted. The researchers identify certain requirements that encourage reliability and that together make high-risk organizations reliable organizations.

Later on, high-reliability processes have also been examined in different types of organizations: the *Columbia* space shuttle (Starbuck and Farajoun 2005), manufacturing (Clarke and Ward 2006), offshore platforms (Bea 2002), aviation (C.S. Burke, Wilson, and Salas 2005), a police force (Roberts et al. 2008), submarines (Bierly, Gallagher, and Spender 2008), wild land and urban firefighting (Bigley and Roberts 2001), and many others (see Weick and Sutcliffe 2007; Roberts 2009).

The requirements of HROs

The logic of reliability, as dealt with here, does not refer only to a particular type of organization, such as nuclear power plants, aircraft carriers, trains, chemical plants, and so on, but increasingly constitutes an organizational requisite for operations in traditional sectors as well, such as automobile production, financial markets, telecommunication and Internet systems, healthcare, and groups operating in extreme conditions. In addition, many of the indications and considerations that emerge from studies of HROs are just as fundamental for organizations and companies that, while not operating in conditions of risk for people and the surrounding environment, find themselves working in highly competitive fields with a high level of uncertainty, and in which managing the unexpected is a vital characteristic (Weick and Sutcliffe 2007). The performances of these organizations increasingly require the quest for reliability through forms of group work, which develop collective mental processes and *heedful interrelating* (Weick and Roberts 1993). It is a problem for not only organizations defined as highly reliable but also for all production and service organizations.

How to improve reliability

Roberts and Libuser (1993; Libuser 1994) develop a management model that includes five processes they believe to be imperative if an organization has to maximize its reliability. They are (1) *process auditing* – a system of ongoing checks to monitor hazardous conditions, (2) *reward system* – expected social compensation or disciplinary action to reinforce or correct behavior, (3) *quality assurance* – policies and procedures that promote high-quality performance, (4) *risk management* – how the organization perceives risk and takes corrective action, and (5) *command and control* – policies, procedures, and communication processes used to mitigate risk.

Studying successful organizations in the context of anticipating events and limiting the unexpected, Weick and colleagues (Weick et al. 1999; Weick and Sutcliffe 2007) identify five characteristics that improve organization reliability:

1. Preoccupation with failure rather than success.
2. Reluctance to simplify interpretations.
3. Sensitivity to operations.
4. Commitment to resilience.
5. Deference to expertise.

The first three regard anticipation – acting beforehand to prevent a negative event. The final two relate to limiting the unexpected and its potentially negative effects. An organization that exhibits these five characteristics is an HRO, an organization that does not possess one or more of them is not: "failure to move towards this type of mindful infrastructure magnifies the damage produced by unexpected events and impairs reliable performance" (Weick and Sutcliffe 2007, p. 2).

1. Preoccupation with failure rather than success

"HROs are distinctive because they are preoccupied with failure" (Weick and Sutcliffe 2007, p. 9). HROs regard close calls and near misses as a kind of failure that reveals potential danger rather than as evidence of their success and ability to avoid danger. HROs treat near misses and errors as information about the health of whole system and try to learn from them. HROs are preoccupied with all failures, especially small ones, because small things that go wrong are often early warning signs of deepening trouble. As Roberts and Bea state (2001, p. 72), "HROs spend disproportionately more money than other organizations training people to recognize and respond to anomalies." Catching problems before they grow bigger, organizations have more possible ways to deal with them. Yet, we have a tendency to ignore or overlook our failures (which suggest we are not competent) and focus on our successes (which suggest we are competent). This can lead to serious problems as people expect success and become *myopic* in regard to potential danger signs that are canceled because of preceding success. Success generates an expectation of success in people and makes it difficult for them to see clearly. Preoccupation with failure and ongoing attention are therefore managerial and organizational attitudes that should be constantly nourished to increase organizational reliability. The analysis of a near miss, for example, is an important moment of verification for an organization's conditions of reliability and safety.

To sum up, HROs deal with failures in two ways. First, they put a tremendous amount of work into the detection of even the smallest examples of failure, since these might be signs of more wide-ranging and catastrophic failures. Second, they also work extremely hard to anticipate and avoid errors that they do not want to commit. Detection of failure is the first step and reporting failure is the second. Learning requires some preconditions: psychological safety (tolerance for mistakes of commission), learning orientation (intolerance for mistakes of omission), and efficacy (belief that we can handle what comes up).

2. Reluctance to simplify interpretations

All organizations tend to ignore many of the things they see in order not to shut down work. This process of simplification implies, however, a phenomenon of *blindness*: organizations ignore those signs that, if caught in time, could be the right key to handling unexpected difficulties. This simplification is, on the one hand, a structural condition (because of rationality and limited information) and necessary for action (otherwise, the outcome is a decisional block). But, on the other hand, it also implies the risk of underestimating the nature of certain problems, thus increasing the likelihood of eventual surprises (Weick and Sutcliffe 2007).

To maintain awareness of simplification, HROs often implement a new form of redundancy, based not only on duplication and backup (Landau 1969; Lerner 1986; Husted 1993), but also on the awareness of the possible fallibility of all human actions. This is a consideration that increases reliability. HROs tend to create the most complete possible picture of the event: "With closer attention to context, more differentiation of worldviews and mind-sets. And with more differentiation comes a richer and more varied picture of potential consequences, which in turn suggests a richer and more varied set of precautions and early warning signs" (Weick and Sutcliffe 2007, p. 53). They take nothing for granted and reject simplifying analysis of events: they see more. They know that the world they must deal with is complex, unstable, unknown, and unpredictable. They also encourage *nuance*, variety of analysis and richness of description through interaction between people with different kinds of expectation. They know that to see some danger signs means not to see other potentially dangerous signs. To counteract the tendency towards simplification, HROs encourage heterogeneity of experience in personnel, creating an organizational climate that fosters variety of analyzes and diversity of opinion and viewpoint. HROs know that "[e]arly warnings signs lie buried in those heterogeneous details. And those signs go undetected when details are lumped into generic categories. That's why HROs simplify slowly, reluctantly, mindfully" (Weick and Sutcliffe 2007, p. 54).

3. Sensitivity to operations

HROs are sensitive to operations. They are particularly sensitive to activities carried out in the frontline, where the real work takes place. Being sensitive to operations involves "seeing what we are *actually* doing regardless of what we were supposed to do based on intentions, designs, and plans" (Weick and Sutcliffe 2007, p. 59). Frontline operators strive to maintain situational awareness, to remain as aware as possible of the current state of operations, to understand the implications of the ongoing situation for future functioning. To follow this objective, frontline operators need to be highly informed about operations as a whole, about how operations can fail, and about strategy for recovery.

As Weick and Sutcliffe state (2007, p. 12), "[t]he big picture in HROs is less strategic and more situational than is true of most organizations. When people have well-developed situational awareness, they can make the continuous adjustments that prevent errors from accumulating and enlarging." As frontline operators must be sensitive to operations, so must managers: they must be sensitive to the experience of their frontline operators, encouraging them to report their experiences and the detection of anomalies.

4. Commitment to resilience

Reliability depends on the lack of unwanted, unanticipated, and unexplainable variance in performance (Hollnagel 2004). Resilience is the attitude to absorb and make use of changes: HROs do not wait for errors; rather, they prepare for inevitable surprises through attention to their prevention and to the limitation of their consequences. Resilience can also be defined as a system's ability to maintain its functions and structure even when faced with significant external and internal changes. A resilient system continues to function despite the failure of some of its parts. HROs are able to reorganize stock actions in new combinations, expanding possibilities in order to face dramatic and dangerous situations. HROs' commitment to resilience "is a combination of keeping errors small and of improvising workarounds that allow the system to keep functioning" (Weick and Sutcliffe 2007, p. 14). No organizational system is error-free: HROs know this better than anybody. They are not exempt from the possibility of committing errors, but errors do not destroy them: such organizations are in fact always ready to confront errors and know how to mobilize when they occur, blocking and limiting their effects and avoiding allowing them to become the starting point for an accident or, even worse, a catastrophe. As Roberts and Bea state (2001, p. 74), "HROs use failure simulations to train everyone to be:

- heedful of the possibility of accidents;
- flexible in their thinking about accidents and solutions;

- able to formulate appropriate responses, avoid decoys, and develop decoupling strategies;
- empowered to fix problems; and
- aware of organizational commitment to accident prevention.

5. Deference to expertise

HROs encourage diversity because it makes it possible for them both to have greater attention in complex environments and to intervene better with regard to the complexity that they identify. To avoid errors committed at higher levels of an organization combining with those committed at lower levels, HROs decentralize the decisional process (Roberts 1990). HROs shift decisions away from formal authority towards expertise and experience independent of rank. HROs have flexible decision-making structures; their networks do not have a fixed central player who can mistakenly assume that she or he knows everything. Decision making migrates to experts at all levels of the hierarchy during high-tempo times: "[d]uring routine operations, members of typical organizations demonstrate deference to the powerful, the coercive, and the senior, forgetting that higher-ups may have had the same experience over and over, were never on the shop floor, were not around when the plant was constructed, or may have acquired their position through politics" (Weick and Sutcliffe 2007, p. 74). Because people in high positions only tend to divulge good news, personnel may think that things are going well and there are no problems. When a problem becomes obvious, it is usually detected by someone low in the hierarchy, and someone in the frontline may be reluctant to speak about it openly. HROs put a lot of work into avoiding this kind of trap and modifying such patterns of deference. HROs foster migrating decisions, both up and down.

Weick and Sutcliffe (2007) prefer the concept of *expertise* to that of *expert*, underlining the crucial fact that *expertise* is *relational*. *Expertise* is in fact conceived of as a combination of awareness, experience, learning, and intuition, elements rarely to be found in one single person. And when it does seem to be the property of a single person, it is only evoked and becomes significant when a second person requires it, shows deference, modifies it, or rejects it. Deference to expertise is a form of *heedful interrelating* (Weick and Roberts 1993).

It is important to remember that the original set of HRO organizations were studied because of their extraordinary operational performance. That is what made them an HRO, not the presence of particular characteristics. Indeed, the five characteristics previously analyzed may be necessary but not sufficient for an organization to achieve remarkable operational reliability.

According to Roberts and Bea (2001, p. 77), "accidents are normal in the sense that they aren't likely to be eliminated on either a system or organizational level. The lessons learned from HROs offer promise that all organizations can benefit from attending to these issues and implementing the lessons learned." If an organization encourages focus on success rather than on attention to failure; on efficiency more than on safety and reliability; on episodic learning rather than on ongoing, systematic learning; on conformity and low diversity rather than on rich differentiation; and on the presence of informational filters with low circulation of information rather than on open communication, the reluctance to acknowledge weak signs of the danger and/or degradation of quality instead of constant quest for anomalies: if an organization does all (or part) of this, then it is not an HRO.

The five features illustrated make it possible to improve organizational reliability, increase organizational resilience, and reduce myopia and the possibility of errors.

High reliability management to avoid organizational myopia

Weick and Roberts (1993) maintain that the logic of reliability requires organizations to promote collective mental processes that are more intense in respect to organizations based on efficiency. This implies that organizations that have to achieve reliability must promote *mindfulness* and *heedful interrelating*. A reliable organization is an intelligent organization. And the intelligence lies in the connections rather than in single nodes. Referring back to psychological research and studies relating to connectionism, Weick and Roberts state that organizations can be represented as minds, with people taking the place of single neurons. The ability of an organization and its reliability therefore depend on the richness of the connections. Ordinary people are able to elaborate highly complex input because of the strength of the interaction developed between them. Organizations can maintain shared mental models in dangerous environments and in conditions of rapid change through the development of a collective mind, in other words, "a pattern of heedful interrelations of actions in a social system. Actors in the system construct their actions (contributions), understanding that the system consists of connected actions by themselves and others (representations), and interrelate their actions within the systems (subordination) ... As heedful interrelating and mindful comprehension increase, organizational errors decrease" (Weick and Roberts 1993, p. 357).

When technical systems are so various as to be beyond the comprehension of a single individual, one of the few ways in which human beings can deal with this wide variety is by forming a network or team involving individuals who are different from one another (Weick 1987). The main implication of this line of reasoning is that to correctly carry out a complex piece of work or a task, it is not sufficient to have careful and diligent personnel: sooner or later, anyone, working alone, can be guilty of distraction. Attention is not therefore just an individual attribute but a collective result. A careful performance is the result of a social action, a group one, and not an individual action. Sharing mental models is a requisite for reliability (Orasanu and Salas 1995). In dealing with complex events, a collective mind is more effective and reliable than many individual minds. In a collective mind, actions are individual, but they are connected through a shared, socially structured field that provides orientation and contributes to the construction of sense. The heedful interaction of a collective mind averts the risk of an accident: it makes it possible for the different actors involved to observe this in a different way and furthermore brings into play the interaction of the various know-how present, connecting them to the different levels of experience possessed by the subjects.

One example is provided by the landing of a plane on an aircraft carrier at night. This is not the result of an individual performance but of the continuous interconnections between a variety of components: the pilot, the airtraffic controller, the expert assistance offered to the pilot, the signal personnel on the carrier, and more besides. The landing is therefore a collective performance in which the reliability lies in the interactions among the members of the collective mind, all involved in dealing with the problem together. This leads on to the idea that reliability exists as part of a cooperative and communicative culture rather than as the action of a heroic individual. Weick suggests that a *macho culture*, which encourages individualism and the heroics of a single person, should be regarded with suspicion, because the performance to be carried out exceeds the ability of a single person, however competent. Reliable performances are possible with reliable collective minds. Organizations that are concerned about problems of reliability have to foster the development of collective minds in order to act in ways that are mindful, heedful, coherent, and intelligent.

One of the most relevant problems regarding the reliability of complex systems is the divergence between dominant approaches to designing systems and the process of managing them. According to Roe and Schulman (2008, p. 5), "the study of reliability in critical systems is the study of strategic balances that must be struck between efficiency and reliability, between learning by trial and error and the prevention of risky mistakes, and between maximizing our anticipation of shocks and maximizing our resilience to recover after them. High reliability management is about how these balances are achieved and sustained." Roe and Schulman studied the reliability professionals at the control center for the newly reorganized California power grid, from 2001 to 2006. Reliability professionals are middle-level personnel who are controllers, dispatchers, technical supervisors, and department heads in the California Independent System Operator (CAISO) that runs most of California's high-voltage electricity grid. They intended to show "that the key to increased reliability for our electricity grids, water supplies, telecoms, transportation systems, and financial services, among others, lies not in the pursuit of optimal designs and fail-safe technologies for large complex systems but, rather, in their careful management" (Roe and Schulman 2008, p. 12). However, the main problem that the authors highlight is that engineers and upper management design the system without taking into account the experience and knowledge of the reliability professionals. Roe and Schulman (2008, p. 217) identify the threats of formal and technical design to high reliability management and, at the same time, point out how operational redesign can improve network relations for better performance: "the promulgation of policy designs that ignore institutional challenges and requirements is not simply narrow and short-sighted; it is irresponsible."

Their analysis suggests three specific design principles:

[1] As a matter of principle, every design proposal should pass that reliability test keyed to the work of these professionals ... [2] As a matter of principle, any design that compels operators to work in a task environment outside their domain of competence in pattern recognition and scenario formulation for prolonged periods of time cannot be expected to produce a reliability system. [3] As a matter of principle, cognitive neutrality should be

followed, in which new variables are introduced into high reliability management only if they pose no net increase in the cognitive requirements of their control room manager. (Roe and Schulman 2008, p. 213)

These principles compel system designers to learn from the cognitive workload of operators and system contingencies that cannot be planned for but which must be managed by these reliability professionals case by case. To assure safety in complex systems, "organizations that must manage critical infrastructures reliably need to be institutions. They need to enjoy public acceptance, because to perform effectively reliability must be embedded in norms at the heart of their culture and the culture of the society around them" (Roe and Schulman 2008, p. 211).

5.2 Detecting weak signs

Scanning the external environment for potential threats and opportunities is one of the most important and challenging tasks for organizations today. They must develop the ability to detect threats and opportunities as soon as possible, in order to be able to react in time and in a suitable manner. These detecting capabilities are increasingly necessary for organizations that operate in hypercompetitive environments in which speed of change is invariably becoming faster and faster. The ability to foresee future events constitutes a highly relevant skill for the survival of organizations – a skill based on the ability to detect weak signs. However, reality demonstrates that many organizations are incapable of detecting warning signs present prior to the onset of damage (Pauchant and Mitroff 1992). As evidenced by a great deal of research, various types of accidents have been preceded by many such warning signs (Vaughan 1996; Reason 1997; Turner and Pidgeon 1997; Catino 2010) that, although recognizable, were never detected.

Ansoff (1975, 1980) is one of the first scholars to introduce the concept of weak signs that point to strategic discontinuities in the organizational environment. These are internal and external signs that can warn an organization of potential threat and opportunity (Dutton and Ashford 1993). Weak signs, in contrast to strong signs, are those ambiguous and controversial bits of information about the complex environment that are typically hidden among the noise. A weak sign is characterized by ambiguous, unclear, and unstructured informational content.

According to Ansoff (1975, 1980), organizations are capable of anticipating strategic discontinuities to the extent that they can receive, interpret, and act on the basis of weak signs; the traditional forms of forecasting, based on historically familiar raw data, are destined to fail in the face of strategic discontinuities in the development of the environment and strategic surprises. Strategic surprises are "sudden, urgent, unfamiliar changes in the firm's perspective which threaten either a major profit reversal or loss of a major opportunity" (Ansoff 1976, p. 131). It is possible to anticipate these strategic surprises through the detection of weak signs and the appropriate response with regard to them.

This, however, is not easy. Rerup (2009) states that organizations may fail to detect weak signs for a variety of reasons: (1) because they do not recognize them as indicators of potential problems (Weick 2005b), (2) because of a lack of attentional resources for this particular aim (Ocasio 1997), and (3) because the signs are detected only by those who are close to them and who may not have either the power or motivation to speak up or act on them (Lampel and Shapira 2001; Edmondson, Bohmer, and Pisano 2001; Bouquet and Birkinshaw 2008).

Diane Vaughan (1996), for example, very effectively demonstrates the difficulty of learning from weak signs with reference to the *Challenger* launch disaster. Early flights of the space shuttle showed that O-rings in the booster rockets had partly eroded. This was an extremely dangerous warning sign, given that this kind of damage might have allowed hot gases to escape, with the consequent destruction of the shuttle. Rather than see the deterioration of the O-rings as a real threat, however, engineers and management considered it as an acceptable risk.

In order to recognize weak signs, organizations must develop organizational attention, defined as "the noticing, encoding, interpreting, and focusing of time and effort by organizational decision makers on both issues: (a) the available repertoire of categories for making sense of the environment – problems, opportunities and threats; and (b) ... the available repertoire of action alternatives – proposals, routines, projects, programs, and procedures" (Ocasio 1997, p. 189).

Rerup (2009) introduces the concept of organizational triangulation. To prevent a crisis, an organization needs to integrate three interdependent dimensions of organizational attention: stability, which refers to sustained attention to issues; vividness, which refers to the complexity of representation of issues; and coherence, which refers to how similar or compatible attention to issues is across levels, units, and people. "Attending to weak cues from the lower levels can help organizations to prevent and learn from rare events" (Rerup 2009, p. 889).

With reference to financial crises, Reinhart and Rogoff (2009) maintain that the signal approach can be an important tool for obtaining early warnings of them. For example, the signals approach described by Kaminsky, Lizondo, and Reinhart (1998) classifies the indicators on the basis of their noise-to-signal relationship. When an indicator sends a signal and a crisis occurs within two years, this can be called an accurate signal. If no crisis follows the signal, then this can be classified as false alarm or noise. The best indicators are those with the lowest noise-to-signal ratio (Kaminsky et al. 1998). This approach is certainly not capable of identifying the exact date on which a bubble will burst, or of providing an obvious indication of the severity of the looming crisis. However, the systematic application of this method can, say the authors, make valuable information available, if the economy is manifesting the classic symptoms that emerge before a severe financial illness develops. The main obstacle to the development and application of this particular tool is not of a practical kind, state Reinhart and Rogoff (2009, p. 281): in fact, "the greatest barrier to success is the well-entrenched tendency of policy makers and market participants to treat the signals as irrelevant archaic residuals of an outdated framework, assuming that old rules of valuation no longer apply."

Cultivating imagination

Reexamining certain cases of unsuccessful military events such as the Israeli information services' inability to forecast the Egyptian and Syrian 1973 Yom Kippur attack, Stech (1979) identifies two characteristics that distinguish failure from success: the secret services' maintenance of a plurality of hypotheses; the use of information and data to distort existing convictions and assumptions – prejudices – rather than confirm reassuring hypotheses. Similar conclusions were reached by the analysis of the 9/11 terrorist attacks: the *9/11 Commission Report* states that the bureaucracy of the organizations charged with internal defense of the United States was the main reason for the failure to

forecast the attack. At the same time, the report says that it is necessary to render the exercise of the imagination routine in some way,
without falling into the trap of bureaucracy and without having to
depend on experts with special skills in divination.

How to combine imagination and organizing? The idea of a hijacking suicide attack had been imagined by Richard Clarke during the
Clinton administration, although in that case the scenario envisioned
was a suicide hijacking involving aircraft *with* explosives, not aircraft
as explosives, as we saw in Chapter 1. The US defense system had not,
however, thought his indication worth following up. It is interesting to
note that many of the ideas concerning domestic vulnerability put forward by Clarke came not from government sources but from reading
the books of political thriller writer Tom Clancy.[1]

Reconciling organizing and imagination, as I said in Chapter 3, is an
organizational dilemma, since the increase in one may result in the reduction of the other: "organizing restricts perception because requirements
for coordination necessitate generalizing. Generalizing can suppress
both recognition of anomalous details and imaginative development
of their meaning" (Weick 2005a, p. 431). Organizing fosters perception based on rigid schemas, deduction rather than abductive reasoning (see Section 1.2), an attitude that is mindless rather than mindful,
the formulation of hypotheses that are imaginative but not realistic
(fancy), rather than an aptitude for the production of plausible scenarios (imagination).[2] Imagination is an antidote to myopia. Not only
an individual quality, it can also be an organizational characteristic. As

[1] "Richard Clarke told us that he was concerned about the danger posed by
aircraft in the context of protecting the Atlanta Olympics of 1996, the White
House complex, and the 2001 G8 summit in Genoa. But he attributed his
awareness more to Tom Clancy novels than to warnings from the intelligence
community. He did not, or could not, press the government to work on the
systemic issues of how to strengthen the layered security defenses to protect
aircraft against hijackings or put the adequacy of air defenses against suicide
hijackers on the national policy agenda" (NCTA 2004, p. 347).

[2] "Imagination" may be defined as the ability to bring together fragmentary
elements into a complete and integrated whole, while the concept of "fancy"
refers to the power to invent something original but not realistic through a
new combination of elements present in reality. For example, the ability of
imagination could have predicted the use of planes as weapons, based on
existing information. Fancy, on the other hand, could have developed a political
thriller narrative that describes the use of planes loaded with explosives as
weapons (Tom Clancy).

Hutchins (1995) states, the cognitive property of human groups may depend on the social organization of individual cognitive abilities.

Imagination is based on that form of abductive reasoning that generates surprise with questions that marshal all the elements in one single instant and present them in a completely different light, a bringing together of items that no one has dreamed of bringing together before (Peirce 1931–1935). With reference to the 9/11 attack, for example, on the one hand, there was the fact that a group of Islamic men were undertaking courses to become pilots and, on the other hand, the use of planes as weapons, in a situation where threats of terrorist attacks on American soil were increasing.

In short, imagination and abductive reasoning are two ways of counteracting organizational myopia. "To counteract failures of imagination is to alter organizing in ways that reduce the demands for coordination, replace deductive thinking with abductive thinking, shift a culture of analysis toward a culture of imagination, and intensify norms of mindfulness" (Weick 2005a, p. 436). Naturally, the individual ability of imagination is not enough: it must be an organizational property aimed at fostering the ability to imagine possible scenarios and events, while at the same time searching for the conditions to transform subjective knowledge of an intuitive kind into objective organizational knowledge, or knowledge that is at least accessible on an intersubjective level.

5.3 Preventing surprises, managing the unexpected

In a survey carried out involving 140 company strategists, two-thirds of them admitted that in the previous five years, their organizations had been taken by surprise by at least three high-impact events, regarding their competitors (Day and Schoemaker 2006). Of those interviewed, 97 percent declared that their own companies were not equipped with any system that could predict this kind of event in the future. Day and Schoemaker (2006) employ the effective metaphor of peripheral vision, with the aim of identifying an approach to building a superior ability in a company, making it possible to recognize weak signs arriving from peripheral areas and enabling action before it is too late. The propensity for peripheral vision is mainly linked to how organizations perceive and act and can therefore be considered a meta-ability, transversal in relation to the operational skills of the organization itself. Day and Schoemaker (2006) identify certain components of the propensity for peripheral vision that are particularly important for an organization that intends to detect weak signs: a mindful management that encourages breadth of vision in relation to the periphery, the adoption of an inquiring approach in the development of strategy, a flexible culture and a company configuration that encourage exploration of the periphery, and systems of knowledge suited to the detection and sharing of weak signs.

In order to deal with the unexpected, predict surprises and contain negative effects it is necessary for organizations to act according to the properties of HROs (Weick and Sutcliffe 2007). As seen in Section 5.1, the five principles specified for HROs increase the ability of an organization to manage unforeseen events and reduce both individual and organizational myopia, fostering increasing levels of mindfulness.

Roberto (2009) affirms that the leaders of present-day organizations must change their principal ability, shifting from being problem solvers to become problem finders, in relation to those problems that may threaten the survival of the organization. Leaders can no longer simply wait for problems to show up and then be solved: the ever-reducing time available for seeking a solution and the seriousness of the problems themselves do not make this feasible. If a leader identifies a problem in its earliest stages, there is time to avert a major catastrophe through the application of those corrective actions required to break the chain of events before it becomes uncontrollable.

Integrating operations and reducing ambiguity

Increasing internal integration through more organic working processes helps strengthen the organization's capacity for rapid response to sudden changes in an uncertain environment. Unifying and integrating operations increases the sharing and management of knowledge, favoring the detection of weak signs and threats.

Groups made up only of specialists are less likely to share information compared to mixed groups consisting of specialists and generalists, who have a variety of experience in different areas (Bunderson and Sutcliffe 2002). Information sharing is not only a matter of collective norms and expectations regarding sharing: it is also a question of individual motivation. If personnel coming from a specific group perceive others as coming from similarly specialized groups, this reduces the propensity to share information and knowledge because the general belief is that neither group can properly understand the other's respective activity.

The culture of information sharing is a powerful antidote to organizational myopia, particularly where it is supported by efficient information and database systems that increase the volume of information available to the decision makers. There are two problems, however: the first regards the quantity of information to evaluate and, the second, informational ambiguity. The latter is a substantial problem: ambiguity, as we saw in Section 2.1, means in fact that the same piece of information may have multiple and sometimes contrary meanings. Environments that are hypercompetitive (in rapid transformation from a social, economic-financial, technological, and political point of view) or high risk (because of the technologies in use or dangerous activity involved) produce signs that are often not very clear, or ambiguous, which can lead people to a variety of plausible interpretations and conclusions while referring to the same objective data. Ambiguity cannot therefore be reduced only through greater amounts of information, since increasing information may only serve to increase confusion and uncertainty (Daft, Bettenhausen, and Tyler 1993). Ambiguity can be solved through group processes, such as meetings and discussions. However, in hierarchical organizations with bureaucratic functioning methods, open discussion is complicated: open organizational structures, flexible and with a culture of information sharing and expertise, are more suited to handling unforeseen situations with ambiguous signs and information.

Extending recovery windows

Roberto, Bohmer, and Edmondson (2006) analyze a series of cases, including the pharmaceutical firm Merck, whose painkiller Vioxx was associated with cardiovascular risks; Kodak, who ignored the first signs of the decline in use of camera film; bicycle manufacturer Schwinn, who underestimated the threat of the mountain bike; and NASA, who underestimated the damage caused by the detachment of insulating material during the *Columbia* shuttle's takeoff. They affirm that organizations that develop a systematic ability to identify, evaluate, and react to ambiguous threats are able to avoid the onset of serious problems far more effectively than are those unable to develop this particular ability. Each risk has its own recovery window, a period from the first warning signs to the manifestation of the event, during which, should one or more members of an organization become aware of these signs, the threat can be prevented or contained. Action taken during this time, this recovery window, means that the negative result can be avoided or contained. This happens in particular if organizations are prepared to deal with the emergency and apply suitable methods.

A recovery window exists when one or more members of an organization become aware of the risk of a serious failure (Edmondson et al. 2005). The duration of a recovery window can be a matter of a few minutes or of days. For example, in the case of the *Columbia* disaster, the recovery window opened approximately two days after the launch and closed sixteen days later, when the shuttle reentered Earth's atmosphere. However, as seen in Chapter 1, the threats and signs were not taken into consideration because of a series of reasons of a mainly organizational nature. With the 9/11 attack, the recovery window opened when the air transport system became aware of the first hijacking and closed less than two hours later. It could also be said, taking a broader view, that the recovery window opened months beforehand, when the first signals emerged regarding possible attacks on US soil.

An effective response in a recovery window consists of two processes: (1) the identification and evaluation of the nature of the threat and (2) the generation of possible solutions or preventive actions. Without identification of the threat, solutions are improbable or at least inadequate.

With respect to the recovery window, organizations can respond in two ways (Edmondson et al. 2005). A response of a confirmatory kind, which reinforces assumptions, the *frame*, and consolidated beliefs, is a passive response, based on *taken-for-granted* ideas, in which individuals believe that past success is a guarantee for success in the future. In uncertain situations, conformity to existing norms and routines is the most logical response. A different response, of an exploratory kind, places acquired certainties constantly in doubt and tends to put existing assumptions to the test. The aim of this second type of response is to learn everything possible about the nature of the threat in order to be able to deal with it.

To fight myopia and block catastrophic errors, organizations must learn to identify the recovery window and make it last for as long as possible, in order to have the necessary time to develop appropriate creative solutions (Roberto et al. 2006). Recovery windows can be an opportunity for learning and improvement: one possible process of this type involves three stages.

1. *Teamwork training under pressure.* In crisis situations, there is not a lot of time available to calmly decide what to do. Stress and anxiety are not conducive to easy decision making. Training involving repeated attempts at reacting to potential threats can be extremely advantageous. Even though it is not possible to try out all possible situations, it is important to develop generic abilities to react during the recovery window, which can then be applied to a wider range of potentially dangerous situations.

2. *Amplify the signs.* Leaders must amplify the pre-alarm warning signs, and companies must equip themselves with mechanisms that promote the creation of recovery windows. For example, certain medical researchers noted that patients who suffered a cardiac arrest all displayed the same symptoms some hours before. From the moment when these symptoms manifest themselves to the *code-red* alarm that activates a reanimation team, there is a period that makes it possible for doctors to intervene in advance rather than wait until the situation is already compromised. Certain hospitals are already employing these tactics, with a reduction in the number of code-red alarms, but there are positive examples of this behavior in other sectors as well, including the Electricité de France electric company, with its fifty-seven nuclear reactors, and Fidelity Investment, with its quality control system for service operations.

3. *Experimentation.* The evaluation of vague threats requires a rapid response: in most cases, there is no time for scientific experiments and an assessment of their results. At the same time, improvised responses may not be suitable. Examples of behavior involving experimentation come from those organizations that study consumer preferences by creating prototypes of new products. These prototypes do not reproduce the whole product but only a part of the experience, which is then used to generate feedback. This system makes it possible for the company to avoid possible failures and reduces the cost of inquiries into any eventual problems, given the high cost of product development and the low probability of success.

Putting these three phases into action, state Roberto, Bohmer, and Edmondson (2006), a company learns to react to threat, favoring both individual and organizational learning.

Exaggerating the evaluation of the negative possibilities of threats and coordinating problem solving and analysis teams to work out remedial action make it possible for managers to handle the unexpected and reduce myopia. At worst, in cases where effective threats are absent, the organization will have wasted time in following up false alarms, but will probably have learnt something useful for the future (Edmondson et al. 2005). Operating in an exploratory rather than confirmatory way, and facilitating dissension and alternative hypotheses, managers, while perhaps not being able to eliminate preconceptions, remain open to the verification of alternative hypotheses regarding possible threats and opportunities. An exploratory response is therefore more suitable in a hypercompetitive environment, in research and development, and in high-risk systems. Exploratory response does not require any particular resources and may not only provoke the expansion of positive effects concerning specific projects but also develop the general ability for organizational learning and ongoing improvement.

Epilogue

Herbert Simon, well over half a century ago, in 1947, introduced a new perspective into organizational behavior, moving away from the economists' theories of rational choice and emphasizing the limits of human rationality in explaining how organizations really make decisions. These human and organizational limits become even more critical in uncertain and unstable environments.

Analyzing the environment in search of potential threats and opportunities is today one of the most important tasks of an organization, which naturally attempts to detect threat and opportunity as early as possible in order to have time to react. This is particularly vital in a world of organizations characterized by a constant increase in interdependence, complexity, and scale (LaPorte 2007a; 2007b).

Crises and catastrophes do not happen out of the blue but are in a sense organized, and often originate in executive failures and in the banality of organizational life (Vaughan 1996). In an era of *normal accidents* (Perrow 1999) and *worst cases* (L. Clarke 2006), the *probabilistic* approach to risk has to be replaced by a *possibilistic* approach. The question can no longer be, *What are the probabilities that a specific event will occur?* but *What will happen when this specific event occurs?* (L. Clarke 2006). One of the most common self-fulfilling behavioral biases, the *Titanic Effect*, is captured by the aphorism: "the thought that disaster is impossible often leads to an unthinkable disaster" (Weinberg 1986, p. 95).

Perrow (2007) highlights the inevitable inadequacy of our efforts in dealing with various types of disaster, whether natural or man-made, tracing this back to the inevitable inadequacy of formal organizations. It follows that the traditional way of protecting ourselves from disasters is insufficient and myopic. Czarniawska (2009) states that there are no easy recipes for organizing in the face of threat and risk. Rather than planning, it is necessary to develop the organization's ability to improvise: "effective organizing does not imply ... that uncertainty must be reduced, but rather that uncertainty must be accepted as part of the human condition and that acting in spite of it is necessary – with the courage that results from a great deal of practice and improvisation" (Czarniawska 2009, p. 168).

Many problems arise for an organization when it fails to be fully aware of the complex interactions among the different organizations and the organizational subunits. The problem, according to Clarke, is that worst cases are, often, unthinkable and, therefore, myopia is inevitable. Schwartz (2003), in contrast, maintains that if, on the one hand, technological innovation, demographic changes, terrorism, ethnic conflict, and other significant developments produce inevitable surprises, then, on the other hand, most of these surprises can be foreseen. In this context, the key task for the policy maker and for the crisis manager is that of establishing institutional procedures and creating the cultural climate to confront these extraordinary threats. An organization's response to risk and unexpected events depends on how these come to be understood and explained. Risk is not always clearly identifiable and manageable, but emerges from, and is produced by, complex and necessarily incomplete processes of organizational attention.

Central to every discussion regarding the relationship between organizations and the management of risk is the subject of regulation (Hutter and Power 2005a; Hutter 2010; Scheytt et al. 2006). Increasing institutional demand for the regulation of corporate risk creates in turn a new type of risk for the organizations providing the regulation. At a world level, there are an increasing number of organizations that offer coordination and guidance for risk management, such as the Basel Committee on Banking Supervision, the World Health Organization, the International Atomic Energy Agency, and the Financial Stability Board, to name just a few. These are *meta-organizations* (Ahrne and Brunsson 2006), that is, organizations whose members are also organizations. Meta-organizations, the new arena for the production of knowledge concerning risk management, have acquired international status, providing global standards of reference for public and private enterprise.

As this present book brings out, organizations that do not worry about failures, especially small ones; that carry out simplifying operations in relation to reality; that do not practice strategies of anticipation; and that place hierarchy over expertise detect a smaller number of details: they often fail to see the first signs of danger and remain more vulnerable to adverse events, recognizing them only when it is already too late. These are myopic organizations. In contrast, organizations that are concerned about failure and complications, and that pay attention to frontline operations, to resilience and to knowledge, are in a better position to detect adverse events earlier, as they are developing, and to correct them, thus avoiding or containing possible disasters or negative consequences.

A variety of ways have been developed over the years to define crises (Rosenthal and Kouzmin 1993; Rike 2003; Gundel 2005), types of future and uncertain events (Tsoukas and Shepherd 2004), and accidents (Perrow 1999). Every classification is a trade-off between analytical rigor and empirical appropriateness. Here, I advance a classification of the various syndromes of organizational myopia, based on the conceptual categories introduced in the previous chapters, namely, the predictability of the event, distinguishing between potentially predictable versus hardly predictable events (as defined in Chapters 2 and 3), and on the possibility of dealing with it, or manageability, either ex ante or ex post (as discussed in Chapters 4 and 5).

1. Predictability

An event is *potentially predictable* if (a) there is a *direct* and *clear* causal link between signs and event and (b) before it takes place, there is an *incubation period* in which signs (weak or strong) make possible its detection.[1]

An event is *hardly predictable* if (a) *no preceding signs exist* whatsoever, (b) there is an *indirect* and *unclear* causal link between signs and event, or (c) the event has never occurred before and there is no model to refer to.

The concept of predictability refers to an event in itself, and not to whether an organization was able to predict and avoid it. In other

---

[1] *Potentially* predictable because, as emphasized more than once, information is not enough. Warning signs are necessary but insufficient condition for organizational awareness. Their presence do not ensure that an organization will become automatically aware of them, and many factors exist that can hinder their detection (see Section 5.2). In order to become aware, an organization must be able to detect signs, to interpret them within a frame that makes sensemaking possible, and to act to avoid or contain their consequences. It is important to know how to connect the dots. Highly Reliable Organizations seem to be more able to do this.

words, the question is not if an organization *should* have predicted and avoided an event (the answer is often yes), but if the event *could* have been predicted and avoided. Finally, despite the fact that here I have used a categorical classification of events (distinguishing between potentially predictable and hardly predictable events), in reality, the predictability of events is better conceived as a continuum.

2. Manageability

Moving to the second dimension, an event is manageable ex ante if there is sufficient time from the first sign of the event's manifestation either to avoid it completely or to contain its damage – in other words, a *recovery window*. For example, in the case of *Challenger*, there were numerous signs that indicated the dangerous condition of the O-rings. These signs, however, because of a process of normalization of deviance (Vaughan 1996), went unheeded by managers and engineers. An event is manageable ex post if it is possible to contain its consequences. The *Columbia* disaster was manageable *both ex ante and ex post*, while the Challenger disaster was manageable *only ex ante*. If there are no preceding signs, or there is too little time involved in the event's occurrence, an event is not manageable ex ante, but it may still be managed ex post. For instance, the Chernobyl nuclear meltdown was manageable *only ex post*.

The two dimensions intersect to provide four forms of organizational myopia (see Table E.1).

Systemic myopia (quadrant 1): the events in this quadrant are *potentially predictable* because there is a *direct* and *clear* causal link between signs and event, and before it takes place, there is an *incubation period* in which signs (weak or strong) make possible its detection. The events were manageable by an organization both ex ante and ex post and the organizations failed (a) to detect signs before the event (failure of anticipation) and (b) to contain its consequences, despite the presence of a recovery window (failure of containment). Myopia here is a systemic condition of an organization, as in the case of man-made disasters (Turner and Pidgeon 1997) and organizational accidents (Reason 1997). For example, in the case of the *Columbia* shuttle, NASA did not draw the right conclusions from the breaking away of the foam insulation, something that had already happened during previous launches. There was no attempt to search for other images of the possible

Table E.1. *Types of organizational myopia*

	Manageability ex ante *and* ex post	Manageability *only* ex ante *or* ex post
Potentially predictable (signs)	Man-made disasters, Organizational accidents (e.g. *Linate* and *Überlingen* air disasters, *Columbia* shuttle disaster, *BP* oil spill) *Enron* financial misconduct Tsunami *Systemic myopia* 1	Man-made disasters, Organizational accidents (e.g. *Challenger* shuttle disaster, *Chernobyl* accident) Disease outbreak *Foresight myopia* 2
Hardly predictable (no signs, unclear signs, no model of event)	4 9/11 terrorist attacks Sudden fires Earthquakes *Preventive and reactive myopia*	3 Normal accidents (e.g., *Three Mile Island*) *Unavoidable myopia*

damage caused to the thermal protection system, the situation was played down, and no remedial measures were taken. The organization failed to anticipate and contain.

Foresight myopia (quadrant 2): the events in this quadrant are *potentially predictable* because there is a *direct* and *clear* causal link between signs and event, and before it takes place, there is an *incubation period* in which signs (weak or strong) make possible its detection. The events were manageable only ex ante (as in the case of the *Challenger's* O-rings) or only ex post (Chernobyl accident, for example). However, the organization failed to detect and make sense of warning signs (failure of anticipation) or take any kind of remedial measure (failure of containment).

Unavoidable myopia (quadrant 3): the events in this quadrant are *hardly predictable* because *no preceding signs exist* whatsoever, or there is an *indirect* and *unclear* causal link between signs and event, or the event has never occurred before and there is no model to refer to. The organization could act only ex ante, or only ex post, and was not able to do so. It is the most justifiable of the four forms of myopia, because there was no opportunity for the organization to implement either mindful preventive action or suitable methods of containment. In this quadrant, we can place a particular kind of accidents: the *normal accidents* that were introduced by Perrow (1999). A normal accident would require that in a system, such as an organization, there were unwitting failures that interacted in a way that could not be anticipated or foreseen. This kind of accident, also, arises when a complex system exhibits complex interactions (when it has unfamiliar, unplanned, or unexpected sequences which are not visible or not immediately comprehensible) and when it is tightly coupled (when it has time-dependent processes which cannot wait, rigidly ordered processes – as in sequence A must follow B). Those events are manageable either *only ex ante* by avoiding some of these high-risk systems (e.g., nuclear weapons) or are manageable *only ex post* by seeking to limit the consequences of inevitable failures.

Preventive and reactive myopia (quadrant 4): the events in this quadrant are *hardly predictable* because *no preceding signs exist* whatsoever, or there is an *indirect* and *unclear* causal link between signs and event, or the event has never occurred before and there is no model to refer to. The organization could have implemented anticipatory preventive measures (for example, forest maintenance, preemptive fires, antiseismic construction, etc.) but did not do so (failure of anticipation). In addition, the organization was also unable to contain the consequences of the event (failure of containment).

This classification scheme does not include those very rare events that are not predictable neither manageable ex ante or ex post. *Epistemic accidents* are an example of this. The epistemic accidents (like the case of Aloha Airlines Flight 243[2]) are "those accidents that occur because a scientific or technological assumption proves to be erroneous, even though there were reasonable and logical reasons to hold that assumption before (although not after) the event" (Downer 2011, p. 752). As

---

[2] The Aloha Airlines Flight accident (1988) is a case of fuselage failure. An 18-foot fuselage section, 35 square meters, had completely torn away from the airframe. The causes were a fateful combination of stress fractures, corrosion, and metal fatigue. According to Downer (2011, p. 750), this accident was inevitable because the "warning signals were visible only in retrospect."

normal accidents, epistemic accidents are unpredictable and unavoidable, because "engineers necessarily build technologies around fallible theories, judgements and assumptions" (Downer 2011, p. 752).

In conclusion, while it is true that it is not possible to completely avoid all accidents and disasters, it is also true that it is possible to reduce their frequency and limit the consequences. Some recommendations for management and organizing are the following:

- To avoid failures of anticipation, it is fundamental for the organizations to increase their ability to track the development of uncertain and unexpected events and halt them from worsening. This can be done by enhancing skills to detect weak signs and make sense of unexpected events, organizational attention, peripheral vision, anticipatory thinking, problem-finding skills, cultivating imagination, and abductive reasoning to connect the dots, knowledge-sharing system, preoccupation with failure and error learning systems, reluctance to simplify interpretations, and sensitivity to operations.
- To avoid failures of containment, it is fundamental to improve resilience and the organization's ability to reconfigure in order to manage unexpected events. This can be done by developing features like ability to cope with the unexpected, extension of recovery windows, error containment, teamwork training under pressure, problem-solving skills, improvisation skills, sensemaking of unexpected events, crisis management, commitment to resilience, and deference to expertise.

Boin and Lagadec (2000) highlight how the preparation for the unexpected involves far more than simply preparing plans for crisis management. It is not a matter only of planning but also of anticipation and the development of strategies to ensure organizational resilience. This is possible if the organizational elite foster resilience through systems of detection of errors and weak signs. In order to predict adverse events, handle the unexpected, and combat myopia, organizations must have a better understanding of the processes of sensemaking in conditions of stress and high environmental pressure, paying particular attention to the involuntary tendency towards simplification that manifests itself when first impressions and information are pooled for collective action (Weick 1995).

As has been specified throughout, it is necessary to be aware that knowledge of the mechanisms of myopia does not in itself guarantee their neutralization. The optimism of reason needs to be moderated regarding the fact that greater knowledge of the processes may assure less myopic decisions. The present study does not intend to impose a superior rationality nor least of all reintroduce irrationality into organizational choices. Its principal objective is to identify mechanisms and processes, often latent and not visible, which foster myopia at various levels of organizational action (micro, meso, macro), creating a broader opportunity for less myopic decisions and helping to bring out choices that are, as far as possible, more reliable on the part of individual organizations or wider institutional contexts.

Bibliography

Abramson, N.R. and Senyshyn, Y. (2010), "Effective Punishment through Forgiveness: Rediscovering Kierkegaard's Knight of Faith in the Abraham Story," *Organization Studies*, 31, 5, 555–81.

Ahrne, G. and Brunsson, N. (2006), "Organizing the World," in M.L. Djelic and K. Sahlin-Andersson (eds.), *Transnational Governance: Institutional Dynamics of Regulation*, Cambridge University Press, pp. 74–94.

Aldrich, H.E. and Ruef, M. (2006), *Organizations Evolving*, Second Edition, Thousand Oaks, CA, Sage.

Allen, D.G. and McDermott, K. (1993), *Accounting for Success: A History of Price Waterhouse in America, 1890–1990*, Boston, Harvard Business School Press.

Allison, G. and Zelikow, P. (1999), *Essence of Decision: Explaining the Cuban Missile Crisis*, Second Edition, New York, Longman.

Ansoff, H.I. (1975), "Managing Strategic Surprise by Response to Weak Signals," *California Management Review*, 18, 2, 21–33.

(1976), "Managing Surprise and Discontinuity – Strategic Response to Weak Signals," *Zeitschrift für betriebswirtschaftliche Forschung*, 28, 2, 129–52.

(1980), "Strategic Issue Management," *Strategic Management Journal*, 1, 1, 131–48.

Argyris, C. and Schön, D. (1996), *Organizational Learning II: Theory, Method and Practice*, New York, Addison-Wesley.

Ashraf, N., Camerer, C.F., and Loewenstein, G. (2005), "Adam Smith, Behavioral Economist," *Journal of Economic Perspectives*, 19, 3, 131–45.

Avery, R.D. and Ivancevich, J.M. (1980), "Punishment in Organizations: A Review, Propositions, and Research Suggestions," *Academy of Management Review*, 5, 1, 123–32.

Babcock, L. and Loewenstein, G. (1997), "Explaining Bargaining Impasse: The Role of Self-Serving Biases," *The Journal of Economic Perspectives*, 11, 1, 109–26.

Bardach, E. (1998), *Getting Agencies to Work Together: The Practice and Theory of Managerial Craftsmanship*, Washington, DC, Brookings Institution.

(2005), "How Do They Stack Up? The 9/11 Commission Report and the Management Literature," *International Public Management Journal*, 8, 3, 351–64.

Baron, R.M. and Misovich, S.J. (1999), "On the Relationship Between Social and Cognitive Modes of Organization," in S. Chaiken and Y. Trope (eds.), *Dual-Process Theories in Social Psychology*, New York, Guilford, pp. 586–605.

Bazerman, M.H. (2006), *Judgment in Managerial Decision Making*, Hoboken, NJ, John Wiley and Sons.

Bazerman, M.H., Loewenstein, G., and Moore, D.A. (2002), "Why Good Accountants Do Bad Audit," *Harvard Business Review*, 80, 1, 97–102.

Bazerman, M.H., Morgan, K.P., and Loewenstein, G.F. (1997), "The Impossibility of Auditor Independence," *Sloan Management Review*, 38, 4, 89–94.

Bazerman, M.H. and Watkins, M. (2004), *Predictable Surprises*, Boston, Harvard Business School.

(2005), "Airline Security: The Failure of 9/11 and Predictable Surprise," *International Public Management Journal*, 8, 3, 365–77.

Bea, R. (2002), "Human and Organizational Factors in Risk Analysis and Management Offshore Structures," *Risk Analysis*, 22, 1, 29–45.

Beck, U. (1986), *Risikogesellschaft: Auf dem Weg in eine andere Moderne*, Berlin, Suhrkamp Verlag.

Berends, H., Boersma, K., and Weggeman, M. (2003), "The Structuration of Organizational Learning," *Human Relations*, 56, 9, 1035–56.

Berger, P.L. and Luckmann, T. (1966), *The Social Construction of Reality*, Garden City, NJ, Doubleday.

Bernoulli, J. (1713), *Ars Conjectandi*, Basel, Switzerland, Thurmisiorum.

Betts, R.K. (1978), "Analysis, War and Decision: Why Intelligence Failures are Inevitable," *World Politics*, 31, 1, 61–89.

(1982), *Surprise Attack*, Washington, DC, Brookings Institution.

(2007), *Enemies of Intelligence: Knowledge and Power in American National Security*, New York, Columbia University Press.

Bierly, P., Gallagher, S., and Spender, J.C. (2008), "Innovation and Learning in High Reliability Organizations: A Case Study of the United States and Russian Nuclear Attack Submarines," *IEEE Transactions in Engineering Management*, 55, 3, 393–408.

Bigley, G.A. and Roberts, K.H. (2001), "The Incident Command System: High-Reliability Organizing for Complex and Volatile Task Environments," *Academy of Management Journal*, 44, 6, 1281–99.

Boh, W-F., Ren, Y., Kiesler, S., and Bussjaeger, R. (2007), "Expertise and Collaboration in the Geographically Dispersed Organization," *Organization Science*, 18, 4, 595–612.

Boin, A. and Lagadec, P. (2000), "Preparing for the Future: Critical Challenges in Crisis Management," *Journal of Contingencies and Crisis Management*, 8, 4, 185–91.

Bouquet, C. and Birkinshaw, J. (2008), "Weight Versus Voice: How Foreign Subsidiaries Gain Attention from Corporate Headquarters," *Academy of Management Journal*, 51, 3, 577–601.

Bourrier, M. (1996), "Organizing Maintenance Work at Two Nuclear Power Plants," *Journal of Contingencies and Crisis Management*, 4, 2, 104–12.

(2005), "The Contribution of Organizational Design to Safety," *European Management Journal*, 23, 1, 98–104.

Bradbury, H. and Lichtenstein, B.M.B. (2000), "Relationality in Organizational Research: Exploring the Space Between," *Organization Science*, 11, 5, 551–64.

Brennan, T.A. (2000), "The Institute of Medicine Report on Medical Errors – Could It Do Harm," *New England Journal of Medicine*, 342, 15, 1123–5.

Brown, J. (1986), *Social Psychology*, Second Edition, New York, Free Press.

Bunderson, J.S. and Sutcliffe, K.M. (2002), "Comparing Alternative Conceptualizations of Functional Diversity in Management Teams: Process and Performance Effects," *Academy of Management Journal*, 45, 5, 875–93.

Burger, W. (1984), *United States vs. Arthur Young & Co.*, vol. 82–687, Supreme Court of United States.

Burke, W.W. (2005), "Gatekeepers," in C.L. Cooper, C. Argyris and W.H. Starbuck (eds.), *The Blackwell Encyclopedia of Management*, Oxford, Blackwell, p. 135.

Burke, C.S., Wilson K.A., and Salas, E. (2005), "The Use of a Team Based Strategy for Organizational Transformation: Guidance for Moving Toward a High Reliability Organization," *Theoretical Issue in Ergonomic Science*, 6, 6, 509–30.

Burns, T. and Stalker, G.M. (1961), *The Management of Innovation*, London, Tavistock.

Burton-Jones, A. (1999), *Knowledge Capitalism: Business, Work and Learning in the New Economy*, Oxford University Press.

Busby, J.S. (2006), "Failure to Mobilize in Reliability-Seeking Organizations: Two Cases from UK Railway," *Journal of Management Studies*, 43, 6, 1375–93.

Cabbage, M. and Harwood, W. (2004), *COMM: The Final Flight of Shuttle Columbia*, New York, Free Press.

CAIB, Columbia Accident Investigation Board (2003), *Report, Volume One*, Washington, DC, National Aeronautics and Space Administration and the Government Printing Office.

Camerer, C.F. (2005), "How Neuroscience Can Inform Economics," *Journal of Economic Literature*, 43, 1, 9–64.

(2007), "Neuroeconomics: Using Neuroscience to Make Economic Predictions," *Economic Journal*, 117, C26-C42.

Camerer, C.F. and Lovallo, D. (1999), "Overconfidence and Excess Entry: An Experimental Approach," *American Economic Review*, 89, 1, 306–18.

Carey, J. (1970), *The Rise of the Accounting Profession: To Responsibility and Authority, 1937–1969*, New York, American Institute of Certified Public Accountants.

Cassidy, J. (2009), *How Markets Fail: The Logic of Economic Calamities*, New York, Farrar, Straus and Giroux.

Catino, M. (2008), "A Review of Literature: Individual Blame vs. Organizational Function Logics in Accident Analysis," *Journal of Contingencies and Crisis Management*, 16, 1, 53–62.

(2010), "A Multilevel Model of Accident Analysis: The Linate Disaster," in P. Alvintzi and H. Eder (eds.),*Crisis Management*, Hauppauge, NY, Nova Science, pp. 187–210.

Chia, R. (2004), "Re-educating Attention: What is Foresight and How is it Cultivated?" in H. Tsoukas and J. Shepherd (eds.), *Managing the Future: Foresight in the Knowledge Economy*, Oxford, Blackwell, pp. 21–37.

Choularton, R. (2001), "Complex Learning: Organizational Learning From Disasters," *Safety Science*, 39, 1, 61–70.

Christianson, M.K., Farkas, M.T., Sutcliffe, K.M., and Weick, K.E. (2009), "Learning Through Rare Events: Significant Interruptions," *Organization Science*, 20, 5, 846–60.

Churchland, P.M. (1989), *A Neurocomputational Perspective: The Nature of Mind and the Structure of Science*, Cambridge, Massachusetts Institute of Technology Press.

Ciborra, C. (2006), "Imbrication of Representations: Risk and Digital Technologies," *Journal of Management Studies*, 43, 6, 1339–55.

Clarke, L. (1999), *Mission Improbable*, University of Chicago Press.

(2006), *Worst Cases: Terror and Catastrophe in the Popular Imagination*, University of Chicago Press.

Clarke, S. and Ward, K. (2006), "The Role of Leader Influence Tactics and Safety Climate in Engaging Employee's Safety Participation,"*Risk Analysis*, 26, 5, 1175–85.

Coffee, J. (2006), *Gatekeepers: The Professions and Corporate Governance*, Oxford University Press.

Cohen, M.D., March, J.G., and Olsen, J.P. (1972), "A Garbage Can Model of Organizational Choice," *Administrative Science Quarterly*, 17, 1, 1–25.

Cohen, S. (2001), *States of Denial: Knowing about Atrocities and Suffering*, Cambridge, Polity Press.

Coleman, J.S. (1990), *Foundations of Social Theory*, Cambridge, London, The Belknap Press of Harvard University Press.

Crossan, M.M., Lane, H.W., and White, R.E. (1999), "An Organizational Learning Framework: From Intuition to Institution," *Academy of Management Review*, 24, 3, 522–37.

Czarniawska, B. (2009), "Conclusion: Plans or Well-Practiced Improvisation," in B. Czarniawska, (ed.), *Organizing in the Face of Risk and Threat*, Northampton, Edward Elgar, pp. 166–9.

Daft, R.L. (2004), *Organization Theory and Design*, Eighth Edition, Mason, OH, South-Western College.

Daft, R.L., Bettenhausen, K.R., and Tyler, B.B. (1993), "Implications of Top Managers' Communications Choices for Strategic Decisions," in G.P. Huber and W.H. Glick (eds.), *Organizational Change and Redesign: Ideas and Insights for Improving Performance*, New York, Oxford University Press, pp. 112–46.

Daft, R.L. and Huber, G.P. (1987), "How Organizations Learn: A Communication Framework," *Research in the Sociology of Organizations*, 5, 1, 1–36.

Daft, R.L. and Lengel, R.H. (1986), "Organizational Information Requirements, Media Richness and Structural Design," *Management Science*, 32, 5, 554–71.

Daft, R.L. and Weick, K.E. (1984), "Toward a Model of Organizations as Interpretation Systems," *Academy of Management Review*, 9, 2, 284–95.

Damasio, A. (1994), *Descartes' Error: Emotion, Reason and the Human Brains*, New York, G.P. Putnman.

Darnton, R. (1984), *The Great Cat Massacre and Other Episodes in French Cultural History*, New York, Basic Books.

Davidson, I. (1991), "Is Probability Theory Relevant for Uncertainty? A Post-Keynesian Perspective," *Journal of Economic Perspective*, 5, 1, 129–43.

Davis, E. (1995), "What's on American Managers' Minds?" *Management Review*, 84, 4, 14–20.

Davis, G.F. (2009), *Managed by the Markets: How Finance Reshaped America*, Oxford University Press.

Davis, G.F. and Powell, W. (1992), "Organization-Environment Relations," in M. Dunnette and L. Hough (eds.), *Handbook of Industrial and Organizational Psychology*, Palo Alto, Consulting Psychologists Press, pp. 315–75.

Day, G.S. and Schoemaker, P.J.H. (2006), *Peripheral Vision: Detecting the Weak Signals That Will Make or Break Your Company*, Boston, Harvard Business School.

Dekker, S.W.A. (2005), *Ten Questions about Human Error*, Mahwah, NJ, Lawrence Erlbaum Associates.

(2007), *Just culture: Balancing Safety and Accountability*, Aldershot, Ashgate.

Dewey, J. (1938), *Logic: The Theory of Inquiry*, New York, Henry Holt.

Diamond, J. (2005), *Collapse: How Societies Choose to Fail or Succeed*, New York, Penguin Books.

Dietz, T., Ostrom, E., and Stern, P.C. (2003), "The Struggle to Govern the Commons," *Science*, 302, 5652, 1907–12.

DiMaggio, P.J. and Powell, W.W. (1983), "The Iron Cage Revisited: Institutional Isomorphism and Collective Rationality in Organizational Field," *American Sociological Review*, 48, 2, 147–60.

Dixon, N.M. (1992), "Organizational Learning: A Review of the Literature with Implications for HRD Professionals," *Human Resource Development Quarterly*, 3, 1, 29–49.

(1994), *The Organizational Learning Cycle: How We Can Learn Collectively*, Maidenhead, UK, McGraw-Hill.

Dodier, N. (1995), *Les Hommes et les Machines*, Paris, Edition Métailié.

Dore, R. (2008), "Financialization of the Global Economy," *Industrial and Corporate Change*, 17, 6, 1097–112.

Douglas, M. (1966), *Purity and Danger*, London, Ark Paperbacks.

(1985), *Risk Acceptability According to the Social Sciences*, New York, Russell Sage Foundation.

(1992), *Risk and Blame: Essays in Cultural Theory*, London, New York, Routledge.

Douglas, M. and Wildavsky, A. (1982), *Risk and Culture*, Berkeley, University of California Press.

Downer, J. (2011), "737-Cabriolet: The Limits of Knowledge and the Sociology of Inevitable Failure," *American Journal of Sociology*, 117, 3, 725–62.

Drabeck, T. and Quarantelli, E. (1967), "Scapegoats, Villians and Disasters," *Trans-action*, 4, 4, 12–7.

Dugan, I.J. (2002), "Depreciated: Did You Hear the One about the Accountant? It's Not Very Funny," *Wall Street Journal*, March 14, p. A1.

Duncan, R. and Weiss, A. (1979), "Organizational Learning: Implications for Organizational Design," in B.M. Staw (ed.), *Research in Organizational Behavior*, Greenwich, CT, JAI Press, pp. 75–123.

Dunning, D., Heath, C., and Suls, J. (2005), *Flawed Self-Assessment: Implications for Health, Education and Business*, Cornell University Working Paper.

Dutton, J.E. and Ashford, S.J. (1993), "Selling Issues to Top Management," *Academy Management Review*, 18, 3, 397–428.

Easterby-Smith, M., Crossan, M., and Nicolini, D. (2000), "Organizational Learning: Debates Past, Present and Future," *Journal of Management Studies*, 37, 6, 783–96.

Eco, U. and Sebeock, T.A. (eds.) (1983), *The Sign of Three – Dupin, Holmes, Peirce*, Bloomington, Indiana University Press.

Edelman, L.B. and Stryker, R. (2005), "A Sociological Approach to Law and Economy," in N.J. Smelser and R. Swedberg (eds.), *The Handbook of Economic Sociology*, Second Edition, Princeton University Press, pp. 527–51.

Edmondson, A.C. (1996), "Learning from Mistakes Is Easier Said than Done: Group and Organizational Influences on the Decision and Correction of Human Error," *Journal of Applied Behavioral Science*, 32, 1, 5–28.

(2002), "The Local and Variegated Nature of Learning in Organizations," *Organization Science*, 13, 2, 128–46.

Edmondson, A.C., Bohmer, R.M., and Pisano, G.P. (2001), "Disrupted Routines: Team Learning and New Technology Implementation in Hospitals," *Administrative Science Quarterly*, 46, 4, 685–716.

Edmondson, A.C., Roberto, M.A., Bohmer, R.M.J., Ferlins, E.M., and Feldman, L.R. (2005), "The Recovery Window: Organizational Learning Following Ambiguous Threats," in W.H. Starbuck and M. Farajoun (eds.), *Organization at the Limit: Lessons from the Columbia Accident*, Malden, MA, Blackwell, pp. 220–45.

Einhorn, H.J. and Hogarth, R.M. (1978), "Confidence in Judgment: Persistence in the Illusion of Validity," *Psychological Review*, 85, 1, 395–416.

Elliott, D. and Smith, D. (2006), "Cultural Readjustment after Crisis: Regulation and Learning from Crisis within the UK Soccer Industry," *Journal of Management Studies*, 43, 2, 289–317.

Elster, J. (1979), *Ulysses and the Sirens*, Cambridge University Press.

(1989), *Nuts and Bolts for the Social Sciences*, Cambridge University Press.

(2000), *Ulysses Unbound: Studies in Rationality, Precommitment and Constraints*, Cambridge University Press.

Engestrom, Y., Kerouso, H., and Kajamaa, A. (2007), "Beyond Discontinuity: Expansive Organizational Learning Remembered," *Management Learning*, 38, 1, 319–36.

Epstein, G. (2005), *Financialization of the World Economy*, Aldershot, Edward Elgar.

Eurocontrol Performance Review Commission (2006), *Report on Legal and Cultural Issues in Relation to ATM Safety Occurrence Reporting in Europe: Outcome of a Survey Conducted by the Performance Review Unit in 2005–2006*, Eurocontrol, Brussels.

Evans, J.S. (1989), *Bias in Human Reasoning: Causes and Consequences*, Hillsdale, NJ, Erlbaum.

Ewald, F. (1991) "Insurance and Risks," in G. Burchell, C. Gordon, and P. Miller (eds.), *The Foucault Effect: Studies in Governmentality*, London, Harvester Wheatsheaf, pp. 197–210.

Farajoun, M. (2005), "History and Policy at the Space Shuttle Program," in W.H. Starbuck and M. Farajoun (eds.), *Organization at the Limit: Lessons from the Columbia Accident*, Malden, MA, Blackwell, pp. 21–40.

Ferguson, J. and Fakelmann, R. (2005), "The Culture Factor," *Frontiers of Health Services Management*, 22, 1, 33–40.

Festinger, L. (1957), *A Theory of Cognitive Dissonance*, Stanford University Press.

Fischhoff, B. (1975), "Hindsight Foresight: The Effect of Outcome Knowledge on Judgment under Uncertainty," *Journal of Experimental Psychology: Human Perception in Action*, 1, 3, 288–99.

Fiske, S.T. and Taylor, S.E. (1984), *Social Cognition*, Reading, MA, Addison-Wesley.

Fligstein, N. (1990), *The Transformation of Corporate Control*, Cambridge, Harvard University Press.

   (2001), *The Architecture of Markets: The Economic Sociology of Twenty-first-Century Capitalist Societies*, Princeton University Press.

Fox, J. (2009), *The Myth of the Rational Market*, New York, HarperCollins.

Freud, S. (1913) [1950], *Totem and Taboo*, New York, Norton.

Friedberg, E. (1993), *Le Pouvoir et la Règle: Dynamiques de l'Action Organisée*, Paris, Edition du Seuil.

Frijda, N. (1986), *The Emotions*, Cambridge University Press.

Gahmberg, H. (1980), *Contact Patterns and Learning in Organizations*, Helsinki, School of Economics.

Galbraith, J.R. (1977), *Designing Complex Organizations*, Reading, MA, Addison-Wesley.

   (2002), *Designing Organizations*, San Francisco, Jossey-Bass.

Garret, T.A. and Sobel, R.S. (2002), *The Political Economy of FEMA Disaster Payments*, St. Louis, Federal Reserve Bank of St. Louis.

Gawande, A. (2002), *Complications: A Surgeon's Notes on an Imperfect Science*, New York, Henry Holt and Co.

Ghepart, R.P., Van Maanen, J., and Oberlechner, T. (2009), "Organizations and Risk in Late Modernity," *Organization Studies*, 30, 2/3, 141–55.

Giddens, A. (1984), *The Constitution of Society*, Berkeley, University of California Press.

   (1990), *The Consequences of Modernity*, Cambridge, Polity Press.

Gigerenzer, G. (2007), *Gut Feelings: The Intelligence of Unconscious*, New York, Viking Penguin.

Gigerenzer, G., Hertwig, R., and Pachur, T. (eds.) (2011), *Heuristics: The Foundations of Adaptive Behavior*, New York, Oxford University Press.

Gigerenzer, G. and Selten, R. (2001), *Bounded Rationality: The Adaptive Toolbox*, Cambridge, Massachusetts Institute of Technology Press.

Gilbert, D.T. and Malone, P.S. (1995), "The Correspondence Bias," *Psychological Bulletin*, 117, 1, 21–38.

Ginzburg, C. (1990), *Myths, Emblems, Clues*, London, Hutchinson Radius.

Glynn, M.A., Lant, T.K., and Milliken, F.J. (1994), "Mapping Learning Processes in Organizations: A Multi-Level Framework Linking Learning and Organizing," in C. Stubbart, J. Meindl, and J. Porac (eds.), *Advances in Managerial Cognition and Organizational Information Processing*, Greenwich, CT, JAI Press, pp. 43–83.

Goffman, E. (1974), *Frame Analysis*, Boston, Northeastern University Press Edition.

Gourevitch, P. (2002), "Collective Action Problems in Monitoring Managers: The Enron Case as a Systemic Problem," *Economic Sociology: European Electronic Newsletter*, 3, 3, 3–16.

Grabowski, M., George, J.C., and Roberts, K. (1997), "Risk Mitigation in Large Scale Systems: Lessons from High Reliability Organizations," *California Management Review*, 39, 4, 152–61.

Granovetter, M. (1985), "Economic Action and Social Structure: The Problem of Embeddedness," *American Journal of Sociology*, 91, 3, 481–510.

Grattan, R.F. (2005), "Strategy in the Battle of Britain and Strategic Management Theory," *Management Decision*, 43, 10, 1432–41.

Greve, H.R. (2005a), "Inter-Organizational Learning and Social Structure," *Organization Studies*, 26, 1, 1025–47.

(2005b), "Interorganizational Learning Before 9/11," *International Public Management Journal*, 8, 3, 383–90.

Gundel, S. (2005), "Towards a New Typology of Crises," *Journal of Contingencies and Crisis Management*, 13, 3, 106–15.

Hackman, J.R. (2004), *Leading Team*, Boston, Harvard University Press.

Handel, M.I. (1980), "Avoiding Surprise in the 1980's," in R. Godson (ed.), *Intelligence Requirements for the 1980's: Analysis and Estimates*, vol. 2, Washington, DC, National Strategy Information Center, pp. 85–111.

Hardin, G. (1968), "The Tragedy of the Commons," *Science*, 162, 3859, 1243–8.

Haunschild, P.R. and Sullivan, B.N. (2002), "Learning from Complexity: Effects of Airline's Heterogeneity of Experience on Learning from Accidents and Incidents," *Administrative Science Quarterly*, 47, 4, 609–43.

Heath, C. and Staudenmayer, N. (2000), "Coordination Neglect: How Lay Theories of Organizing Complicate Coordination in Organizations," *Research in Organizational Behavior*, 22, 1, 155–93.

Hedberg, B. (1981), "How Organizations Learn and Unlearn," in P. Nystrom and W. Starbuck (eds.), *Handbook of Organizational Design*, Oxford University Press, pp. 3–27.

Heiner, R. (1983), "The Origin of Predictable Behavior," *American Economic Review*, 73, 4, 560–95.

Helsloot, I. (2007), *Beyond Symbolism: On the Need for a Rational Perspective on Crisis Management*, Boom Juridische Uitgevers, Den Haag, The Netherlands.

Hirschman, A.O. (1967), *Development Projects, Observed*, Washington, DC, Brookings Institution.

Hogarth, R.M. and Makridakis, S. (1981), "Forecasting and Planning: An Evaluation," *Management Science*, 27, 2, 115–38.

Hollnagel, E. (2004), *Barriers and Accident Prevention*, Aldershot, Ashgate.

Hood, C., Jones, D., Pidgeon, N., Turner, B., and Gibson, R. (1992), "Risk Management," *Chapter 6 of The Royal Society Risk: Analysis, Perception and Management*, London, The Royal Society, pp. 135–92.

Huber, G.P. (1991), "Organizational Learning: The Contributing Processes and the Literatures," *Organization Science*, 2, 1, 88–115.

Husted, B.W. (1993), "Reliability and the Design of Ethical Organizations," *Journal of Business Ethics*, 12, 10, 761–9.

Hutchins, E. (1995), *Cognition in the Wild*, Cambridge, Massachusetts Institute of Technology Press.

Hutter, B. (2005), "Ways of Seeing: Understandings of Risk in Organizational Settings," in B.M. Hutter and M. Power (eds.), *Organizational Encounters whit Risk*, Cambridge University Press, pp. 66–91.

(ed.) (2010), *Anticipating Risks and Organising Risk Regulation*, Cambridge University Press.

Hutter, B. and Lloyd-Bostock, S. (1990) "The Power of Accident: The Social and Psychological Impact of Accidents and the Enforcement of Safety Regulations," *British Journal of Criminology*, 30, 4, 453–65.

Hutter, B. and Power, M. (eds.) (2005a), *Organizational Encounters with Risk*, New York, Cambridge University Press.

Hutter, B. and Power, M. (2005b) "Organizational Encounters with Risk: An Introduction," in B. Hutter and M. Power (eds.), *Organizational Encounters with Risk*, New York, Cambridge University Press, pp. 1–32.

Ingram, P. (2002), "Interorganizational Learning," in J.A.C. Baum (ed.), *The Blackwell Companion to Organizations*, Oxford, Blackwell, pp. 642–63.

Janis, I. (1982), *Groupthink*, Boston, Houghton Mifflin.

Jasanoff, S. (2005), "Restoring Reason: Causal Narratives and Political Culture," in B. Hutter and M. Power (eds.), *Organizational Encounters with Risks*, Cambridge University Press, pp. 209–32.

Kahneman, D. (2002), *Rationality for Economists? Maps of Bounded Rationality: A Perspective on Intuitive Judgment and Choice*, Nobel Lecture, December 8, The Nobel Foundation.

(2003), "A Psychological Perspective on Economics," *The American Economic Review*, 93, 2, 162–8.

Kahneman, D., Slovic, P., and Tversky, A. (1982), *Judgment under Uncertainty: Heuristics and Bias*, Cambridge University Press.

Kahneman, D. and Tversky, A. (1979), "Prospect Theory: An Analysis of Decision under Risk," *Econometrica*, 47, 2, 263–91.

(1998), *Choices, Values and Frames*, Cambridge University Press.

Kam, E. (1988), *Surprise Attack: The Victim's Perspective*, Cambridge, Harvard University Press.

Kaminsky, G.L., Lizondo, J.S., and Reinhart, C.M. (1998), "Leading Indicators of Currency Crises," *International Monetary Fund Staff Papers*, 45, 1, 1–48.

Kelman, S. (2005), *Unleashing Change: A Study of Organizational Renewal in Government*, Washington, DC, Brookings Institution.

Kenning, P. and Plassmann, H. (2005), "Neuroeconomics: An Overview from an Economic Perspective," *Brain Research Bulletin*, 67, 5, 343–54.

Keohane, R.O. (1988), "International Institutions: Two Research Programs," *International Studies Quarterly*, 32, 1, 379–82.

Kettl, D.F. (2003), "Contingent Coordination: Practical and Theoretical Puzzles for Homeland Security," *American Review for Public Administration*, 33, 1, 253–7.

Keynes, J.M. (1921), *A Treatise on Probability*, London, Mcmillan.

Kim, T-Y., Hongseok, O. and Swaminathan, A. (2006), "Framing Inter-Organizational Network Change: A Network Inertia Perspective," *The Academy of Management Review*, 31, 1, 703–20.

Klimecki, R. and Lassleben, H. (1998), "Modes of Organizational Learning: Indications from an Empirical Study," *Management Learning*, 29, 4, 405–30.

Knight, F. (1921), *Risk, Uncertainty and Profit*, Boston, Houghton Mifflin.

Knutson, B., Rick, S., Wimmer, G.E., Prelec, D., and Loewenstein, G. (2007), "Neural Predictors of Purchases," *Neuron*, 53, 4, 147–56.

Koberg, C.S. and Ungson, G.R. (1987), "The Effects of Environmental Uncertainty and Dependence on Organizational Structure and Performance: A Comparative Study," *Journal of Management*, 13, 4, 725–37.

Kuhn, T. (1962), *The Structure of Scientific Revolutions*, University of Chicago Press.

Lægreid, P. and Serigstad, S. (2006), "Framing the Field of Homeland Security: The Case of Norway," *Journal of Management Review*, 43, 6, 1395–413.

Lagadec, P. (1993), *Preventing Chaos in Crisis: Strategies for Prevention, Control and Damage Limitation*, London, McGraw-Hill International.

Lampel, J., Shamsie, J., and Shapira, Z. (2009), "Experiencing the Improbable: Rare Events and Organizational Learning," *Organization Science*, 20, 5, 835–45

Lampel, J. and Shapira, Z. (2001), "Judgmental Errors, Interactive Norms and the Difficulty of Detecting Strategic Surprises," *Organization Science*, 12, 5, 599–611.

Landau, M. (1969), "Redundancy, Rationality and the Problem of Duplication and Overlap," *Public Administration Review*, 29, 4, 346–58.

LaPorte, T.R. (1988), "The United States Air Traffic System: Increasing Reliability in the Midst of Rapid Growth," in R. Mayntz and T. Hughes (eds.), *The Development of Large Scale Technical Systems*, Boulder, CO, Westview Press, pp. 215–44.

(1996), "High Reliability Organizations: Unlikely, Demanding and at Risk," *Journal of Contingencies and Crisis Management*, 4, 2, 60–71.

(2007a), "Anticipating Rude Surprises: Reflections on 'Crisis Management' Without End," in L. Jones (ed.), *Communicable Crises: Prevention, Management and Resolution in the Global Arena*, New York, Elsevier, pp. 25–44.

(2007b), "Critical Infrastructure in the Face of a Predatory Future: Preparing for Untoward Surprise," *Journal of Contingencies and Crisis Management*, 15, 1, 60–4.

LaPorte, T.R. and Consolini, P. (1994), "Working in Practice but not in Theory: Theoretical Challenges of High Reliability Organizations," *Journal of Public Administration Research and Theory*, 1, 1, 19–47.

(1998), "Theoretical and Operational Challenges of 'High-Reliability Organizations': Air-Traffic Control and Aircraft Carriers," *International Journal of Public Administration*, 21, 6/8, 847–52.

Latané, B. and Darley, J.M. (1970), *The Unresponsive Bystander: Why Doesn't He Help?*, New York, Appleton-Century-Crofts.

Lawrence, P.R. and Lorsch, J.W. (1967), *Organization and Environment*, Boston, Harvard Business School Press.

Lerner, A.W. (1986), "There Is More than One Way to Be Redundant: A Comparison of Alternatives for the Design and Use of Redundancy in Organizations," *Administration and Society*, 18, 1, 334–59.

Levitt, T. (1960), "Marketing Myopia," *Harvard Business Review*, 28, 1, 24–47.

Levitt, B. and March, J.G. (1988), "Organizational Learning," *Annual Review of Sociology*, 14, 1, 319–40.

Lewin, K. (1947), "Frontiers in Group Dynamics: Concepts Method and Reality in Social Science, Social Equilibria and Social Change," *Human Relations*, 1, 1, 5–41.

Libuser, C. (1994), "Organizational Structure and Risk Mitigation," *Dissertation in Partial Satisfaction of the Requirements for the Degree of Doctor of Philosophy in Management*, Los Angeles, University of California.

Lindenberg, S. (2000), "The Extension of Rationality: Framing versus Cognitive Rationality," in J. Baechler, F. Chazel, and R. Kamrane (eds.), *L'Acteur et ses Raisons: Mélanges en l'honneur de Raymond Boudon*, Paris, Puf, pp. 168–204.

Lipshitz, R. and Barak, D. (1995), "Hindsight Wisdom: Outcome Knowledge and the Evaluation of Decisions," *Acta Psychologica*, 88, 1, 105–25.

Luhmann, N. (1991), *Soziologie des Risikos*, Berlin, Walter de Grutyer.

(2000), *Organization und Entscheidung*, Opladen, Wiesbaden, Westdeutscher Verlag GmbH.

Lupton, D. (1999), *Risk*, London, Routledge.

Mack, A. and Rock, I. (1998), *Inattentional Blindness*, Cambridge, Bradford Books.

Mahler, J.G. (2009), *Organizational Learning at NASA: The Challenger and Columbia Accidents*, Washington, DC, Georgetown University Press.

Manns, C. and March, J.G. (1978), "Financial Adversity, Internal Competition and Curriculum Change in a University," *Administrative Science Quarterly*, 23, 4, 541–52.

March, J.G. (1978), "Bounded Rationality, Ambiguity and the Engineering of Choice," *Bell Journal of Economics*, 9, 2, 587–608.

(1988), *Decisions and Organizations*, Oxford, Blackwell.

(1994), *A Primer on Decision-Making*, New York, Free Press.

March, J.G. and Levinthal, D.A. (1993), "The Myopia of Learning," *Strategic Management Journal*, 14, Winter Special Issue, 95–112.

March, J.G. and Olsen, J.P. (1975), "Organizational Learning under Ambiguity," *European Journal of Policy Review*, 3, 2, 147–71.

March, J.G. and Olsen, J.P. (eds.) (1976), *Ambiguity and Choice in Organizations*, Bergen, Germany, Universitetsforlaget.

March, J.G. and Olsen, J.P. (1983), "Organizing Political Life: What Administrative Reorganization Tells Us about Governing," *American Political Science Review*, 77, 2, 281–96.

(1989), *Rediscovering Institutions: The Organizational Basis of Politics*, New York, Free Press.

March, J.G. and Shapira, Z. (1987), "Managerial Perspectives on Risk and Risk Taking," *Management Science*, 23, 11, 1404–18.

March, J.G. and Simon, H.A. (1993), *Organizations*, Second Edition, Cambridge, Blackwell.

Marcus, A. (1995), "Managing with Danger," *Industrial and Environmental Crisis Quarterly*, 9, 2, 139–52.

Martin, J. (1992), *Cultures in Organizations*, New York, Oxford University Press.

Mason, R. (2004), "Lessons in Organizational Ethics from the Columbia Disaster: Can a Culture Be Lethal?" *Organizational Dynamics*, 33, 2, 128–42.

Mayer, J. (2002), "The Accountants' War," *New Yorker*, April, 64–72.

Mayntz, R. and Sharpf, Z. (1975), *Policymaking in the German Federal Bureaucracy*, Amsterdam, Elsevier.

Merry, A. and Smith, A.M.C. (2001), *Errors, Medicine and the Law*, Cambridge University Press.

Merton, R.K. (1936), "The Unanticipated Consequences of Purposive Social Action," *American Sociological Review*, 1, 6, 894–904.

Merton, R.K. and Barber, E.G. (1992), *The Travels and Adventures of Serendipity: A Study in Historical Semantics and the Sociology of Science*, Princeton University Press.

Messick, D.M. and Sentis, K.P. (1979), "Fairness and Preference," *Journal of Experimental Social Psychology*, 15, 4, 418–34.

Meyer, J.W. and Rowan, B. (1977), "Institutionalized Organizations: Formal Structure as Myth and Ceremony," *American Journal of Sociology*, 83, 2, 340–63.

Milan Court, (2008), *Sentenza Parmalat (Parmalat Sentence)*, 18 December (dep. 5 May 2009), n. 14344, unedited.

Miller, D.T. (1992), "The Icarus Paradox: How Exceptional Companies Bring about Their Own Downfall," in B. De Wit and R. Meyer (eds.), *Strategy, Process, Context, Content*, St. Paul, MN, West, pp. 454–67.

Miller, D.T. and Ross, M. (1975), "Self-serving Biases in the Attribution of Causality," *Psychological Bulletin*, 82, 2, 213–25.

Milliken, F.J. (1987), "Three Types of Perceived Uncertainty about the Environment: State, Effect and Response Uncertainty," *Academy Management Review*, 12, 1, 133–43.

(1990), "Perceiving and Interpreting Environmental Change: An Examination of College Administrators' Interpretation of Changing Demographics," *Academy of Management Journal*, 33, 1, 42–63.

Milliken, F.J., Lant, T.K., and Bridwell-Mitchell, E.N. (2005), "Barriers to the Interpretation and Diffusion on Information about Potential Problems in Organizations: Lessons from the Space Shuttle Columbia," in W.H. Starbuck and M. Farajoun (eds.), *Organization at the Limit: Lessons from the Columbia Accident*, Malden, MA, Blackwell, pp. 246–66.

Mintzberg, H. (1994), *The Rise and Fall of Strategic Planning*, New York, Prentice Hall.

Mintzberg, H., Ahlstrand, B., and Lample, J. (1988), *Strategy Safari*, London, Prentice Hall.

Mizruchi, M. and Stearns, L. (2001), "Getting Deals Done: The Use of Social Networks in Bank Decision-Making," *American Sociological Review*, 66, 5, 647–71.

Mohamedou, M.M.O. (2007), *Undestanding Al Qaeda: The Transformation of War*, London, Pluto Press.

Moore, D.A., Tetlock, P.E., Tanlu, L., and Bazerman, M.H. (2006), "Conflicts of Interest and the Case of Auditor Independence: Moral Seduction and Strategic Issue Cycling," *Academy of Management Review*, 31, 1, 10–29.

Morrison, E.W. and Milliken, F.J. (2000), "Organizational Silence: A Barrier to Change and Development in a Pluralistic World," *Academy of Management Review*, 25, 4, 706–25.

Mutti, A. (2010), "Heterodox Reflections on the Financial Crisis," *Economic Sociology-European Electronic Newsletter*, 11, 2, 39–43.

Narayanan, V.K. and Fahey, L. (2005), "Invention and Navigation as Contrasting Metaphors of the Pathways to the Future," in H. Tsoukas and J. Shepherd (eds.), *Managing the Future: Foresight in the Knowledge Economy*, Oxford, Blackwell, pp. 38–57.

NCTA, National Commission on Terrorist Attacks Upon United States (2004), *The 9/11 Commission Report, Final Report of the National Commission on Terrorist Attacks upon United States*, New York, Norton.

NCCFC, National Commission on the Causes of the Financial Crisis in the U.S. (2011), *Final Report*, New York, Public Affairs, Perseus Book Group.

Nohria, N. (1992), *Is a Network Perspective a Useful Way of Studying Organizations?*, in N. Nohria and R.G. Eccles (eds.), *Networks and Organizations*, Boston, Harvard Business School Press, pp. 1–22.

Nonaka, I. (1994), "A Dynamic Theory of Organizational Knowledge Creation," *Organization Science*, 5, 1, 14–37.

Nonaka, I. and Takeuchi, H. (1995), *The Knowledge-Creating Company*, Oxford University Press.

North, D. (1990), *Institutions, Institutional Change and Economic Performance*, Cambridge University Press.

(2005), *Understanding the Process of Economic Change*, Princeton University Press.

Nystrom, P.C. and Starbuck, W.H. (2005), "To Avoid Organizational Crises, Unlearn," in K. Starkey, S. Tempest, and A. McKinlay (eds.), *How Organizations Learn*, Second Edition, London, Thompson, pp. 100–11.

Ocasio, W. (1997), "Towards an Attention-Based View of the Firm," *Strategic Management Journal*, 18, Summer Special Issue, 187–206.

Olson, M. (1965), *The Logic of Collective Action*, Boston, Harvard University Press.

Orasanu, J. and Salas, E. (1995), "Team Decision Making in Complex Environments," in G.A. Klein, J. Orasanu, R. Calderwood, and C.E. Zsambock (eds.), *Decision Making in Action: Models and Methods*, Norwood, Ablex, pp. 327–45.

Ostrom, E. (1990), *Governing the Commons: The Evolution of Institutions for Collective Actions*, Cambridge University Press.

Palmer, D. and Mahler, M. (2010), "A Normal Accident Analysis of the Mortgage Meltdown," in M. Lounsbury and P.M. Hirsch (eds.), *Markets on Trial: The Economic Sociology of the U.S. Financial Crisis, Part A. Research in the Sociology of Organizations*, Bingley, UK, Emerald, pp. 219–56.

Parker, C.F. and Stern, E.K. (2005), "Bolt from the Blue or Avoidable Failure? Revisiting September 11 and the Origins of Strategic Surprise," *Foreign Policy Analysis*, 1, 3, 301–31.

Pauchant, T.C. and Mitroff, I. (1992), *Transforming the Crisis-Prone Organization, Preventing Individual Organizational and Environmental Tragedies*, San Francisco, Jossey-Bass.

Peirce, C.S. (1931–1935), *Collected Papers, Vol. 1–6*, Cambridge, Harvard University Press.

Perrow, C. (1986), *Complex Organizations: A Critical Essay*, Third Edition, New York, Random House.

 (1999), *Normal Accidents: Living with High-Risk Technologies*, Second Edition, New York, Basic Books.

 (2002), *Organizing America: Wealth, Power and the Origin of Corporate Capitalism*, Princeton University Press.

 (2007), *The Next Catastrophe: Reducing Our Vulnerabilities to Natural, Industrial and Terrorist Disaster*, Princeton University Press.

 (2010), "The Meltdown Was Not an Accident," in M. Lounsbury and P.M. Hirsch (eds.), *Markets on Trial: The Economic Sociology of the U.S. Financial Crisis, Part A. Research in the Sociology of Organizations*, Bingley, UK, Emerald, pp. 309–30.

Perrow, C. and Guillén, M.F. (1990), *The Aids Disaster*, Yale, Yale University Press.

Peters, T.J. and Waterman, R.H. (1982), *In Search of Excellence: Lessons from America's Best-Run Companies*, New York, Harper and Row.

Pfeffer, J. and Salancik, G. (1978), *The External Control of Organizations: A Resource Dependance Approach*, New York, Harper and Row.

Pidgeon, N., Kasperson, R.E., and Slovic, P. (2003), *The Social Amplification of Risk*, Cambridge, Cambridge University Press.

Platt, J. (1973), "Social Traps," *American Psychologist*, 28, 8, 641–51.

Popper, K.R. (1963), *Conjectures and Refutations: The Growth of Scientific Knowledge*, London, Routledge.

(1984) [1994], *In Search of a Better World*, London, Routledge

Porter, L. and Roberts, K. (1976), "Communication in Organizations," in M.D. Dunnette (ed.), *Handbook of Industrial Organizations Psychology*, Chicago, Rand McNally, pp. 1553–89.

Porter, M.N. (1985), *Competitive Advantage: Creating and Sustaining Superior Performance*, New York, Free Press.

Posner, R.A. (2006), *Uncertain Shield*, Oxford, Rowman and Littlefield.

Powell, W.W. and DiMaggio, P. (eds.) (1991), *The New Institutionalism in Organizational Analysis*, University of Chicago Press.

Power, M. (1997), *The Audit Society: Rituals of Verification*, Oxford University Press.

(2007), *Organized Uncertainty: Designing a World of Risk Management*, Oxford University Press.

Preston, T. and Hart, P.T. (1999), "Understanding and Evaluating Bureaucratic Politics: The Nexus between Political Leaders and Advisory Systems," *Political Psychology*, 20, 1, 49–98.

Rajan, R.G. (2005), *Has the Financial Development Made the World Riskier?*, NBER Working Paper No. 11728, Issued in November, available at http://www.nber.org/papers/w11728.

(2010), *Fault Lines: How Hidden Fractures Still Threaten the World Economy*, Princeton University Press.

Rangel, A., Camerer, C.F., and Montague, R. (2008), "A Framework for Studying the Neurobiology of Value-Based Decision-Making," *Nature Reviews Neuroscience*, 9, 7, 545–56.

Rasmussen, J. (1990), "Human Error and the Problem of Causality in Analysis of Accidents," *Philosophy Transactions of the Royal Society*, B 327, 449–62.

(1997), "Risk Management in a Dynamic Society: A Modelling Problem," *Safety Science*, 27, 2/3,183–213.

Reason, J. (1990), *Human Error*, Cambridge University Press.

(1997), *Managing the Risk Organizational Accidents*, Aldershot, Ashgate.

(2008), *The Human Contribution: Unsafe Acts, Accidents and Heroic Recoveries*, Aldershot, Ashgate.

Reinhart, C.M. and Rogoff, K.S. (2009), *This Time Is Different*, Princeton University Press.

Rerup, C. (2009), "Attentional Triangulation: Learning from Unexpected Rare Crises," *Organization Science*, 20, 5, 876–93.

Rike, B. (2003), "Prepared or Not ... That Is the Vital Question," *The Information Management Journal*, 37, 6, 25–33.

Risen, J. and Gilovich, T. (2007), "Informal Logical Fallacies," R.J. Sternberg, D. Halpern and H. Roediger (eds.), *Critical Thinking in Psychology*, New York, Cambridge University Press, pp. 110–30.

Ritov, I. and Baron, J. (1990), "Reluctance to Vaccinate: Omission Bias and Ambiguity," *Journal of Behavioral Decision Making*, 34, 3, 263–77.

Roberto, M.A. (2009), Know *What You Don't Know: How Great Leaders Prevent Problems Before They Happen*, Upper Saddle River, NJ, Wharton School.

Roberto, M.A., Bohmer, R.M.J., and Edmondson, A.C. (2006), "Facing Ambiguous Threats," *Harvard Business Review*, 84, 11, 106–13.

Roberts, K.H. (1990), "Some Characteristics of High Reliability Organizations," *Organization Science*, 1, 2, 160–77.

Roberts, K.H. (ed.) (1993), *New Challenges to Understanding Organizations*, New York, Macmillan.

Roberts, K.H. (2009), "Book Review Essay: Managing the Unexpected: Six Years of HRO-Literature Reviewed," *Journal of Contingency and Crisis Management*, 17, 1, 50–4.

Roberts, K.H. and Bea, R. (2001), "Must Accidents Happen? Lessons from High-Reliability Organizations," *Academy of Management Executive*, 15, 3, 70–8.

Roberts, K.H. and Libuser, C. (1993), "From Bhopal to Banking, Organizational Design Can Mitigate Risk," *Organizational Dynamics*, 21, 4, 15–26.

Roberts, K.H., Madsen, P.M., and Desai, V.M. (2005), "The Space between in Space Transportation: A Relational Analysis of the Failure of STS-107," in W.H. Starbuck and M. Farajoun (eds.), *Organization at the Limit: Lessons from the* Columbia *Accident*, Malden, MA, Blackwell, pp. 81–97.

Roberts, K.H. and Rousseau, D.M. (1989), "Research in Nearly Failure-Free, High-reliability Systems: Having the Bubble," *IEEE Transactions on Engineering Management*, 36, 1, 132–9.

Roberts, K.H., Stout, S.K., and Halpern, J.J. (1994), "Decision Dynamics in Two High Reliability Organizations," *Management Science*, 40, 1, 614–24.

Roberts, K.H., Yu, K.F., Desai, V., and Madsen, P. (2008), "Employing Adaptive Structuring as a Cognitive Decision Aid in High Reliability Organizations," in G.P. Hodgkinson and W.H. Starbuck (eds.), *The Oxford Handbook of Organizational Decision Making*, Oxford University Press, 194–210.

Rochlin, G.I. (1993), "Defining High-Reliability Organizations in Practice: A Taxonomic Prologue," in K.H. Roberts (ed.), *New Challenges to Understanding Organizations*, New York, Macmillan, 11–32.

Rochlin, G.I., LaPorte, T.R., and Roberts, K.H. (1987), "The Self-Designing High Reliability Organizations: Aircraft Carrier Flight Operation at Sea," *Naval War College Review*, 40, 4, 76–90.

Rochlin, G.I. and Von Meier, A. (1994), "Nuclear Power Operations: A Cross-Cultural Perspective," *Annual Review of Energy and the Environment*, 19, 1, 153–87.

Roe, E. and Schulman, P.R. (2008), *High Reliability Management: Operating on the Edge*, Stanford University Press.

Roll, R. (1986), "The Hubris Hypothesis of Corporate Takeovers," *Journal of Business*, 59, 2, 197–216.

Ron, N., Lipshitz, R., and Popper, M. (2006), "How Organizations Learn: Post-Flight Reviews in an F-16 Fighter Squadron," *Organization Studies*, 27, 8, 1069–89.

Rosenthal, U. and Kouzmin, A. (1993), "Globalizing an Agenda for Contingencies and Crisis Management: An Editorial Statement," *Journal of Contingencies and Crisis Management*, 1, 1, 1–12.

Ross, L. (1977), "The Intuitive Psychologist and His Shortcomings," in L. Berkowitz (ed.), *Advances in Experimental Psychology*, vol. 10, New York, Academic Press, pp. 173–220.

Ruitenberg, B. (2002), "Court Case against Dutch Controllers," *The Controller*, 41, 4, 22–5.

Russell, B. (1918), "On the Notion of Cause," *Proceedings of the Aristotelian Society*, 13, 1–26.

Sagan, S.D. (1993), *The Limits of Safety*, Princeton University Press.

Samuelson, I.A. (1969), "Classical and Neoclassical Theory," in R.W. Clower (ed.), *Monetary Theory*, London, Penguin, pp. 403–32.

Samuelson, W.F. and Zeckhauser, R. (1988), "Status Quo Bias in Decision Making," *Journal of Risk and Uncertainty*, 1, 1, 7–59.

Savage, L.J. (1954), *The Foundations of Statistics*, New York, John Wiley and Sons.

Sawyer, J.E. (1952), "Entrepreneurial Error and Economic Growth," *Explorations in Entrepreneurial History*, 4, 1, 199–204.

Schelling, T. (1960), *The Strategy of Conflict*, New Haven, CT, Yale University Press.

Scheytt, T., Soin, K., Sahlin-Andersson, K., and Power, M. (2006), "Introduction: Organizations, Risk and Regulation," *Journal of Management Studies*, 43, 6, 1331–7.

Schulman, P.R. (1993a), "The Analysis of High Reliability Organizations: A Comparative Framework," in K.H. Roberts (ed.), *New Challenges to Understanding Organizations*, New York, Macmillan, pp. 33–54.

(1993b), "The Negotiate Order of Organizational Reliability," *Administration and Society*, 25, 1, 352–72.

Schwartz, P. (2003), *Inevitable Surprises: Thinking Ahead in a Time of Turbulence*, New York, Gotham.

Scott, R.W. and Davis, G.F. (2007), *Organization and Organizing: Rational, Natural and Open System Perspectives*, Upper Saddle River, NJ, Pearson International Edition.

Shapiro, S.P. (1987), "The Social Control of Impersonal Trust," *American Journal of Sociology*, 93, 3, 623–58.

Sheth, J.N. (2007), *The Self-Destructive Habits of Good Companies: And How to Break Them*, Philadelphia, WhartonSchool, Pearson Education.

Shrivastava, P. and Schneider, S. (1984), "Organizational Frames of Reference," *Human Relations*, 37, 10, 795–809.

Short, J.F. and Clarke, L. (eds.) (1992), *Organizations, Uncertainties and Risks*, Boulder, CO, Westview Press.

Sikka, P. (2009), "Financial Crisis and the Silence of the Auditors," *Accounting, Organizations and Society*, 34, 6/7, 868–73.

Simon, H.A. (1947), *Administrative Behavior*, New York, Free Press.

 (1955), "A Behavioral Model of Rational Choice," *Quarterly Journal of Economics*, 69, 1, 99–118.

 (1956), "Rational Choice and the Structure of the Environment," *Psychological Review*, 63, 2, 129–38.

 (1957), *Models of Man*, New York, John Wiley and Sons.

 (1991), "Organizations and Markets," *Journal of Economic Perspectives*, 5, 2, 25–44.

 (1992), "The Bottleneck of Attention: Connecting Thought with Motivation," in W.D. Spalding (ed.), *Nebraska Symposium on Motivation*, vol. 41, Lincoln, University of Nebraska Press, pp. 1–21.

 (1999), "The Potlatch between Political Science and Economics," in J. Alt, M. Levi, and E. Ostrom (eds.), *Competition and Cooperation: Conversations with Nobelists about Economics and Political Science*, Cambridge University Press, pp. 112–9.

Simons, D.J. and Levin, D.T. (1997), "Change Blindness," *Trends in Cognitive Science*, 1, 7, 261–7.

 (2003), "What Makes Change Blindness Interesting?", in D.E. Irwin and B.H. Ross (eds.), *The Psychology of Learning and Motivation*, vol. 42, San Diego, Academic Press, pp. 295–322.

Simons, D.J. and Rensink, R.A. (2005), "Change Blindness: Past, Present and Future," *Trends in Cognitive Sciences*, 9, 1, 16–20.

Sinn, H.W. (1984), "Common Property Resources, Storage Facilities and Ownership Structures: A Cournot Model of the Oil Market," *Economica*, 51, 1, 235–52.

Sitkin, S.B. (1992), "Learning through Failure: The Strategy of Small Losses," in L.L. Cummings and B.M. Staw (eds.), *Research in Organizational Behavior*, Greenwich, CT, JAI Press, pp. 231–66.

Slovic, P. (2000), *The Perceptions of Risk*, London, Earthscan.

(2001), *Smoking: Risk, Perception and Policy*, Thousand Oaks, CA, Sage.

Slovic, P., Fischhoff, B., and Lichtenstein, S. (1977), "Cognitive Processes and Societal Risk Taking," in H. Jungermann and G. De Zeeuw (eds.), *Decision Making and Change in Human Affairs*, Dordrecht, Riedel, pp. 7–36.

(1982), "Facts versus Fears: Understanding Perceived Risk," in D. Kahneman, P. Slovic, and A. Tversky (eds.), *Judgment Under Uncertainty: Heuristics and Biases*, Cambridge University Press, pp. 463–89.

(1984), "Behavioral Decision Theory on Risk and Safety," *Acta Psychologica*, 56, 1, 183–203.

Smith, A. (1759) [2002], *The Theory of Moral Sentiment*, Cambridge University Press.

Smith, D. and Elliott, D. (2007), "Exploring the Barriers to Learning form Crisis," *Management Learning*, 38, 5, 519–38.

Smith, R.J. (1981), "Resolving the Tragedy of the Commons by Creating Private Property Rights in Wildlife," *CATO Journal*, 1, 1, 439–68.

Snook, S.A. (2000), *Friendly Fire: The Accidental Shootdown of U.S. Black Hawks Over Northern Iraq*, Princeton University Press.

Snowden, D.J. and Boone, M.E. (2007), "A Leader's Framework for Decision Making: Wise Executives Tailor their Approach to Fit the Circumstances they Face," *Harvard Business Review*, 85, 11, 69–76.

Stacey, R.D. (2001), *Complex Responsive Processes in Organizations: Learning and Knowledge Creation*, London, Routledge.

Starbuck, W.H. and Farajoun, M. (eds.) (2005), *Organization at the Limit: Lessons from the* Columbia *Accident*, Malden, MA, Blackwell.

Starbuck, W.H. and Milliken, F.J. (1988), "*Challenger*: Fine-Tuning the Odds until Something Breaks," *Journal of Management Studies*, 25, 1, 319–40.

Staw, B.M. (1976), "Knee-Deep in the Big Muddy: A Study of Escalating Commitment to a Chosen Course of Action," *Organizational Behavior and Human Performance*, 16, 1, 27–44.

(1981), "The Escalation of Commitment to a Course of Action," *Academy of Management Review*, 6, 4, 577–87.

Stech, F.J. (1979), *Political and Military Intention Estimation*, Bethesda, MD, Mathtech.

Stern, E. (1999), *Crisis Decisionmaking: A Cognitive Institutional Approach*, Stockholm University Press.

Stern, E. and Verbeek, B. (1998), "Wither the Study of Governmental Politics in Foreign Policymaking: A Symposium," *Mershon International Studies Review*, 42, 1, 205–55.

Stern, N. (2006), *Stern Review on the Economics of Climate Change*, October 30, available at http://www.hmtreasury.gov.uk/independentreviews/stern.

Stevens, M. (1981), *The Big Eight*, New York, Collier.

(1991), *The Big Six: The Selling Out of America's Top Accounting Firms*, New York, Simon and Schuster.

Stinchcombe, A.L. (1990), *Information and Organization*, Berkeley, University of California Press.

Strang, D. and Soule, S. (1998), "Diffusion in Organizations and Social Movements: From Hybrid Corn to Poison Pills," *Annual Review of Sociology*, 24, 1, 265–90.

Sunstein, C.R. (2000), *Behavioral Law and Economics*, Cambridge University Press.

Taleb, N.N. (2007), *The Black Swan*, New York, Random House.

Tamu, M. and Harrison, M.I. (2006), "Improving Patient Safety in Hospitals: Contributions of High-Reliability Theory and Normal Accident Theory," *Health Services Research*, 41, 4, 1654–76.

Taylor, S.E. (1989), *Positive Illusions: Creative Self-Deception and the Healthy Mind*, New York, Basic Books.

Taylor-Gooby, P. and Zinn, J.O. (eds.) (2006), *Risk in Social Science*, Oxford University Press.

Thagard, P. and Shelley, C.P. (1997), "Abductive Reasoning: Logic, Visual Thinking, and Coherence," in M.L. Dalla Chiara, K. Doets, D. Mundici, and J. Van Benthem (eds.), *Logic and Scientific Methods*, Dordrecht, Kluwer, pp. 413–27.

Thompson, J.D. (1967), *Organizations in Action*, New York, McGraw-Hill.

Toft, B. and Reynolds, S. (1997), *Learning from Disasters*, Second Edition, Leicester, Perpetuity Press.

Tsebelis, G. (2002), *Veto Players: How Political Institutions Work*, New York, Russell Sage Foundation.

Tsoukas, H. and Shepherd, J. (eds.) (2004), *Managing the Future: Foresight in the Knowledge Economy*, Oxford, Blackwell.

Tsoukas, H. and Vladimirou, E. (2001), "What is Organizational Knowledge?" *Journal of Management Studies*, 38, 7, 973–93.

Tucker, A.L. and Edmondson, A.C. (2003), "Why Hospitals don't Learn from Failures: Organizational and Psychological Dynamics that Inhibit System Change," *California Management Review*, 45, 2, 1–18.

Turner, B.A. (1976), "The Organizational and Interorganizational Development of Disasters," *Administrative Science Quarterly*, 21, 3, 378–97.

(1978), *Man-Made Disasters*, London, Wykeham.

Turner, B.A. and Pidgeon, N.F. (1997), *Man-made Disasters*, Second Edition, Oxford, Butterworth-Heinemann.

Tversky, A. and Kahneman, D. (1973), "Availability: A Heuristic for Judging and Probability," *Cognitive Psychology*, 5, 2, 207–32.

(1974), "Judgment under Uncertainty: Heuristics and Biases," *Science*, 185, 4157, 1124–231.

(1981), "The Framing of Decisions and the Psychology of Choice," *Science*, 211, 4881, 453–8.

Van der Heijden, K. (1996), *Scenarios: The Art of Strategic Conversation*, Chickester, NY, John Wiley and Sons.

Varian, H. (1992), *Microeconomic Analysis*, New York, London, Norton.

Vaughan, D. (1996), *The Challenger Launch Decision: Risk Technology, Culture and Deviance at NASA*, University of Chicago Press.

(1999), "The Dark Side of Organizations: Mistake, Misconduct and Disaster," *Annual Review of Sociology*, 25, 1, 271–305.

(2005), "System Effects: On Slippery Slopes, Repeating Negative Patterns and Learning From Mistake," in W.H. Starbuck and M. Farajoun (eds.), *Organization at the Limit: Lessons from the* Columbia *Accident*, Malden, MA, Blackwell, pp. 41–59.

Vera, D. and Crossan, M.M. (2004), "Theatrical Improvisation: Lessons for Organization," *Organization Studies*, 25, 5, 727–49.

Vertzberger, Y. (1990), *The World in Their Minds: Information Processing, Cognition and Perception in Foreign Policy Decisionmaking*, Stanford University Press.

Vince, R. and Saleem, T. (2004), "The Impact of Caution and Blame on Organizational Learning," *Management Learning*, 35, 2, 131–52.

von Clausewitz, C. (1832) [1984], *On War*, Second Edition, Princeton University Press.

Von Neumann, J. and Morgenstern, O. (1947), *Theory of Games and Economic Behavior*, Princeton University Press.

Von Winterfeldt, D.V., John, R.S., and Borcherding, K. (1981), "Cognitive Components of Risk Rating," *Risk Analysis*, 13, 1, 277–87.

Wagenaar, W.A. and Groeneweg, J. (1987), "Accidents at Sea: Multiple Causes and Impossible Consequences," *International Journal of Man-Machine Studies*, 27, 587–98.

Walsh, J. and Ungson, R. (1991), "Organizational Memory," *Academy of Management Review*, 16, 1, 57–91.

Wason, P.C. (1960), "On the Failure to Eliminate Hypotheses in a Conceptual Task," *Quarterly Journal of Experimental Psychology*, 20, 1, 273–83.

Weber, M. (1922), *Wirtschaft und Gesellschaft*, Tübingen, Mohr.

Weick, K.E. (1969), *The Social Psychology of Organizing*, Reading, MA, Addison-Wesley.

(1987), "Organizational Culture as a Source of High Reliability," *California Management Review*, 29, 2, 112–27.

(1993), "The Collapse of Sensemaking in Organizations: The Mann Gulch Disaster," *Administrative Science Quarterly*, 38, 4, 628–52.

(1995), *Sensemaking in Organizations*, Thousand Oaks, CA, Sage.

(2005a), "Organizing and Failures of Imagination," *International Public Management Journal*, 8, 3, 425–38.

(2005b), "Making Sense of Blurred Images: Mindful Organizing in Mission STS-107," in W.H. Starbuck and M. Farajoun (eds.), *Organization at the Limit: Lessons from the* Columbia *Accident*, Malden, MA, Blackwell, pp. 159–77.

Weick, K.E. and Roberts, K.H. (1993), "Collective Mind in Organizations: Heedful Interrelating on Flight Decks," *Administrative Science Quarterly*, 38, 3, 357–81.

Weick, K.E. and Sutcliffe, K.M. (2007), *Managing the Unexpected: Resilient Performance in an Age of Uncertainty*, San Francisco, Jossey-Bass.

Weick, K.E., Sutcliffe, K.M., and Obstfeld, D. (1999), "Organizing for High Reliability: Processes of Collective Mindfulness," in B. Staw and R. Sutton (eds.), *Organizational Behavior*, Stanford, CA, JAI Press, pp. 81–123.

Weinberg, G.M. (1986), *The Secrets of Consulting*, New York, Dorset House.

Weitzel, W. and Jonsson, E. (1989), "Decline in Organizations: A Literature Integration and Extension," *Administrative Science Quarterly*, 34, 1, 91–109.

Westrum, R. (1995), "Organizational Dynamics and Safety," in N. McDonald, N.A. Johnston, and R. Fuller (eds.), *Application of Psychology to the Aviation System*, Aldershot, Averbury Aviation, pp. 75–80.

Whitehead, A.N. (1967), *Adventures of Ideas*, New York, Free Press.

Wilensky, H.L. (1967), *Organizational Intelligence: Knowledge and Policy in Government and Industry*, New York, Basic Books.

Wilson, G.C. (1986), *Supercarrier*, New York, Macmillan.

Wilson, J.Q. (1989), *Bureaucracy: What Government Agencies Do and Why They Do It?*, New York, Basic Books.

Wohlstetter, R. (1962), *Pearl Harbor: Warning and Decision*, Stanford University Press.

Wong, P.T.P. and Weiner, B. (1981), "When People Ask 'Why' Questions and the Heuristics of Attributional Search," *Journal of Personality and Social Psychology*, 40, 4, 650–63.

Woods, D. and Cook, R.I. (1999), "Perspectives on Human Error: Hindsight Biases and Local Rationality," in R.S. Durso (ed.), *Handbook of Applied Cognition* New York, John Wiley and Sons, pp. 141–71.

(2002), "Nine Steps to Move Forward from Error," *Cognition, Technology and Work*, 4, 2, 137–44.

Wright, P. (1974), "The Harassed Decision-Maker: Time Pressure, Distractions and the Role of Evidence," *Journal of Applied Psychology*, 59, 5, 555–61.

Zaccuri, G. (1993), *L'organizzazione invisibile: Il caso della prima guerra mondiale*, Milano, Il Sole 24Ore.

Zakay, D. (1993), "The Impact of Time Perception Processes on Decision-Making under Time Stress," in O. Svenson and J. Maule (eds.), *Time Pressure and Stress in Human Judgment and Decision-Making*, New York, Plenum Press, pp. 59–72.

Zakay, D., Ellis, E., and Shevalsky, M. (1998), *Do Managers Learn from Experience? The Negative Outcome Bias*, Tel Aviv University.

Zegart, A.B. (2007), *Spying Blind: The CIA, the FBI and the Origins of 9/11*, Princeton University Press.

Zhao, B. and Olivera, F. (2006), "Error Reporting in Organizations," *Academy of Management Review*, 31, 4, 1012–30.

Zollo, M. (2009), "Superstitious Learning with Rare Strategic Decisions: Theory and Evidence from Corporate Acquisitions," *Organization Science*, 20, 5, 894–908.

Index

Printed in the United States
by Baker & Taylor Publisher Services